Le Manifeste du Choréographe (Ed. Etoile, 1935)

Du Temps où J'Avais Faim (Ed. Stock, 1935)

Troisième Fête de Pouchkine (Ed. Etoile, 1937)

La Danse (Ed. Denoël, 1938)

Carlotta Grisi (Ed. Albin Michel, 1941)

Giselle (Ed. Albin Michel, 1942)

Terpsichore dans le Cortège des Muses (Ed. Lagrange, 1943)

A l'Opéra (with P. Valéry and Jean Cocteau. Ed. Champrosay, 1943)

Pensées sur la Danse (Preface by Paul Valéry, illustrations by Aristide Mailliol, published by Bordas, 1946)

A l'Aube de mon Destin. Sept ans aux Ballets Russes (Albin Michel 1948)

Traité de Danse Académique (Bordas, 1949)

Histoire du Ballet Russe Academy Prize (Nagel, 1950)

Vestris, Dieu de la Danse (published by La Revue Choréographique, 1952)

Traité de Choréographie (Bordas, 1952)

Méditations sur la Danse (published by La Revue Choréographique, 1952)

Dix Ans à l'Opera 1929–1939 (Comoedia, December, 1953)

La Livre de la Danse (J.M.F., 1954)

Serge de Diaghilev. Preface by J. L. Vaudoyer. (Editions du Rocher, 1954)

La Musique par la Danse (R. Laffont, 1955)

Bulletin No. 1 de l'Institut Choréographique (Ed. I. Ch. 1957)

Les Trois Graces du XXe Siècle (Correa, 1957)

Bulletins Nos. 2, 3 and 4 of the *Institut Choréographique* (Ed. I. Ch. 1957)

Au Service de la Danse (A la recherche d'une science: choréologie: Ed. Univers Danse, 1958)

La Danse Académique et l'Art Choréographique (Ed. Gonthier, 1965)

Ma Vie (Ed. Julliard, 1965)

Bulletins 5 and 6 *de l'Institut Choréographique* (Ed. U.D. 1968)

SERGE LIFAR

Ma Vie
FROM KIEV TO KIEV

AN AUTOBIOGRAPHY TRANSLATED BY
JAMES HOLMAN MASON

THE WORLD PUBLISHING COMPANY
New York and Cleveland

Published by The World Publishing Company
2231 West 110th Street, Cleveland, Ohio 44102

First World Printing—1970

Published in Great Britain in 1970 by
Hutchinson of London

Library of Congress Catalog Card Number: 74–88592

PRINTED IN GREAT BRITAIN

To my country—Russia

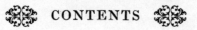 CONTENTS

ILLUSTRATIONS

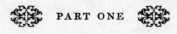

PART ONE

ART AND LIFE

1

KIEV, 1905

A year of troubles and upheavals. My country, Russia, was at war. From far-off Siberia came news of disasters. Port Arthur had surrendered and our army had been beaten. Our fleet had been captured or sunk. Defeat. But before the dismal climax disorders had broken out inside Russia itself. Strikes. The fusillades on 'Red Sunday' . . . it was not until the Tsar had vacillated, ceded at first that reaction had triumphed. This was the year of the mutiny on board the *Potemkin*.

However, it was not yet the age of revolution although there were already the signs pointing to all the revolutions of this century. The course of human history seemed to be secretly subject to a profound change. Freud published his theory of sexuality. Debussy wrote *La Mer*, impressionist music. The Fauves' paintings provoked indignant hostility. In St. Petersburg, Serge de Diaghilev organised his great exhibition of 18th and 19th century art—and then left Russia for ever. Einstein discovered photons. All the forces that were to mould the 20th century were at work. A new world was being born.

I was born on 2nd April, 1905, at Kiev where I spent all my childhood.

As is the case with every child, I suppose, the figures that stand out are those of my father and mother—as well as those of my brothers and sister. We lived all together in a large house near the University. My father was a civil servant in the Department of Waterways and Forests and in my eyes he represented Authority with all that word suggests—confidence, but also dignity, remoteness. My mother—her name was Sophia—was

very beautiful and much closer to us. But, I must be truthful
and say it was only much later that I came to realise how deeply
she loved us and to what an extent she would sacrifice herself
for us.

My parents were both still young and lived their own life—
one in which, as was natural enough, I did not take much part—
neither did I in the lives of my sister, Eugenia, or my brothers
Vassili and Léonide. Maybe I would have felt more in sympathy
with my sister but she was a good deal older than myself and
took scarcely any notice of me. For her I was just a little boy
and rather a nuisance until I was old enough to be a companion.
My brothers were, it is true, nearer to me in age (I was the
youngest of the family) but their characters and their interests
kept us apart. In fact, as is not so unusual it seems to me, we
all liked each other well enough but without being very closely
intimate.

I already had that feeling of solitude—even when among
those closest to me—that has haunted me all my life.

It was perhaps in my childhood that I was the most isolated
from those of my own age, but this did not make me at all sad.
I had other companions who took up my time, companions that
were more inspiring and dearer to my heart—the places where
I lived, the great city of Kiev and the countryside around it.

My city of Kiev was very beautiful and the vision of what it
then was remains very vivid in my memory. In those days
the capital of the Ukraine was already a large modern city and
after St Petersburg perhaps the most westernised of all Russian
towns. However, Kiev had still a rather oriental look. The
influence of old Byzantium was still strong enough to be felt.
The gilded domes of the St Sophia cathedral dominated the
city while a multitude of belfries and onion-shaped cupolas
spread out in an unforgettable sky-line. And the bells of Kiev!
I have only to shut my eyes and I can hear deep down within
me the peals ringing out all over the city. They accompanied
me and they thrilled me as I walked home through the old
streets and near the wooden houses.

Another memory is inseparable from the Kiev of my childhood—horses. Kiev seemed to me to be the home of horses. I
can still see the barouches, the carts, the wagons—and the
drivers in their padded box-coats. Everywhere the noise of
horses' hooves, quick and rattling or heavy and jerky, it was the

constant companion of our days now that I come to think of it.
However, a greater joy for me was the sight in the city's heart
of camel-caravans led by almond-eyed Tatar merchants. Here
was another way of life, strange animals in the middle of a city.
Here was something to delight the mind of a child—and to
offer him a taste of the natural life he needs, that I needed very
much.

I loved my city of Kiev where everything seemed to me to be
on a huge scale—the Opera House, the theatre I was not yet
allowed to visit, the University I was one day to attend, the
avenues, the lights, the whirlpool of activity and the feeling
that one was part and parcel of it all. But a city was not, in
those days, and maybe especially in Russia, entirely cut off
from the countryside. Four distinct seasons divided our years
and marked our lives. The winters were severe. How well I
remember the whistling winds, the fur-clad pedestrians hurrying
along the streets. At that time of year we lived in a house with
double, padded windows and heated by great porcelain stoves
and lighted with oil-lamps.

But then came the spring. Dull, rumbling explosions which
are linked in my mind with ideas of renovation. The mighty,
beautiful Dnieper river, which borders the city, was splitting
its icy armour. Under the force of the stream, more powerful
since the beginning of the break-up, the floes crashed against one
another.

The Kreshchatik was in those days still only a provincial
highway with wooden dwellings and leading to a district lined
with parks and gardens. Much later on I was to see this as an
avenue, a Kievan Champs-Elysées, bordered with tall apartment-
houses and fine, large, modern shops. But in my childhood's days
we would follow the Kreshchatik so as to get down from our
hilly city to the river-side.

A statue of St Vladimir, cross in hand, dominated the river's
loop. The sails of the Yacht Club vessels would move gracefully
in the fresh wind.

The Dnieper rolls a majestic flood. How apt are Gogol's
words:

'The Dnieper is very splendid when the weather is calm for
then it rolls its water with an easy, placid grace. The Dnieper
does no work. It disturbs not the stillness of forest or hill.'

Long, flat islands, covered with reeds, emerge from the great

stream. The one they call the Turkhanov was my favourite.
One of my childhood's delights was to get hold of some old
fishing-boat and make my way over to this island. And there,
amid the tall grasses and brakes, I would lie down at full length
on the sand . . . then I was off for the great adventures of my
dreams. The water around me was like a threatening presence.
I was encircled. Never should I be able to escape. I would have
to invent a new life where everything would have to be discovered,
a life on a finer and more heroic scale. I would gaze at the masses
of logs floating ceaselessly past. Sometimes there would come
a long raft, the home of the lumbermen who guided the drifting
masses of timber. And I would dream of lives also wafted along.
My isle became a raft gliding away to infinity.

I would remain thus for hours. I was not of course really
thinking, but visions, images, informed me. I was possessed.
I would become absorbed watching the flight of birds—vultures
and eagles. When they glided or hovered before they swooped
down to earth, I was impelled to muse on the intoxication of
space. I would remain lying on the sands until evening so that
I could gaze again at the stars which in the sombre sky promised
me access to other worlds.

I spent all my childhood at Kiev. I did not even accompany
my mother when she and all the household went to stay in the
Crimea. I left the city only when we all went to pay a visit to
my grandfather's country estate. Our house had a very large
garden where I felt very much at home. I still remember the
gigantic lime-tree there. I adored that tree.

What joy and excitement there were when we set out for my
grandfather's house. It lay about forty miles from Kiev and was
a real country seat, almost a *château*, and was surrounded by its
farms. It was situated, moreover, on the ancient caravan-
route linking east to west. My mother's ancestors had, in former
days, worked some of the Caspian Sea salt-deposits and salt
was carried by ox-cart to the interior of Russia and towards
western Europe. All this, for our childish imagination, was a
world full of adventure while the vast, boundless countryside
heightened our sensitiveness to impressions. My grandfather
had, a number of years before, done much to modernise his
farms since he was remarkably well aware of what the future
would demand. He had delivered to him German machines—the
first—and neighbouring landowners would come and borrow

these as they had formerly borrowed horses and oxen. Each time we arrived for the holidays we would admire afresh these marvellous machines.

Twelve uncles and aunts composed a company of grown-ups and they added to our childish pleasures. I can still see four young maid-servants engaged in dressing my aunts' hair for some party or other.

It was in this setting that I experienced no doubt the most vivid emotions of my childhood. It was then that became fixed in my mind an unforgettable picture of our country—the vast plain, the fields of wheat dotted with cornflowers and poppies and stretching to infinity ... the long waning of the days and the melancholy. I can still hear the singing of the girls as they came in from the fields when the day's work was over and then there were the voices of the young men echoing after supper and from afar off in the night. I would stay for long listening to these. My heart was full of passionate longings fumbling to find their purpose.

Then there was the life of the forest—silence and murmurings—what a lot I discovered there! And the wind on the plain and the scents that so attracted me, scents of the countryside wafted along by every breeze—honey and wild camomile flowers—a mingled odour I can never forget. And above all there was the immense presence of the earth itself which I fancied breathed like a living thing.

One exceptional event cast a supernatural light over my welter of emotions. One evening my father came and carried me out onto a balcony where my mother and my brother Leonide were. Without saying a word my father pointed up to a sky spangled with a myriad stars and where I soon noticed a star larger and more brilliant than any other. It was a flaming mass with a streaming tail rushing across the celestial vault. I was immediately filled with awe akin to sacred terror. We said not a word. At other balconies down below the house everyone was watching, masters and servants. Far off a dog howled. I was five years old and can still remember the fear that gripped me, a sort of communion with the terror of the earth itself, of trees and beasts and men. Panic terror, if such there be, at a sign born of the earth but which nonetheless announced some reality of this earth. The star vanished behind the forests of fir and oak that on the horizon merged into the black night. It was much later on I heard that I had witnessed the passage of Halley's comet. Its orbit should bring it back in 1986. Sometimes I feel sure I shall see it again.

I already suspected there was at my side the fairy that has accompanied me all my life long. A generous fairy that bears gifts but that also harries me as much as she spoils me.

2

LOVE AND DEATH

Later on, much later on, when I was already in France I came across a picture-book for young people. The impression this book made on me remains vivid in my memory. It was an impression that aroused a feeling of uneasiness and at the same time struck me as revealing the tragedy of a whole generation. The volume was made up of a number of articles, coloured illustrations representing various scenes of daily life—a view of a living-room in the evening, a return from hunting—peaceful family-life in fact. At the foot of each page was the word 'continue' and then you had to raise a flap that covered only the middle register of the picture. The upper and lower parts of course remained unchanged but when the flap was turned up, you suddenly passed from one world to another. The leggings of the happy sportsman showing his bag to the assembled company were transferred into those of a soldier confronted with his ravaged, deserted home. Then, again, the curl of smoke that denoted a cheerful home life was transmuted into fumes rising from ruins. The tractor's tracks became those of a tank crushing out a joyful past. At the foot of each new scene was the word 'After'. By such pictures children were learning of war—'Before' and 'After'—the ruin of happiness and childhood.

If I remember this picture-book so well it is because it reflected my own childhood. I have said it was happy, and so it was until, in August 1914, some angel turned the page. The setting remained the same but the whole scene was abruptly distorted. War. It was as though this one word had sufficed suddenly to change all the colour of our days. A shadow fell across what had been carefree existence. A menace with an alien face hovered over our happiness. Oh, things did not at once take a tragic turn. The unknown horror, as a matter of fact, lent a new thrill to our lives. As though the better to stress what was to follow, we all agreed to meet our confused fears with exaltation, with enthusiasm.

As Raymond Radiguet—whom I was to know later on—said so aptly in *Le Diable au Corps*: for those who are quite young, war-time is first and foremost vacation-time. The trammels of everyday life are loosened. Older people are so preoccupied with other cares that they lessen their vigilance. Dreams at long last may become realities. We had been so excited by the departure of the grown-ups that my brother Vassili and I determined to follow their example. So we set off on an escapade which we hoped would lead us to the armies. In great secrecy and after thrilling searches we got together a collection of objects we thought indispensable for our exploit—biscuits, Finnish knives, water flasks and some Austrian bayonets—first trophies from the front . . . then I was caught crouched pitifully in a train just as it was leaving. I was taken back and there, for the first and last time, thoroughly thrashed.

During those fine autumn days my new liberty sometimes weighed down so heavy on me that I felt out of things. Older people had their own world, their enthusiasms, their anxieties, their tasks. I had nothing but immense, vague longings. Then I would climb up to the Terrace of the Tsars or go near to the Vydubetski monastery on a sheer cliff beside the Dnieper's banks. There I would remain gazing at the river. By now a new passion had seized on me and was holding me enthralled—a passion for books and reading. I would repeat to myself, and in various versions according to my fancy, the *byliny*, the Russian medieval verse-chronicles which are more or less our *chansons de geste*. These *byliny* were about the only subjects that interested me at school.

The first convoys of wounded were now beginning to arrive from the front. Everything took on a different face. The streets were filled with officers and men, on crutches, their heads bandaged. Our school was turned into a base-hospital. Enthusiasm died down when stark reality showed itself. Real war and its ugly visage had now impinged upon our daily life. The tram-cars were used to transport the wounded. It was decided we should remain after school-hours both to make bandages and to help as far as we could in caring for the wounded. The first soldier I saw with gaping wounds made me want to vomit. I was not yet ten years old. Bad news began to trickle through from the front. Our armies had been checked and were in retreat. Austro-German troops were approaching Kiev. Confusion spread. I tried to escape from all these dreadful happenings—and indeed from all thought of them—by taking refuge in music. After playing the violin I had taken to the piano that year and alone at this instrument I would give myself up entirely to those emotions, void of any precise content, which are typical of a soul in formation.

The murder of Rasputin in December 1916 was hailed with joy. All well-disposed people were now quite sure that the Tsar and Russia would be freed from the evil spirit that had been responsible for all the confusion, all the reverses. I thought Prince Yusupov who had done the deed was a hero, the instrument of destiny. Now our country would tread the road to victory. Alas, the ills were too deep-rooted. Revolution was inevitable.

This is no place to recount the story of the Russian Revolution. But I would like to say something of the sights and sounds that impressed the mind and moved the heart of a quite young boy. The news of the first revolution and of the Emperor's abdication was greeted with delight. I can still remember the beaming faces. Strangers would embrace one another in the streets as at Eastertide. The *Marseillaise* blared out everywhere. Everyone thought we were on the eve of a new era. We were proud that no bloodshed had marred a revolution in which all classes were united. It would lead Holy Russia to victory.

Once again all these hopes were swept away by harsh reality.

The government was disorganised both by Kerensky's severe decrees and by his feebleness in the face of Lenin's exhortations to systematic violence . . . then came the October revolution effected by the workmen's and soldiers' soviets. And this time there was bloodshed. Panic and anarchy reigned. The first actual proofs we saw of these were when hordes of soldiers came streaming back from the front. Like an irresistible lava-flow they swept over the country. They had slaughtered their officers and filthy, famished and tattered they poured in eager to obey the objurgations Lenin had bellowed at them. 'Steal what has been stolen' resounded from the official platforms. The peaceable citizens of Kiev began to realise that the changes were to be much more radical than they had ever dreamt of . . . fear gripped the population.

Gangs of soldiers whose units had fled from what had been once the front, straggled about all over Kiev. They were the masters of the situation. They were certain of immunity and spent most of their time in debauchery and brutal assaults. One day as I was on my way home from school I met a gang of soldiers who had long since ripped off their epaulettes. They shouted at me to pull off at once the silver badge we wore on our caps. It was the imperial eagle with intertwined oak-leaves. For them a Tsarist symbol. The coarseness of their language, and also a feeling of loyalty to my school, made me abruptly refuse. In fact, I still felt in the bottom of my heart loyalty to the Tsar and the Tsarevitch of whom I had once caught a glimpse when I was quite small. The soldiers beat me up and tore off the badge. I managed to get home but I was covered in blood.

In the space of two years our beautiful city, so proud of its history, changed masters no less than eighteen times. First there were the Germans and then the Bolsheviks; after that Petliura's People's Autonomous Ukrainians; these were followed by the aristocratic Ukrainian autonomists, then the Tsarist Whites, Wrangel's and Denikin's United Russia forces, and finally the Poles. All, in their turn, seized and ceded the city. With each change of course there were pillage, reprisals, executions. The reprisals however did not last long. If one hid for a few days one was saved. At the beginning sometimes some enthusiasm was excited—most often aroused by a hope that the worst horrors that had ravaged Petrograd and Moscow might be spared us—that some reason for going on living might be found. Then, with the passing of time and from bitter experience, the inhabitants of Kiev adopted a simple philosophy which might be summarised thus: any troops whatever they might be that occupied the city had only one aim and object—pillage and murder. The sole problem for each of us was the problem of how to keep alive. From then on things were worse in a general atmosphere of depression, resignation and universal corruption.

It was at this time I saw Trotsky. What struck me most about him was his physical type—a very marked profile, a black and

fuzzy head of hair, thick, cruel lips, a straggly beard—and a
beribboned pince-nez. But even more than his physical appearance what I remember most vividly was the ardour, the tenacity
with which he egged on the people to murder. They called him
the 'Red Napoleon'. By very harsh measures—going as far as
decimation—he did, however, establish an appearance of order
amid anarchy.

To add to all the other miseries, sickness now began to spread.
Epidemics broke out. Typhoid fever took a terrible toll. The
hospitals had to turn away patients and it was no uncommon
thing to see wraith-like figures writhing in agony and dying in
the streets.

I am not recalling these scenes because of any morbid taste for
horrors. I mention them in order to convey to what an extent
death became familiar and contact with the dead a daily occur-
rence.

My grandfather was arrested and imprisoned at the Cheka
headquarters in Sadovaya Street. One day when my mother and
I went there I wandered off to explore the upper floors. On
peering out of a window I saw something I have never forgotten.
In the courtyard, Chekists, looking like conscientious workmen,
were piling up bloody corpses of their victims into a truck that
was already half-filled. The truck would then be driven quite
openly through the streets where no one would pay the slightest
attention to it. So resigned had the people of Kiev become and
so inured to such sights.

And, as a commentary on these atrocious scenes, I will just
state that out of about two hundred comrades of my own age
who were the companions of my youth, three only survived the
tragedy of the revolution. Cerna, one of them, now, strange to
say, sells dancing-shoes in Paris. Then there were my brother
Vassili—who later on sought refuge in France—and myself.
And I may add that these terrible memories date from a time
when I was from twelve to sixteen years of age.

Those corpses piled up like logs of wood, my grandmother
burned alive in her home, the tears of mothers, death always at
one's elbow and encountered every minute—such was the setting
of my youthful days. At an age when, it is true, one is fortified
by the obstacles one surmounts, death was my companion.

So close a companion indeed that sometimes death seemed to
be but an illusion. For instance, one day I was in a concert-

hall and well hidden in a crowd of civilians and bedraggled soldiers. We were watching a conjuror's act. The man was in evening-dress and was firing a pistol at his wife. She, of course, was never touched by the bullets. Sitting next to me was a young sailor, a very good-looking lad with bare chest. He wore only sailor's trousers and a jacket that did not hide his tattoo-marks. On his head was a little hat and he had on his arms a number of gold bracelets. He sat staring at the stage and apparently fascinated by the act. Suddenly he pulled out his revolver and, as though to prove whether the apparent miracle was a real one or not, he shot the woman dead. The crowd did not budge, it seemed stupefied, while the sailor, his eyes quite expressionless, seemed little by little to realise what he had done. Just out of curiosity he wanted to make sure whether he was really witnessing a miracle or not . . . such must have been his derisory self-justification for his deed. Finally, in nightmare silence, he got up and left the hall.

But love went with death. Fourteen, fifteen, sixteen years of age amid the licence and frenzy of civil war. As I think back to what I was then, love seems to me to have been like a great realm of purity amid the follies of war and bloodshed. It is easy to imagine what a place love occupied in the life of a lad . . . all this, I must confess, rather astonishes me now. But the urge to love was not clearly understood by me. It was just life itself in all its essential purity surviving amid the omnipresence of death.

One day, however, a young officer I knew came to visit my father. Then all at once I perceived beside him a figure, a face and two blue-green eyes gazing with mute interrogation at me. It was a slender graceful figure like a vision in some fairy-tale. From then onwards the image of the Countess Julie Pagot, that was her name, took up its abode in me. Her gaze watched over me, she was like a light always there in the days and nights —the long nights of blood. She seemed completely inaccessible and I think it was her very inaccessibility that aroused me and attracted me to her. She was very exactly the lady of my thoughts and dreams—for whose sake I set myself tasks and tests.

We spent long evenings together destroying family papers which might have served to excite the Bolsheviks' fury against us. When I was near her I felt profoundly agitated. Julie, who certainly sensed this turmoil in me, pretended to notice nothing.

But on those evenings when we were going to meet she was enough of a coquette to deck herself in finery. She used a subtle perfume that went to my head. I realised well enough why I was so agitated. But who can say how timid a fifteen-year-old boy can be—and how sensitive also?

The other feminine figure of my adolescence was Assia. She was quite different from Julie and was the wife of a Soviet official who had been billeted on us. She was dark and pale of skin whereas Julie was fair and diaphanous. Assia was a typical—and beautiful—Ukrainian of the people. She had been ripened under the rays of a southern sun. But sometimes her face was disfigured by an expression of almost cruel greed. Desire burned within me. I began to dread sleep that exhausted me with dreams in which she came to torture me. While her bodily exuberance strongly attracted me, that look of greed frightened me. I was both provoked and repelled by the violence of her physical passions. I was torn by the twofold emotion which makes us desire what we despise. There is no great mystery about that for anyone who knows what torments are undergone by the sensitive. Furthermore, as regards both women, Julie and Assia, my upbringing had taught me that I was in danger of mortal sin, so I avoided contact with both and wrapped myself in that instinctive reserve which has been mine all my life long with regard to those who it seemed must make me lose my secret vigour.

So two influences were already my companions. One—black—death for ever present in my life, pursuing me and yet avoiding me. The other—white—love—as yet vague it is true—will to live, energy, impetus. All I had to do now was to give this influence shape and form . . . I was about to go and meet them.

3

THE DANCE FOR EVER

'The bells of his carriage sounded still more muted than they had six weeks earlier. Now on every side was shade and thick foliage. The young firs themselves had joined in the general harmony. Now their delicate and downy green serrated shoots did not detract from the beauty of the whole.'

Dreams open up paths different from those of real life which still evades young people. When I was young and surrounded on all sides by bloody atrocities I found refuge in reading. When the cruelties around me became too dreadful to bear, I had recourse to my truest and dearest friends.

One day the Soviets issued an order that all young men—no further details were given—born in the years 1903, 1904 and 1905 must present themselves on such and such a day, at such and such a time, on the Dnieper landing-stage. I was assigned to the vessel *Sverdlov*, formerly *Emperor*, but after some hours of navigation I was beset with a sombre presentiment. It did not deceive me. A little later the ship blew up and sank with all its young passengers. I jumped into the water and tried to swim to the bank. For a long time I struggled against the current in an effort to reach one of the long, rush-fringed sandy beaches that bordered the river. Finally I did touch land and sank down exhausted. When I finally did rise to my feet I saw I was quite close to a sandy hillock. It aroused my curiosity. I went over to it, scratched about a little—and then in my hands there was a human head. A Cossack's head shaven but for one lock of hair. A head freshly severed it seemed, since it had been preserved by the sand. For some minutes I stood there, petrified and with the head that might have been Taras Bulba's in my hands. I was quite alone with the sky, the water and the reeds. I was fifteen years of age.

It was at this time too that music invaded my soul. While I was at the University I had attended classes at the Conservatory of Music. But it was now that my musical taste was formed. Mozart I placed in the forefront of all composers. His music is mingled adolescence and maturity. Chopin, however, puzzled me. I was attracted by what I called the sensuality of his music, but because of this very quality, I put him on one side. I discerned in him a tendency to strike too high a note, too shrill. It was not music as I understood it in my heart but rather, I thought, passages from his private diary. But when I played Chopin, or listened to him being played, I no longer criticised. He was in me and I in him. I loved him.

I once wrote, and I think it is still true, that from my earliest childhood I had been nourished on Glinka and Borodin, but that the Russian composers left me indifferent. I did not fail to respond to some passages in *Boris Godunov*, but, generally speaking, Mussorgsky, Borodin and Rimsky-Korsakov were all alien to me. I think I did not find in them what ravished me in Pushkin and Mozart—that is a freedom from restraint, a luminosity of which I stood in such need at the age I was then. And what seems to me strange enough is that it is only today that I think I know them and really love them.

I had loved music from my earliest years and one of my great joys was to sit at my piano and play, for hours on end, some of the pieces I liked best. In music, as in books, I found a complete exhilaration that real life did not afford me. For long I thought of making a career as a musician, but then one day, after the occupation of the city by White troops, the Bolsheviks attacked again. The Tsarist forces had to fall back, but fifty pupils of our school, including myself, all in Sokol uniform, were attached to the 34th Siberian regiment of the White forces. It was a regiment which had had the honour of being decorated by General Bredov who awarded it the St George's Cross, our highest military distinction for valour. General Dragomirov intended to use us in the fighting. The Bolshevik machine-guns rattled and clattered. A hail of lead was mowing down everything living. Then at a few paces from us came the deafening thunder of an exploding shell. I was so stupefied by the violent shock that I hardly realised I had been half-buried in the sand that was spurting up all around. But there was a very sharp pain in my right hand and I saw it was all red, sticky with blood. It was my brother Vassili who saved me from the holocaust in which most of our comrades perished, beheaded by the Cossacks who charged with brandished sabres across the St Sophia square. When the first fear had died down in me all my thought was for my injured hand. . . . My hand . . . shall I ever be able to play the piano again? Shall I be mutilated for life?

When the city had capitulated I was, secretly, treated with such medicaments as were available. One could not risk any interrogations as to how I managed to get wounded. The shell splinter had cut so deep a furrow that my hand had to be stitched. Then just as I was beginning to get well again, gangrene set in. The wound had to be opened and the treatment began all over again. When I look at the scars I still bear, my mind goes back to the day which no doubt decided my future. I had to give up all thought of becoming a musician. My piano (and with what emotion I sat down to it once more) was henceforth just to be a friend.

Paradoxical as it may seem, our city of Kiev, so harassed by war in the years 1919 and 1920, was nevertheless from the artistic point of view rather favoured. This state of things was due, in the first place, to the past. Kiev, the chief city of the Ukraine, had always gloried in being a miniature capital of the arts. In my parents' eyes the theatrical season presented temptations likely to be harmful to youthful spectators. Therefore I remember all the more vividly the first play I was allowed to see. It was *Kean*. The first opera I was permitted to hear was Tchaikovsky's *Queen of Spades*. I also attended some of the concerts the great Chaliapin gave in our city. I was submerged by a flood of sound and colour. I was carried away by enthusiasm.

In the spring of 1920, my father, my brother Vassili and I —both of us having served in the White Army—had the best of reasons for fleeing from the Cheka, or at least for putting ourselves temporarily out of circulation. So we took refuge in the forests a good way off from the city. We lived in a wild countryside where an oppressive silence reigned. We wore unbleached linen shirts and let our hair grow long. It was only from time to time that I made furtive expeditions to the city—so as to keep in touch with the family.

One evening we got to a little township called Tarashcha. A detachment of Red cavalry was halted there. For their own amusement and that of the villagers, the soldiers held evening dances. These were accompanied by an orchestra of wind instruments and ended with carousels and deep potations.

The Great Russians would spring into frenzied *kamarinskaia* and the Ukrainians would leap into a wild *gopak*. I was thrilled. I followed each movement closely. Here then, were folklore dances performed with energy and skill, dances which later on the Moiseiev ballets were to reveal to the world. The leaps, the swoops, the human tops whipped around as though by a whirlwind, set my heart aflutter. Then, quite suddenly, the man-made tempest would die down into slow, graceful measures. I was enthralled as I watched each step. Something was at work within me. I was undergoing a transformation—though I did not realise it—at the sight of all these instinctive movements as yet unrefined by art.

Thus it was that little by little I moved forward to meet my real self. A feeling of power built up within me and the more it increased the greater became my distress. Not when I was alone with my friends the books or with my piano, but when I was plunged into what others called 'real life', for never had it appeared to me duller and more despicable.

However, the Russian state was being organised and Russia was becoming the USSR. The Bolsheviks had gained control of the whole country. The last White troops had laid down their arms and there was no more fighting after they left the Crimea. We, who hoped against hope for help from the Western Powers, were abandoned to ourselves. There was more emigration than had ever before been known in history. And now I was drafted into the Red Army and was to become the youngest *kraskom* to serve under the supreme command of Lenin.

I was nearly overcome with despair. I spent most of my time smoking. I rolled my own makeshifts and smoked and smoked until I was dizzy. For days on end I would roam about the streets of Kiev—often with some comrade or other. One day my companion said 'Suppose we go in?' as we passed the dancing-school of Bronislava Nijinska, the ballet-mistress of the Kiev Opera. 'It seems the girls are pretty and you'll see my sister dance.'

As I had nothing better to do, I said yes. . . .

I was dazzled. There before me in red-starred uniforms were Mme Nijinska's pupils, accompanied by a piano, and dancing to the music of Chopin and Schumann. I will not go into the details of the scene but say only that the memory of what I saw remains most vivid after a long lifetime. I had stepped out of a broken world where all was clamour and rage and fury and I was finding order and harmony, a real discipline my soul and spirit needed.

On my way home my thoughts were in a whirl. One thing however was clear. There was but one decision for me to take. I must join Mme Nijinska's school, the school of the great Nijinsky's sister. The next day she refused to have me. Her voice was harsh and her words few. But I was advised to apply to the conductor and musical director of the Kiev Opera, the accommodating Steiman whom the Soviet authorities regarded with a favourable eye. He was then very influential.

'Don't worry, Comrade Lifar,' Steiman told me; 'even if she won't have you in her school, you could work much better here. In fact, it is Mme Nijinska who directs my opera ballet.'

You can hardly imagine the odd crowd there was at this State ballet-school—young workmen, young villagers come from no one knew where, 'young ladies from the Kreshchatik, famished 'intellectuals' lured by some will-o'-the-wisp—such a collection could hardly be matched anywhere else in the world.

During my first try-out, Mme Nijinska wrote opposite my name on the report for the jury the word 'Hunchback'. This pitiless little word danced before my eyes long after I had produced a medical certificate attesting that I stood perfectly upright. The certificate had been drawn up by my regimental authorities when they detached me for artistic or university studies.

Though I worked ardently, eagerly, desperately, Mme Nijinska seemed of set purpose, to take no notice of me. But for her I felt not only respect and fear but even veneration from the moment I realised she was the sole possessor of a treasure I was determined at all costs to seize. I realised this still more acutely when, after a few months, whispered rumours began to circulate among the pupils. Mme Nijinska, with all her family, were planning to flee from the Soviet yoke and settle somewhere outside Russia. And, in fact, she did go off and leave us to ourselves. Were my chances of becoming a dancer once more in jeopardy? But I would not give up, and because I would not give up my union with the Dance was sealed for ever.

Bronislava Nijinska was the first woman creator and choreographer in the history of the Dance. Isadora Duncan had, indeed, touched on the principles of the aesthetic of the Dance but not on composition.

Bronislava, like her brother Nijinsky (for whom she was in addition to Diaghilev always the mistress of method, the spiritual guide, the directing intelligence), had belonged to the Imperial Dance School. In 1921 she left Russia and until 1924 she directed, as choreographer, the evolution of the *Ballets Russes*. During this period came the great revelations of Stravinsky's *Noces* (in 1923) and in 1924 of Poulenc's *Les Biches*. Then in 1925, but no longer for the *Ballets Russes*, there came the *Etudes* to Bach's music, the *Variations* of Beethoven and Chopin's *Concerto*. Among her discoveries, Bronislava influenced such outstanding dancers as Massine and Balanchine, and as far as I am concerned I must admit that it was not, at least initially, from Diaghilev, Massine or Balanchine but certainly from Bronislava Nijinska that I received the first 'sign' which is the origin of my faith in the Dance.

Bronislava, by her *method*, united closely form and emotion —and she was the first to do this. Under her direction gestures became signs, symbols. The Dance thus conquered its independence. It became a harmony of movement, something quite different from that produced by the traditional school technique.

In 1921 the 'New Economic Policy' made its appearance in Kiev. Commerce revived. The cafés opened their doors again. It was the heyday of the petty speculator. But Kiev seemed to live once more. However, this factitious restoration resulted really only in the city looking like a painted corpse. I longed to escape from such an existence and to find in the Dance 'the far-off cloister of activity and gentle passions'.

I worked alone and as a man possessed. Still, I did get encouragement from Nussia Vorobieva, Mme Nijinska's first pupil, and also from Davydoff, the great actor. For fifteen months I lived in fear. I forced myself to a most rigorous asceticism. I practised without respite. Alone in front of my looking glass, I competed with my double which, turn and turn about, I both hated and admired. It was the master and I was always the apprentice. Long before I met Cocteau, who was to become my friend, I was familiar with the theme of the mirror that attracted him so much, with the verity also of the artist and his double.

All this time, however, I was making progress.

I absorbed myself, too, in the history of the Dance. I followed it avidly from its sacred and informative origins—linked with Man's earliest lyric creations—right up to Serge de Diaghilev's *Ballets Russes* (rumours of whose triumphs in western Europe had filtered through to us) and to Nijinsky, Pavlova and Karsavina, the idols of European audiences. I imagined I was the first to know all this, to understand the Dance as an art related to Man's whole being and to his connection with the infinite and the divine. This belief of mine served to reinforce my resolve. So it was, in fact, through an illusion, through a deception, that I attained to my own verity!

One day our school was in a hubbub. Mme Nijinska had just sent a telegram which I have kept. It read:

'S. P. Diaghilev asks for Mme Nijinska's five best pupils to complete his troupe.'

They were chosen. But the fifth did not turn up. I was so enthusiastic that I managed to carry the day for myself. I was to leave with the others.

I will not attempt to describe the hardships we underwent, nor the anxiety and the dangers.

I will pass over all these things which my friend Joseph Kessel has depicted in his book *La Faim au ventre*.[1] In fact I will not recount the story of my flight. It was as nothing since I now had an object in life.

On 13th January I was in Paris—and stood before Serge de Diaghilev.

I had told only one person I was leaving—my mother. It was to be the last time I was ever to see her. At the moment of farewell she blessed me. In her eyes was so agonised a look that it was to haunt me. It was a look so candid, so sad, so disquieting, that it strangely resembled the gaze of a doe that, when I was quite a small boy, I had killed with a gun surreptitiously borrowed from my father. She had been drinking quite close to me. Hers was the only life I have ever taken, for I shall never forget that, at the moment of death, and with her eyes veiled in tears, she licked my hand.

[1] Of which I have also told in my book *Du Temps où j'avais faim*.

✿ 4 ✿

DIAGHILEV AND THE *BALLETS RUSSES*

My life's prologue was over. It seems to me that even then, though I was swept along by the flood of events, I realised this in a confused sort of way, and I also felt that my existence would be like a performance which would be carried along by its lyric quality but which an interior dramatic power would organise into quite distinct acts.

I can still visualise that winter morning. Paris. After all we had lived through, only the heedlessness and the fervent curiosity of youth enabled us to support such contrasts. Only yesterday the Soviet world behind its barbed wires, then the great hubbub of the journey, death always present, and now in the milky, cold dawn an inscription in huge white letters on a sheet of blue enamel—Paris—Gare du Nord. . . . The Paris of those days, as I remember it more grey and white than now. The dark crowd milling along to work, the colourless sky, the icy streets, the trace of breaths in the air. Our fatigue. But peace. An unknown world. A slight apprehension. But we were ready for anything and hopeful. We were at once the objects of kind attentions we had not expected. The solicitude that surrounded us overcame the solitude of the immense city and the feeling I feared of being lost in an ocean of indifference.

In Poland I had joined up with Nijinska's other four pupils who were, with me, to enter Diaghilev's troupe. At five o'clock we were to appear before him. Until then we could collect ourselves.

At five o'clock we met in the Hôtel Continental where the Master had his headquarters. Everything there, even the green

M.V.—C

plants in the hall, dazzled me and appeared as the summit of
luxury and distinction.

Walter Nouvel, charming, simple and obliging, Diaghilev's
manager and collaborator, whom I was to get to know so well
later on, was waiting for us.

'Sit down gentlemen, Sergei Pavlovitch is coming.'

Sit down! I could not stay still in one place. I was shivering.
I was seventeen years old. I had come right across Europe. I
knew that all my future was in the balance.

In a small group of people walking towards us I made out a
man in a fur overcoat, a soft hat on his head. He seemed a
giant to me. He came forward swinging his walking-stick. A
Russian *barin* of a past age. In his rather fleshy face, under white
locks reminding one of a St Bernard dog, shone two friendly
brown eyes, eyes that expressed at one and the same time
vivacity, mildness and a kind of sadness. It was Diaghilev.
One could not doubt that for an instant. It is difficult to say
what this man meant for us. He was art incarnate. A man with
the power to change life, to transmute reality. The inventor,
the man we dreamed of having as master.

Diaghilev sat down and said a few words. Such was the
embarrassment I felt that I could not make out anything of his
little speech but the light in his strangely limpid and youthful
eyes set me at my ease when he made us speak. He asked for our
impressions of the country we had just left and which seemed to
us already at the other end of the world. However, while we
spoke to him of the Russia now closed to him for ever he sat
motionless. His eyes wore a far-away look, gazing beyond the
barbed wires of the Soviet frontier.

Then he brightened up. He seemed to have put behind him all
thoughts except those of the future, that is to say of work.

'The task is to astonish Europe,' he told us. 'What for instance can you do?' he asked the oldest of us. 'Can you do two
tours?'

They all wanted to speak at once, describe their abilities. I
kept silent.

'And you, young man, Mme Nijinska hasn't told me anything
about you.'

His velvety eyes rested on me. I could not utter a syllable.
It was my comrades who came to my assistance.

'Oh, he can do everything.'

The conversation then turned on financial questions. Diaghilev proposed a salary of 800 francs a month—times were hard—instead of the 1300 he had promised us. But, on the other hand, he made us a present of the money which had been advanced to us at Warsaw. Some of my comrades tried to get into a discussion, but with a vague and regal gesture accompanied by a distant yet beguiling smile, he cut short the discussion as unworthy of us.

'Trust me,' he concluded in a lordly tone, 'and tomorrow leave for Monte Carlo.'

Mimosas, palms, orange-trees bathed in sunlight. The sea. The boundless view. The paradise of the *dolce vita*. It is not worth while describing how excited a young man could be on discovering all this after an escape from hell. So different was the present from anything I had known in my far-away home, even before the war, that I just could make no comparisons. I did not think of the past. And then the future was before me and the beauty of my surroundings incited me to enthusiasm and to work.

There was, however, one thing that made me sad—the jealousy of my comrades, the lack of warmth in their welcome. I realised soon enough that the troupe was a very tightly closed little society and even the decision of the great Master did not suffice to get one adopted into it. The members of the company were used to living in close contact with each other and newcomers were treated as intruders. In fact they still lived under the old regime.

One day Mme Nijinska, before watching me begin my exercises, asked me:

'Tell me, Lifar, can you really dance?'

What? had all my efforts at Kiev been useless? Did she not remember them at all? Was I just insignificant or was she indifferent, even hostile? I was on the brink of despair.

But I clenched my teeth. There was work to be done. I must take advantage of Diaghilev's absence to prepare for the examination he would put us through. Alone, since that was what my fate seemed to decree, I slaved away.

When three weeks had passed, Diaghilev arrived and he soon asked to see the newcomers. We had hoped very much to perform our exercises before him alone, but no, the whole troupe got permission to come with him. He was seated on a flap-chair in the middle of the studio, the members of the company farther away behind him.

The Master's face at once darkened. Hardly had the first of us presented ourselves before him than he got up abruptly, let his seat slam back behind him and in a dead silence left the hall.

We heard only some explosions of his baritone voice.

'Crass ignorance . . . you've fooled me . . . let them go back to Russia . . .' he bawled out at Mme Nijinska who had followed him. All the same he let himself be calmed down and agreed to come back and watch the second part of our exercises. He looked on with a sulky face. Now it was my turn. A little glint came into his eyes. When I had finished, there was a few moments' silence. Then Diaghilev declared:

'All right, let them stop then. I am sorry for this boy and I've got faith in him.'

It was, perhaps, the first time for a long while that a weight was lifted from my breast. At last I seemed to breathe more freely.

Then, as he got up, he added, as though to himself, and in a lower tone of voice which, all the same, sounded through the studio:

'He'll be a dancer.'

'He'll be a dancer', and it was Diaghilev who had said that, who had said it publicly—about me.

This is no place to paint a full-length portrait of Serge de Diaghilev whose life, works and legend I have recounted in another book.

But it is known that this incomparable individual was then in full possession of his powers and in all his glory. He was for us, as I have said, Art personified. When he was a young man he produced the following admirable sketch of himself in a strikingly just description he wrote to his step-mother:

'I am   (1) A charlatan but one full of vivacity.

          (2) A great charmer.

          (3) An insolent individual.

          (4) A man of much logic and few principles.

          (5) A being afflicted, it would seem, with a total lack of talent.

'Furthermore, I think I have found my real vocation—to be a Maecenas, and for this I have everything needful except money, but that will come.'

Diaghilev was, first and foremost, a man who awakened in others sensitiveness, talents, forms of art, a taste for creation, for collaboration the better to create.

He had been a patron of Russian art. He had left his country where he was not understood. He originated the famous *Ballets Russes*. He travelled all over the world and carrying with him new artistic thrills. He was the renovator of the Dance. He revealed such incomparable dancers as Fokine, Nijinsky, Karsavina, Pavlova, Massine, Spessivtzeva. He was determined not to allow the Dance to remain the simple amusement it had been at the end of the last century. His desire was to make the Dance an artistic spectacle complete in itself. He associated with it musicians (he discovered Stravinsky and Prokofiev) and painters. He was the first to commission décors from such artists as Braque, Picasso, Derain and Matisse. He associated poets with the Dance. From Cocteau he took the theme of *Le Dieu bleu*.

We did not, of course, know all this in detail, nor were we aware of the thunder-clap which had resounded over Europe when he arrived in Paris after having left Russia, where he had been refused permission to put on the *art nouveau* spectacle he had prepared ... the first performance of which was to take place on 17th May 1909 at the Châtelet theatre in Paris. But we did catch some echoes of his fame and we were convinced that since this fame was a living thing all around us, the sole hope for an artist to express himself vividly was to adopt the conceptions of this man.

So I stayed on at Monte Carlo, the second cradle of the *Ballets Russes*. My childhood, which had been so puerile, had come to an end and now, guided by Diaghilev, I entered upon a new period of my existence—adolescence. When I now compare the seven years I was to live with the *Ballets Russes* (from 1923 to 1929) with those endured during the torments of revolution (from 1917 to 1923) I can discover one fundamental difference. The spirit of adventure which had been, earlier on, maybe my most marked trait, became little by little alien to me. For a time, at least, I made myself more docile, less independent, less daring perhaps, or at any rate daring in a different manner.

Diaghilev's few words had given me confidence. But there remained the solitude, the daily task—and day after day when

sometimes doubt would creep back. In the eyes of all the troupe
Diaghilev was a sort of inaccessible divinity, kindly and irritable by turns. He was feared. Sometimes, accompanied by
his suite, he would come and watch our rehearsals. He would
sit down, look at us dancing—and express his dissatisfaction.
Praise from him was exceedingly rare . . . then he would go off.
We had no other contact with him. His orders were transmitted
either through Boris Kochno, his secretary, through Grigorieff
the stage-manager, through Walter Nouvel, our director, or,
again, through Kremnev, the oldest member of the company.
They formed part of the court around the sovereign. A court I
was to get to know better later on, but whose members then
kept themselves at a far distance from the *corps de ballet* and
seemed to us aureoled with glory in a world we could not
reach.

I however did not want to sink myself into the bosom of the
company, as did my comrades in evasion. No doubt this reserve
on my part might be attributed to misplaced pride, but perhaps
one might try to understand the sensitiveness of a youth who
had already seen so much, had taken part in so many experiences calculated to upset the balance of a youth and who had
chosen a personal means of expression and who furthermore
most certainly had the ambition to stand one day on his own
feet. Maybe the others cherished like aspirations but they were
either older or did not react in the same way—and that was all.
In any case, to tell the truth, from the technical and professional
point of view they were all in the same boat. However, judged
by professional standards the troupe was on a very high level,
though it was far from being what I had imagined at Kiev.
Customs borrowed from the days of serfdom still prevailed.
The leading dancers made the boys of the *corps de ballet* run
their errands for them! This veritable free city, the company of
the *Ballets Russes*, had its own life peculiar to it and the members when they were not rehearsing thought only of gambling,
drinking and flirting in the most commonplace manner imaginable. The only event lending some animation to this existence
would be the marriage of a *danseuse* followed by her departure
and the appearance of a new face. As soon as the neophyte
entered the troupe they had to know all about him. His good
qualities and his defects were analysed and his very soul must
be probed often in the most incongruous fashion. Was such a life

in common really essential for the uniformity of a troupe? I had formed quite another idea of our art and of the manner of living of those who might serve it.

Diaghilev, after having encouraged me in the way I have described, paid no more attention to me than to my comrades. Mme Nijinska thought nothing more of us once we had been definitely accepted as her pupils and she left us to our own devices. M. Grigorieff showed nothing but indifference.

The members of the troupe looked condescendingly down upon us. We had come from Soviet lands and it seemed to them that we did not know how to dance at all—which was quite true.

I was eighteen and all I had was memories. I was so lonely and desperate that I began to ask myself why I did not go back to Kiev. But I soon put such thought away from me. This loneliness was good for me, it was no longer a banishment, but a way out, something I was going to utilise. Thus I was forced to devote myself to my only real mistress, the Dance. And I threw myself into it with all the strength I had. After I had looked at the tomb of the Antibes dancer during an outing I said to myself, 'At least I would like to dance *one* day . . .' (see p. 322).

The first ballet I had to study was *Noces* by Stravinsky and the work was by no means easy. What I had to depend on first of all was my will-power and it served to excite my enthusiasm. I strove with all my might to discover the meaning of the music which, however, pleased me, spoke to me . . . and luckily my natural sense of rhythm came to my aid.

Sometimes Diaghilev appeared and watched the rehearsals. He was capable of ordering the same step to be repeated twenty times . . . we were all plunged into apprehension . . . he was the wall against which leaned the ladder, up which those could climb who wanted to view life from higher up.

I was determined anyway to produce an impression on Sergei Pavlovitch, to play at least decently the modest role I had been given. And to this end I formed the habit of going alone each night to rehearse on the point of Monaco rock. The lighthouse beams sweeping the black sky transformed the night into a Faustian laboratory as huge as the universe. The beams kept time with my movements and crackled a spark of madness over my head. The sea was there to remind me of Kiev, of the mirror in which I used to confront myself.

The *Noces* rehearsals took place under the supervision, indeed under the direction, of Stravinsky himself. At first he would give a few hints of a general nature; then, gradually, he would liven up, take off his coat and sit down at the piano. While he played he sang in a cracked voice. One might think that this would have been disagreeable, but it enchanted us. He managed to get over to us his own excitement, the sense of his creative power—and we set to work to dance in earnest.

The first time I saw Stravinsky was in the low, dark, damp rehearsal-room of the *Ballets Russes*. I was astonished by his appearance. He was thin and he stooped. His head was rather bald and his great forehead betokened intelligence. I wondered who such a monkey could be—he wriggled about, thumped the keys, panted, made up for missing chords by kicks on the pedal . . . or to keep up the tempo he would bring his elbows crashing down on the piano.

It was fascinating. Sometimes he would abruptly break off . . . and then the storm of sound would start up again louder than ever . . . it was miraculous, it was diabolical . . . it was very Russian also. As the artists could make out only with great difficulty the sounds and accents of the score he had a barrel-organ sent down from Paris and on its rolls was inscribed the music of the ballet. We then had the extraordinary spectacle of an accompanist transformed into a mechanic and turning the handle!

Later on, I often visited Stravinsky either at Nice, or in Paris, rue Saint-Honoré, or again at London in Albemarle Street. What struck one most about him was something which was all at once bourgeois, mystical, and monarchistic. On the walls would be ikons and portraits of the Emperor Nicholas II and his august children.

Sometimes I would go and spend the evening in his studio at the Salle Pleyel. And there, surrounded with brass and percussion instruments, he would compose. I used to feel I was in Faust's laboratory and was amazed at his experiments with accords, dissonances, harmonies and counterpoint. I was carried away into an ecstasy I have never experienced elsewhere save in Picasso's studio.

Stravinsky was very satisfied with the choreography of *Noces*. Mme Nijinska had won at the expense of Mme Goncharova. It was the former's stylised conception of Russian folklore which had been adopted and this was to become a lasting influence on our company. The aesthetic of *Noces* was composed of a combination of brusque movements at right or acute angles with harmonious groupings. The leading theme of the ballet and maybe its most happy revelation was a *pas de bourrée* which the artists danced on the tips of their toes, thus achieving a longer silhouette while the man danced stressing the accents of the music. The slow Botticelli-like undulation of the groups was very successful.[1] Diaghilev took notice of my work and one day said to me as I passed near him after a rehearsal:

'Very good, young man, go on like that, work in the right way.'

So I became more and more eager. On 13th March and in his presence I did a *double tour* in the air. On 22nd March an *entrechat-six*. I caught a look of approbation in his eye. My hopes were growing that one day I might get somewhere. A little later Diaghilev suggested I be given a role and as Mme Nijinska objected, he replied:

'All right, let Slavinsky dance. I agree with you. Lifar has still got plenty to learn, but it will soon be his turn. You'll see, Bronia, it's another Nijinsky we've got there.'

We went back to Paris. I took a room in a small hotel, rue aux Ours. I lived in the simplest possible way. Later, when I was lodging in another little room in the rue de la Victoire, there could be no question of my doing any exercises at all there, so I would go down and work on the pavement. In the rue Taitbout the ladies in the brothels would peer at me from behind their shutters and call out encouragements; they were at first a little astonished and then delighted. Indeed, I worked all the harder so as to elicit their bravos. These 'boarders' composed my first public which I was delighted to please. After all, it was a Parisian public and Paris was in my eyes already the sole and unique capital where one might meet success—or dire failure.

I earned eight hundred francs a month and I had to buy the uniform we wore. It was composed of black golf-knickers with five buttons up the sides, a white shirt with sleeves turned up at the elbows, white stockings and black dancing-shoes.

[1] The sketches which Goncharova made after the creation of this ballet caused her later on to be credited with this stylisation of folklore. The truth is, however, as I have stated, that she was opposed to this stylisation and only reproduced by her pen the version that Nijinska wanted.

These latter were supplied by the management at the rate of one pair every fortnight.

At the time I am referring to, the Paris season was at its height and *Noces* met with considerable success at the Gaité-Lyrique where our company danced. We rehearsed at the theatre but the musical renderings often took place in the salons of the Princesse Edmond de Polignac. The season's programme included, in addition to *Noces, Pétrouchka* and the *Danses polovtziennes*. One rehearsal of *Pétrouchka* stays in my mind. In the first tableau I had improvised the role of an urchin with a concertina and I did it maybe with some skill since Alexandre Benois came up to me and said:

'I have come to greet you and to compliment you on that role, since for an artist there is no insignificant part.'

I thought for one instant that the doors to Diaghilev's court stood half-open before me.

So I kept on trying. Sergei Diaghilev appeared at times to take some interest in me, but my extreme shyness prevented me from replying as I should have done on the few occasions when he deigned to speak to me. One day when he hailed me as I was on my way back from Monte-Carlo plage, I moved away. He broke out:

'If I stopped you, young man, and if I want to speak to you, it is not in my own interest, believe me, but in yours. I have been noticing you for some time now and you've got more talent and enthusiasm than your comrades. I want to help you to develop that talent, but you won't recognise this and you shy away from me like a wild animal. Take your choice. Do you imagine that I am going to implore you? You are making a mistake, young man. Well, what are you waiting for? You can go home.'

How solitary my life was! And now I had found the means of alienating Diaghilev who no longer glanced at me and whom I now met solely in the company of the 'Englishman' Anton Dolin who had just joined the troupe. And all this had happened without my winning the favour of the other dancers who regarded me with increased indifference the more progress I made. But I worked hard. I felt in an obscure way that my hour would come and several events contributed, moreover, to convince me of this.

I got the impression Diaghilev was testing me. He gave me

the role of the dying slave in *Shéhérazade*. My delight was great. On the day of the performance I got to the theatre extra early. I joined up with the supers and rehearsed with them.

The brief episode of the slave's death was to be a whole pantomime in which I wanted to express bravery and contempt of death. Towards the end of the ballet I went on the stage, moved through the group of sabre-armed supers and made a gigantic bound, entered the Negroes' tent, came out on the other side, went on up the staircase and then instead of dying on the steps I rolled down the whole flight—to the great alarm of the audience—and came to expire near the footlights. Hardly had I got back into the wings when I saw Grigorieff running towards me. 'I'll never forgive you for that bit of clowning. Just try once again to spoil the roles of two artists . . . and wait a little to see what Sergei Pavlovitch is going to say to you, he's furious and you know what sort of a man he is.'

So that was how it was. Then Diaghilev appeared but he seemed more pensive than angry.

'What you've just done, young man, is entirely unartistic, very immature, very callow. I'm sorry you used your talents to wreck the ensemble instead of supporting it by exercising rigorous self-discipline.'

Then he went on to talk about the significance of the action of the whole ensemble. He made some pertinent remarks about the theatre in general . . . such as this: 'The artist with a secondary role must play his proper part; he may play it to perfection but in the background and without trying to eclipse the leading roles and to attract the attention of the audience away from the main action.'

He chided me indeed, but what I heard most was the phrase 'your talents' and what I noticed most was the observant look he gave me. And there was something else that did not deceive me. Diaghilev's collaborators began to take notice of me, to treat me with vigilant attention. And this was at once the cause and the consequence of the confidence which, little by little, I was gaining deep down within me.

There has remained engraved in my memory one incident that happened in the theatre. We were not allowed into the auditorium during a performance. But one day when I was sitting in the stalls with Cocteau, Auric, Darius Milhaud, Braque and Picasso, Diaghilev suddenly appeared. He adjusted his eye-

glass, raised his other eyebrow and a nervous twitching contracted the right side of his face. He came towards us and said
to me in an icy tone:

'Unless I am much mistaken, young man, you have been a
member of my troupe for the last year and you might have
learned by now that paid places in the theatre are reserved
for members of the public, and not for artists of the *corps de
ballet.*'

During the interval I met him again in the hall. He thrust
me aside rudely:

'Once and for all, I forbid you to appear in the auditorium.
If you do not want to obey my orders, you are free to leave the
Ballets Russes, and then, if you wish to, you can come to the
theatre with M. Cocteau every night. I do not force anyone to
remain in my company.'

At first I was at a loss to understand Diaghilev's rage, especially as he was, at that time, giving me my first little role—
that of an officer in *Les Fâcheux,* a ballet by Georges Auric
based on Molière's play, and with scenery by Georges Braque.
But then I remembered Sergei Pavlovitch's annoyance when one
day as I was rehearsing alone some friends had come and were
overwhelming me with enthusiastic compliments.

A few days later Sergei Pavlovitch asked me to have myself
photographed in *Les Fâcheux*—for some book or other. And he
kept three of my photographs for himself. At nineteen years of
age one would have to be devoid both of intuition and sensitiveness not to have an inkling of a kind of power possessed, of
charm exercised—and I did not lack the one or the other.
And then, I had some taste for playing a part and without
that no one is an actor—or, in consequence, a real dancer.

We went off to Spain and were to give eleven performances at
Barcelona. I discovered Spanish music and it enchanted me.
In spite of the harassing days (in the afternoons we rehearsed
for the next Paris season and in the evenings we appeared on
the stage), at night I wandered about in the cabarets where
there was dancing and singing. In some of them, such as the
Casa Rosa, the Cuadro Flamenco and the Sevilla, one could
hear real artists. One evening three well-known figures came
into the Sevilla—Diaghilev with Dolin and Kochno. Sergei
Pavlovitch advised me to learn the dances of the country on
the spot.

After Spain we went to Holland. In Amsterdam I had another strange encounter with Diaghilev. On the very day of our arrival I rushed off to the Rijksmuseum. I was, as one often is at that age, devoured with a veritable passion for learning, for knowing . . . and there at last I beheld 'The Night Watch', 'The Lesson in Anatomy', 'The Syndics of the Cloth Hall'. Suddenly, there in front of the Frans Hals pictures were Diaghilev, Dolin and Kochno. When Sergei Pavlovitch noticed me, he could not hide his surprise. This lad from the *corps de ballet* had come alone, of his own accord, whereas Diaghilev had had to induce his companions to accompany him. Had I in some vague way counted on meeting him there? I do not think so. In any case I was already convinced that significant meetings come about only through art—and chance.

By May 1924 we were back again in Paris. We rehearsed at the Théâtre de Paris and it was there I made the acquaintance of Misia Sert and of Mlle Chanel who, with the Princesse de Polignac and Picasso, played decisive parts in the history of the *Ballets Russes*.

One day while we were rehearsing *Le Train Bleu*—music by Darius Milhaud and the theme Cocteau's—Misia Sert, Coco Chanel and Picasso noticed me dancing:

'That little Russian is charming,' said Misia Sert.

'There's your dancer,' added Coco Chanel, turning to Diaghilev.

Picasso opined: 'Your little dancer's figure is of ideal proportions.'

In those days I had but a slight inkling of the importance such remarks might have coming from such eminent persons.

'Oh, indeed, you don't think he dances too badly . . . your godson?' replied Diaghilev with feigned indifference. But all the same he turned a gaze full of pride towards me. From then on Coco Chanel and Picasso became my godmother and godfather in art.

Picasso's creative genius is of life's very essence.

Each time that I visited Picasso's studios—in the rue de la Boëtie, on the quai des Grands Augustins in Paris, or on the Californie at Cannes or at Notre Dame de Vie—I always found a convent-like or cathedral-like atmosphere where this new Faust's magic never failed to dazzle me. And I myself have been able to move Picasso who has always enthusiastically supported me in my choreographic experiments.

On 20th June, 1924, was the first performance of *Le Train Bleu*.
It was a well-merited triumph for Dolin. Before the dress rehearsal I had met Diaghilev at the Théâtre des Champs-Elysées.
He talked about me, over-praised me and assured me that I
was the most gifted of all his dancers, that I must keep my
career always in mind and therefore work very hard.

'I want to make you my leading dancer and I will manage it,
but, for the present, not a word of this to anyone.'

On 24th June I went to the meeting I had asked for; I had
not been able to sleep at all the night before . . . Diaghilev was
waiting for me in the hall. He was kindly and very pleasant.
His smile was one of goodwill. Tea was served.

'Well, what have you got to tell me?'

'Sergei Pavlovitch . . . I wanted . . . I wanted to thank you
. . . and say goodbye . . . I am leaving next week. . . .'

'Excellent, and where are you thinking of spending your
holidays?'

'Sergei Pavlovitch, it isn't that I am going off for two months
. . . but for good . . . I am leaving the *Ballets Russes*. . . .'

Diaghilev's face got scarlet . . . he grabbed hold of the tea-
table and threw it over amid a frightful crash of broken crock-
ery. Then without paying the slightest attention to the people
around us, he began to yell out:

'What have you got the nerve to tell me? I get you out of
Russia, I teach you how to dance, and now that I am counting
on you, you come and calmly tell me that you are going away.
You're nineteen years of age, you are just beginning to live. I
have told you that you have it in you to become *premier danseur*,
but you are mightily mistaken if you think you are already one.
Your future depends upon me . . . but what's the good? You
can go off, I don't like ungrateful people . . . you can go to hell!'

I was flabbergasted, for I realised that this anger was the
anger of someone in whose eyes one was of some importance.

He calmed down, was less harsh, talked about raising my
salary. . . .

'No, Sergei Pavlovitch, I haven't come to ask you for anything, but just to thank you and say farewell, I am going to
enter a monastery.'

Then something happened that was terribly distressing, Sergei
Pavlovitch let his head slump down on the table and he broke
into tears.

'There he is, the real Aliosha, for you are Aliosha, Aliosha Karamazov, my poor lad. And because of this silly and crazy hot-headedness of yours I like you all the more. But what's really the matter? Why bury yourself alive? Why say goodbye to life, to your abilities?'

I told him of my doubts, of my apprehensions, that I was only a zero, as he had just told me.

'Forget all that, I've got confidence in you, it was not for nothing that I spotted you from the very first. You'll be *premier danseur*. I'll do everything for that. I am ready to do anything for you—or rather for myself. At present you are the only person to keep me attached to the Ballet. Had it not been for you I would have already disbanded the troupe. . . . I want you to be another Nijinsky.'

I was much touched. There I was following my destiny once more . . . I would say as in a dream.

'Sergei Pavlovitch, if you think I am good for anything, send me to Italy, to Cecchetti, the man who taught Nijinsky and Pavlova. I want to try that out. If it does not come off, well then, so much the worse.'

Diaghilev leapt up. He was delighted.

'That's a stroke of genius!'

During the next few days he fitted me out from top to toe. He bought me books and even a straw hat that made people compare me ironically with Maurice Chevalier. Then he gave me a ticket for Turin and my passport with a visa. He had asked Mussolini for it. The Duce in his journalistic days had written articles on Diaghilev and the two men had kept in close touch.

Just at this time Diaghilev, on meeting Mme Nijinska one day, told her he was sending me to Cecchetti. She was much annoyed.

'Mark my words, never—you understand, never—will Lifar be *premier danseur* or even solo dancer.'

'Ah, you think so? Well, I'll tell you he *will* be *premier danseur* and in fact also choreographer.'

'Will you bet on it?'

They wagered a case of champagne. Diaghilev won, but he never got the wine. Nijinska had left the *Ballets Russes*.

I set off on 6th July. I spent the night packing and had no time to sleep. About five o'clock in the morning my door opened and in came Diaghilev, his heavy walking-stick in his hand.

We went out to have coffee. Then we drove to the station.
Diaghilev came into my compartment.

'Now, don't say anything for a minute or so . . . collect your
thoughts . . . and I'll give you my blessing . . . for your studies
and for all good things.'

He made a hurried sign of the cross over me . . . and then
left me alone. I saw him move away . . . disappear. Once more
I was by myself, faced with the unknown.

❧ 5 ❧

PARIS AND THE SEAL OF SUCCESS

Those were months I remember as a tangle of work, solitude, travelling and sunlight. The first thing I did when I got to Turin was to call on Cecchetti. I went to the theatre and there I found a little old man, all white and not at all imposing. He was the great, the only real, dancing master still living, the creator at St Petersburg of the Blue-bird in Petipa's ballet, the *Sleeping Beauty* of Tchaikovsky. I went up to Cecchetti and told him I was the pupil Diaghilev had sent him. At Diaghilev's name he smiled at me. It was the smile of a happy child. He told me to wait until his lesson was over. I remained and was able to witness a curious spectacle. The mild maestro became all at once a choleric old man who whistled the melody under his breath while he used his baton to beat time—and his pupils. They reacted by respectfully kissing the hand that struck them.

The very next day my life got organised around the lessons. Cecchetti told me I must work three hours a day—one hour alone and two in his class. Nijinska had not accustomed me to such long lessons and during the first few weeks I literally dropped from fatigue. From my first lessons I got back covered with bruises. Cecchetti was appalled by my hands. His teaching was that disarticulation of the arms and hands was just as necessary as that of the legs.

So there I was, nineteen years old and once again in an unknown city and alone—with my work. I knew absolutely no one and when the lessons were over I walked about a good deal all over the city. But, still, I spent most of my time in my own room. And even there I would have had nothing to do had it not been for the books Diaghilev had given me before I left Paris. Among them, in addition to Chekhov and Aksakov, there were copies of all the best contemporary Russian authors —Block, Ehrenburg, Remizov, Essenin and an essay by Stchegolev on the duel and death of Pushkin. This interested me very much and took me back in imagination to my childhood when I used to read and muse by the tumultuous waters of the Dnieper. At Turin, indeed, I lived as on a 'small island' pitilessly burned by the sun. I still have a vivid memory of those days of mingled boredom and passion drenched in sunlight while I devoured the novels from my far-off native land.

Little by little Cecchetti became attached to me and, I thought, began to consider me as a well-loved disciple on whom he founded great hopes. He knew that his own end was not far off and that with him would disappear all the old classical traditions, therefore he wanted to inspire me with them and thus succeed in perpetuating his science of the ballet.

Cecchetti was not a very cultivated man anyway in the general sense of the word. His sole interests were the Dance and his orchard. Nevertheless he had evolved very precise ideas about his art.

'Never forget,' he would say to me, 'that in this art we adore, to be persevering and even a little obstinate is a good thing. All the same exaggerated zeal turns into mania. Always work with devotion and strength of will, but never with exaggeration.'

He never allowed me, during the exercises, to push myself 'right to the end' but warned me always to keep a 'reserve' and to use this on the stage and only on the stage. He was very reserved about the 'soul' and 'sentiment' and considered that any 'exteriorisation of the soul' on the stage was a matter that demanded much delicacy and spiritual tact.

'Learn as I want you to,' he would often say, 'and dance as you can—as you yourself want.'

A week after my arrival I got a first letter from Diaghilev and I imagined that all at once Sergei Pavlovitch was with me, had come to join me in this unknown city.

'I got to Venice only yesterday and found your kind letter. I am very pleased by everything you tell me. There is only one point about which I am not pleased and that is the matter of your meals which you say dissatisfy you. You must eat well.

Pay attention to this. Write and tell me if you do any reading, if you have already sent any books back to Paris so that they can be exchanged for others and also whether you are receiving the [Russian] newspapers. Three-hour lessons are obviously a little long but you must strike the iron while it is hot. You have not much time. I would like to have news of you.'

Diaghilev was as preoccupied about my general education, the formation of my artistic taste in all fields, as he was about my progress in the art of the Dance. And it was with the view to my progress in both directions that Diaghilev had had the idea of my stay in Italy.

Later I got this note that made me jump for joy:

'Dear Serge, I shall be in Milan on Tuesday March 29th—I will leave in the morning at 9.25 and shall arrive in the afternoon at 3.5. You will take a second-class ticket and leave Turin at 10.50 in the morning and you will be at Milan at 1.30 in the afternoon. You can have luncheon at the railway-station and then wait for me. I am sending you today a money-order for the expenses of your journey. Reply at once and tell me that you have received this letter. I got yours all right. Thank you. And we meet soon. Yours S.P.'

We were happy to be in Milan. The immense Victor Emmanuel Gallery, the Cathedral, the church of Santa Maria della Grazia with Leonardo da Vinci's 'Last Supper', the Brera Gallery, the Scala . . . Diaghilev wanted me to see all the beauties of that endlessly beautiful city. I was often tired, overwhelmed by the countless new impressions, and I did not always dare to let myself go and express what spontaneously came into my mind, so intimidated was I by Sergei Pavlovitch's personality.

He was wearing his summer outfit, short and narrow white trousers (they reached only to his ankles), white shoes, straw hat which he often lifted to sponge his forehead, black jacket with a camellia in the buttonhole, eyeglass dangling against his waistcoat. His shirt-collar was stiffly starched (never even in the hottest weather would he consent to wear a soft collar). He leaned on his walking-stick and constantly moved his head about as though he was trying to escape from the collar.

I was sad to return to Turin. Milan had taught me much. I had had Diaghilev and it seemed to me I had disappointed him, had given him the impression I was not capable of rising to the

height he expected. So I wrote to him. I wanted everything to
be quite clear between us. Some days later I got a reply that
restored my self-confidence. The letter was, moreover, very
characteristic regarding Diaghilev's views on an artist's
education.

'Dear Seriozha: Your letter displeases me very much. It is
melancholic and contains unfinished expressions which are
perfectly useless. My impression, however, is excellent. If you
wish to become a real artist I think it useful, even necessary, for
you to find out in this way some of the most beautiful things
the world contains. I would very much have liked to show you
Florence which was where Massine's artistic activity took its
start. It was there that he recognised and felt that something
which made him a creator. I hope that such a visit will be
possible between the 15th and 20th of August. For the moment
I can promise nothing but I will write.'

After that Diaghilev announced that I would be receiving a
package. At Milan, indeed, he had mentioned he was going to
give me a surprise. God knows what I dreamt of while waiting.
When the parcel from Florence did arrive, I hesitated for quite
a time before opening it and so joyfully prolonged the pleasure
of anticipation. What could it be? Some knick-knacks? Ties?
Something to help me relax after my hard work with Cecchetti?
I put an end to my suspense, opened the package and found . . .
pamphlets containing reproductions of paintings by about
twenty famous artists. It is difficult to imagine how disappointed
I was. I was like a child robbed of his toys. It would have been
so much better not to have announced anything at all than to
have provoked a cruel deception of my dream. A letter inside
the parcel read:

'I would ask you to study very carefully these reproductions
in order that you may understand the differences which exist
between the various Florentine masters. In that way you will
not find yourself in quite unfamiliar surroundings. You must
bring these brochures along with you . . . write to tell me you
have received them together with your dancing-shoes. I am
glad to hear that you often go to the maestro's house and that
you help him with his gardening. It is a very innocent occupation.'

Such solicitude enraged me. I had been deprived of a pleasant
surprise, had been reminded of work and told to be a good boy.

I was being made a fool of . . . still I looked through the booklets but did not understand one thing about them. The pictures all looked alike to me—the same Virgins from Giotto to Tiepolo, always the same Christs, the same faces, and I could not make out at all clearly what were the distinguishing characteristics of any style or school. But when my anger had died down I did set to work so as not to cut too wretched a figure in Diaghilev's eyes.

I tried to read the introductions but they were written in Italian and my knowledge of that tongue was still too rudimentary for me to get any coherent ideas about the pictures. But Diaghilev continued to write to me.

'Did you get the brochures? Did they interest you? Write me a long and detailed letter.' So at last I summoned up my courage and sent him a letter in which I tried as well as I could to sort out and express my feelings. Then I awaited an explosion. Diaghilev did not answer. It was only much later on that he told me I had seized on the essentials and that some of my remarks (generally those I had made without at all reflecting on what I was saying) had pleased him and that he had begun to believe in me as a personality and see me as 'a real artist'. This caused me as much embarrassment as I have ever felt in my life. But this cruelty did help to awaken my mind. My culture, which paradoxically enough had begun with Stravinsky and Picasso, must go back to origins.

But at the time all I got after a long silence was a telegram: 'I have sent you 500. Settle up everything at Turin. Be Wednesday evening with all your luggage Milan Hotel Cavour.'

I did not have much trouble in clearing up everything at Turin. All I had there was the maestro Cecchetti. We took a very affectionate farewell of each other. I ended up with having worked a great deal with this lover of the Dance who since he had been more an outstanding acrobatic dancer than an artist was an admirable teacher. He was passionately devoted to his art and its techniques, and he was the last to use a little violin as did the dancing masters of bygone days. I had, during my months of solitude, become a familiar guest in his home where he always welcomed me with the greatest generosity. It was as a son of the family that I took leave of him and not before I had made him promise to come to Monte Carlo that winter.

Hardly had I met Diaghilev in Milan than we started off

for Venice where we arrived in the evening. When we got out
of the train Sergei Pavlovitch asked me:

'Would you like us to take a cab or a gondola?'

I begged him to take a gondola. He burst out laughing. It
was 20th August, 1924. The weather was perfect. A deep blue
sky was reflected on the dark surface of a hardly murmuring
Grand Canal. In all about us was a sort of sense of sweet joy,
peaceful, pure, contemplative. Everything, it seemed to me, had
changed, including Diaghilev himself. He had become another
man, such as I had never seen him before, but as he always was
in Venice. He was a Venetian Doge, proud and happy to show
the splendours of his 'native city'.

We stayed five days in Venice. Diaghilev was smiling all
the time. He knew everyone. He liked to sit in the Piazza San
Marco and it was evident that he felt as much at home as in
his own drawing-room. I looked at him. His joy was infectious.
I seemed to be relieved of an immense weight. I knew that I
had found in him a sure and firm supporter.

From Venice we made a short pilgrimage to Padua. One
special experience links me with Padua; it was in the city of
St Anthony that I communicated—once and for all it seemed to
me—profoundly in Italian art, in art in general. There it was
that my destiny was sealed. All that I had felt as vague expec-
tation in Milan Cathedral, was realised when I gazed on Giotto's
frescoes. Diaghilev experienced the same feelings. Our two souls
met together more than ever in an upsurge towards the Beautiful.

Sergei Pavlovitch was not a pious man, nor indeed, in the
usual sense of the word, a believer. But he had a religious sense
with regard to everything beautiful. He also liked the solemn
majesty of ritual. He experienced moments when the soul
mounts up as though to encounter a God still unknown.
Sometimes he had a tendency towards superstition linked with
religious rites. He had a great respect for St Anthony of Padua
and paid his devotions to this saint whom he looked upon as
his patron. In one of Diaghilev's waistcoat pockets there was
always a trinket with St Anthony's image. On this occasion,
after we had both knelt at St Anthony's shrine, Sergei Pavlovitch
said he had faith in me and that henceforth he would take charge
of me and back me up in my career. From that day our friendship became stronger. I felt now that I had really been received
into the heart of the artistic world, that I was no longer just

myself but the member of something much greater, something
I must serve with all my powers.

We had, in this same town of Padua, an interview that increased both my hopes and my desires. Diaghilev said to me:

'I've no longer any doubt at all about having won my bet. I
know you'll soon be the choreographer of the *Ballets Russes*.
I long to see you at work, to be proud of you and of myself.'

At that moment there sparked in me an urge to create that has
never since left me.

Then we parted. Diaghilev went off to Monte Carlo and I
returned to Paris where the troupe was to reassemble on 1st
September.

Diaghilev got to Paris on 31st August accompanied by Anton
Dolin and Boris Kochno. I felt at once that a living wall was
going to arise between Diaghilev and me and separate us for a
long time. I would catch sight of him but our private meetings
were finished. After those delightful months when I had had
him all to myself, there I was once more plunged in solitude
which was harder to bear than it had been before I had gone
away.

Boris Kochno, who had been Soudeikine's secretary and who
had recommended him to Diaghilev, was a sort of secretary to
the director of the *Ballets Russes*, and was by way of being a poet.
Diaghilev, just to please him, allowed him to put his signature
to some ballet scenarios. This young man, who was handsome
and intelligent, appeared—I do not know why but probably
from jealousy—to be suspicious of me. He had known how to
get round Diaghilev and he was not at all disposed to allow
someone who had not been approved of by him to come and
undermine his influence. He did his best then to push me on one
side, to keep me at a distance.

On 1st September all the troupe was assembled in Paris.
My comrades were at once struck by the change in me; the
rather brusque and rough bear's cub of a short time before
had become an elegant and courteous young man. Besides, no
one knew anything of my work with Cecchetti. They were all
stupefied at the progress I had made. When I put myself to the
bar I felt I had become a real dancer, that my whole body *sang*.
All the rest of the troupe remarked on this. 'It's a miracle,'
they said. I at once took my place at the head of the class and
everyone thought this perfectly normal. But it was on Diaghilev

that I produced the most profound impression. No sooner had he seen me work than he considered me as his *premier danseur*. He gave me a part in *Cimarosiana* as well as that of Borée in *Zéphyr et Flore*. My teachers now were Egorova and Trefilova, formerly star dancers of the Imperial Ballet in St Petersburg.

We went off to dance in Germany—Munich, Leipzig, Chemnitz, Berlin, Breslau, Hamburg, Frankfurt, Cologne and Hanover saw us in turn. At each place I made off to the museums to admire the Memlings, the Dürers, and the Cranachs.

After a short stay in Paris we were in London for the winter season—November 1924, and there I made my début as a choreo-author—a very memorable event for me. In December Diaghilev gave me the role of Boreé in *Zéphyr et Flore*, a ballet by Doukelsky which Sergei Pavlovitch regarded as very important and about which he had spoken enthusiastically to me in Venice. Nijinska had charge of the choreography but she was piqued because Diaghilev had given me the role of Borée and she left.

What was my surprise when Sergei Pavlovitch turned to me before the whole troupe and told me I was to undertake the choreography of *Zéphyr et Flore*.

If Diaghilev puts me in charge of the choreography of this ballet, I said to myself . . . it's because . . . and my head turned.

I set eagerly to work. I would lie awake at night thinking up new steps, new attitudes. I did so much of it indeed that a doubt began to creep into my mind. I did not want to devote myself entirely to a job I was far from knowing thoroughly. Choreography might make me lose signs of my real objective— the Dance. I did not want to sacrifice time I needed to become a dancer, to an occupation in which I might never be anything but a very poor creator. So this doubt soon induced a decision. So I asked Diaghilev to relieve me of the responsibility and I suggested he should turn over the work to Massine whom I had got to know in London and who now, after his quarrel with Sergei Pavlovitch, was to rejoin the troupe. Diaghilev was furious at my decision but to this day I have not ceased to congratulate myself on the step I took.

This début of 1925 was the most trying period for me. During a rehearsal at Monte Carlo of *Zéphyr et Flore* I had sprained both my feet. Diaghilev, who must put on the performance, wanted to give the part to another dancer. But I told him I had made up my mind to appear—'otherwise I will kill myself'—

and I did dance but at the price of a veritable torture. The dancer was very nearly never born. Picasso, as a testimony to my will-power that evening, signed and gave me one of the twelve drawings he had made of me.

In June, during our week's performance at the Gaité-Lyrique, *Les Matelots* was created—music by Georges Auric and scenario by Boris Kochno—and *Zéphyr et Flore* was danced for the first time in Paris.

Dolin's career with the *Ballets Russes* was drawing to its close and he was about to leave the troupe. The Parisian news-papers were speaking of the forthcoming season as *my* season. It was my decisive victory. Diaghilev, who was generally so reticent about showing his feelings, wrote on my programme: 'For the first among the youngest, to the youngest among the first.' And that was a statement I took as my real letters patent.

Our last performance in Paris was on 20th June and then it was that Dolin said good-bye to the *Ballets Russes*. He bore me no grudge for taking his place and very courteously, before the performance, came into my dressing-room and placed Borée's wreath on my head. And then, with tears in his eyes, he danced.

The second London season began on 22nd June. I had, without anyone questioning, assumed the rank of leading artist of the troupe. At Mrs Mathias' house, Gershwin entertained Diaghilev with the *Rhapsody in Blue* music and begged him to stage a ballet for this music which should be interpreted by me.[1]

I was made much of, overloaded with wreaths and flowers, especially by Diaghilev. A new epoch was beginning for the *Ballets Russes*.

[1] I did put on this ballet—for Béjart and Solange Schwarz—under the name 'Sunlight', in 1945, but it was not created until then.

6

NIJINSKY'S SUCCESSOR

The year 1925, for me, was not the year of the Rif war or of Hindenburg's election to the presidency of the German Republic, or of the consolidation of Mussolini's power in Italy. It was not even the year of the revelation of the Exhibition of Decorative Arts, or of the publication of T. E. Lawrence's *Seven Pillars of Wisdom*, it was not the year of Bernard Shaw's Nobel Prize or of Charlie Chaplin's *Gold Rush* or of the *Rue sans Joie* with Greta Garbo. It was not even the year when the Negro Review with Josephine Baker took the town by storm at the Champs-Elysées. The appearance of Josephine Baker was for me just a music-hall event. I did, indeed, guess that, coming as it did after Picasso's Negro Period, Negro influence—and syncopation—from Harlem would assume a considerable importance in the history of the Dance. And this influence was to continue with Cole Porter and Gershwin and lead up to the new Expressionism of today . . . a movement in fact on the fringe of the theatrical Dance which nevertheless did have a great effect on the ballet—as had had in a preceding period Isadora Duncan's attempts at 'free dancing'.

No, for me the year 1925 was that of my close friendship with Diaghilev, though this friendship, which ended only with his life, became more and more a silent one.

It is a constant feature of human relationships that when two beings come together they reveal themselves fully to each other only at the beginning of their acquaintance. Long conversations, confessions, are but the prelude to a friendship—the door that opens onto thought in common. Little by little the confidences become less frequent, since a hint suffices for understanding . . . then they cease.

If this constant observation holds good in most cases, then it was particularly true regarding Diaghilev . . . he felt no need to confess himself to anyone, though his friendships were tyrannical for those he liked, whatever his relations with them were. His friendship assumed quite absurd forms in the case of people he was very fond of or who were close to him. He was jealous —one must use that word—concerning everything and everyone —about my childhood's dreams, girl dancers, my partners, people I met casually . . . and even my success as an artist. One day when I was beginning to rehearse with a *danseuse* who had been engaged in our company, Diaghilev gave this order—luckily soon countermanded—to Grigorieff: 'Throw that girl out of the troupe, she's making eyes at Lifar. . . .'

Sometimes he made real scenes. The first took place soon after we had left London. We had gone off for a trip to Italy where Diaghilev wanted to show me Stresa and Lake Maggiore. We stayed for several days at the Villa d'Este on Lake Como. He was happy about the excellent season we had had and he surrounded me with charming attentions. I found our life on Lake Como most enchanting. However, it nearly came to an end owing to one of Diaghilev's fits of jealousy. At Cernobbio, and not far from us, lived the Demidoffs and the beautiful Madame Demidoff invited us to supper.

During the meal she talked only with Sergei Pavlovitch, though she kept an eye on me. I noticed that he was getting angrier and angrier and having difficulty in controlling himself.

After supper Countess Demidoff suggested we should go out in a boat on the lake. Diaghilev, who had a superstitious dread of water since some fortune-teller had predicted in his youth that he would die on water, refused.

'No, no, take Serge, I'll go home.'

We were about half an hour on the lake, chatting gaily. The shores of the lake, the beauty of my hostess, her conversation —and then she could talk Russian which she could not very often —made me forget Sergei Pavlovitch's stormy looks. Anyhow, what could be the reason for them? I accompanied my hostess to her villa and then with nothing on my mind I went off to the hotel. The concierge stopped me as I was making my way to Diaghilev's room.

'M. Diaghilev has left and asked me to tell you that you can spend all your holiday here.'

I pushed the door open. No Sergei Pavlovitch. He had gone and taken all his luggage with him. I was not long in guessing where he had gone to—surely Milan. I packed my bags, set off for Milan and then made straight for the Hotel Cavour where he always stayed.

'M. Diaghilev?'

'M. Diaghilev arrived ten minutes ago.'

I had no need to convince Sergei Pavlovitch, the rapidity of my departure spoke volumes.

We went to Venice, then to Florence and Rome, which Diaghilev revealed to me with great care—above all Florence, his Florence, his 'holy city', where I was overwhelmed by the majesty of Michelangelo. I remember an excursion to Fiesole. We did no sight-seeing, we just sat chatting during the evening at a table on a restaurant terrace. We gazed out to the far distance while a soft transparent night veiled little by little the lights of the city down beneath us . . . this visit to Florence lives in my memory as one of the most marvellous interludes in my life. Moreover, the year 1925 was one of the happiest in Diaghilev's existence as it was in mine. I had become a leading dancer, 'The Dancer'.

The year that was approaching proved, on the contrary, to be full of worry for Sergei Pavlovitch, worries of all sorts that served to detach him more and more from the *Ballets Russes*.

From 22nd December to 6th January we danced in Berlin— *Les Biches, Les Matelots, Le Tricorne, La Boutique fantasque, Zéphyr et Flore* and *Carnival*. The Press praised us to the skies. But despite this the *Kunst Theater* where we performed was, all the time, three-quarters empty and the *Ballets Russes* suffered a financial fiasco which affected them very seriously. Sergei Pavlovitch was gay and in good form only on Christmas Eve. On that day I bought a little Christmas tree and put it in his bedroom. He was very touched and told me that it was the first Christmas tree he had had since his childhood's days. His mind filled with memories. He talked about his parents, of his childhood spent at Perm, of his years at high school. He could not think of Russia without shedding tears. But such effusions were beginning to be infrequent between us.

In the early part of 1926, after the Berlin fiasco, Diaghilev fell into a state of deep depression. He had to busy himself with preparations for the forthcoming season in London and Paris. He was short of money and had not much hope of finding any. During the opera season at Monte Carlo he stayed in his bedroom. He was prostrated and a prey to sinister thoughts. In addition the pains he suffered from became worse and worse and almost intolerable.

It was at this time that I got him to do something which made me not a little proud. Diaghilev used to snuff cocaine. But on the other hand he did not smoke and disliked tobacco. I had indeed given up smoking cigarettes so as to please him but I asked in return that he should give up cocaine.

One morning he declared:

'You know, Seriozha, a queer thing happened to me this morning. I woke up and felt all at once that cocaine disgusted me, as though I had never had the habit of snuffing it. I decided to give it up—and I'll do that without difficulty.'

A little time later on he finally managed to get financial support from Lord Rothermere who not only took a great interest in the artists of our ballet but who also took a particular interest in three of our *danseuses*. But what difficulties Diaghilev encountered before promise of financial help was translated into reality! And furthermore this matter caused an estrangement between one of the *danseuses* and Diaghilev, since her caprices had been aggravated.

Sergei Pavlovitch set to work hurriedly to prepare the season. First of all it was *Roméo et Juliette* with the score by Lambert who proceeded at once with the arrangements to make a ballet out of it. During the whole month of February I was absent from Paris as I had gone to study with Cecchetti at the Scala. I got back only in March. Diaghilev had at first been in touch with Mme Kschissinska and had asked her to dance the *Lac des Cygnes* but the negotiations broke down. Then he got Karsavina and Nijinska to come and create *Roméo et Juliette*. But when Nijinska heard that I was to dance with Karsavina, she at once declared:

'I demand that Lifar pass an examination and without it I refuse to give him the role of Romeo.'

My indignation may be imagined. When had a *premier danseur* ever had to pass an examination? What sort of conduct was this—treating him as someone quite unknown?

Diaghilev consoled me:

'Don't be angry, Seriozha, since Nijinska wants, in her capacity as choreographer of the company, for there to be an examination. Let her have one.

The 'examination' lasted half an hour, I do not remember having ever danced so well. Nicholas Legat, the company's dance professor, who was at the piano, gave me easy little variations which he then complicated when he saw with what ease I did *vols* and made twelve pirouettes and three *tours en l'air. Entrechats-huit, petites batteries, cabrioles* and *grands jetés* followed each other brilliantly. The 'examination' was over. M. Legat got up and came over to embrace me. Diaghilev also embraced me and in his turn congratulated me. 'We will begin no later than tomorrow.' Nijinska was confounded. The next day I started to rehearse with Karsavina.

So I was going to dance with the great, the celebrated Tamara Karsavina! At the first performance I fell in love with my partner. Karsavina was very sweet to me and paid me plenty of compliments. During the first performance of *Roméo et Juliette* I danced with great fire. The success was considerable. Encores, bravos, a mass of roses. I had a bouquet from Diaghilev and roses from Karsavina with this note: 'All my heartiest good wishes for your success. Tamara Karsavina.' I went back to my room at the Hôtel de Paris, arranged the roses in a vase on my table, then went back to the theatre, for I was to take Karsavina to supper. Then I ran up against Diaghilev:

'What are you doing here?'

'I am waiting for Tamara.'

Diaghilev said nothing but I could see he was furious. Karsavina appeared and we went off to supper together. Afterwards I accompanied her to where she was staying and then went back to the Hôtel de Paris and in a very good humour. What did I see? Karsavina's roses were no longer on my table. I opened the window and—there they were down below in the courtyard.

Was it possible that Sergei Pavlovitch had dared to throw my roses out of the window? The roses of my triumph and of my Karsavina?

I tied my sheets together and made a rope so that I could go

and find my roses. I had hardly got one leg over the window-sill
when my door opened violently. Diaghilev grabbed me by the
hair and forced me back into the room.

Then there was a horrible row that kept the whole hotel
awake for quite a considerable time.

'This can't go on,' he bawled aloud, 'all this debauchery you
are carrying on with members of my company ... I'll soon fling
out all these women who cling on to my artists in front of everyone. Oh, yes, he's a handsome fellow my leading dancer who is
in raptures because someone has smiled at him. I'll kick the
pair of you out of my troupe and you can go off and get your
amusement elsewhere.'

Thereupon he slammed the door so loudly that the noise
resounded all over the landing.

The next day things were all right again.

On 9th May we gave the last evening performance of our
Monte Carlo season. On the 13th we left for Paris where four new
ballets were to be created—*Barabau* by Rietti with scenery
by Utrillo; *Jack in the Box*, with Erik Satié's music orchestrated
by Darius Milhaud, choreography by Balanchine and scenery
by André Derain: *Pastorelle* with music by Georges Auric, and
Roméo et Juliette 'rehearsal without scenery'. The first three
were completely put in the shade by the last, whose creation
gave rise to a first-class row. There had been a good many rumours about this new surrealist ballet with scenery by Ernst
and Miró. The police warned Diaghilev that the surrealists
and Communists were preparing a demonstration during which
Diaghilev, the 'bourgeois', together with Ernst and Miró 'traitors
brought up by the bourgeois', were to be manhandled. The
18th May arrived. Excitement was at its height. I asked Diaghilev for permission to summon all the troupe on the stage and
then I organised a little crash commando all ready to counter-
attack if or when the demonstrators tried to rush stage.

The Théâtre Sarah-Bernhardt was sold out. The first part of
the performance went off quietly enough. After the interval
suddenly there was a blowing of whistles that drowned the
orchestra. Soon none of the audience had their eyes on the stage
any more. Fanatics up in the gallery were pelting down showers
of surrealist tracts signed by Aragon and Breton which fluttered
all over the theatre. I saw Lady Abdy, a great friend of Diaghilev, box a man's ears. Then the police rushed in and ejected

the disturbers of the peace. After that we could start and the ballet was danced with marked success, whereas *Les Matelots*, the last piece of the evening, secured a real triumph.

This row was enough, for all Paris chattered about the new ballet with a consequence that the house was sold out and plenty of people had to be turned away when the ballet was put on again.

The critics as with one accord praised the choreographers and the dancers, but comment was more reserved about the ballets themselves. They were compared with those of former seasons and were judged decidedly inferior, especially as regards the music which was held to be 'not very danceable'. 'The composers forced our ballet-masters to have recourse to gimmicks which were tending to make the *Ballets Russes* develop into displays of clowning, into a combination of circus, music-halls, and gymnasium for physical culture.' As for Diaghilev himself, he was accused of being little disposed to meet the tastes of the day and of striving mainly to 'be ahead of the times'.

In July it was Italy once more and in October I was again working with dear old Cecchetti. In November and December 1926 there were seasons with new ballets in both London and Paris. Diaghilev had fallen back on Massine and had asked him to take over the choreographic direction of the company. He also engaged a new *première ballerina* Olga Spessivtzeva, 'the Divine', who from then onwards was to dance with me the whole of our classical and modern repertoire.

From the very first moment I was enthusiastic about her genius and her distinction. Diaghilev had often said to me, 'Your dancing-partner should be Spessivtzeva' . . . and now I was with her. A great affection sprang up between us.

The year 1927 was marked by the creation of *Pas d'Acier* with music by Prokofiev. Now, although Diaghilev might have been a revolutionary in the field of art, he was certainly not one in other directions. He might well have had within him an anarchical, even a nihilistic streak, quite in the Slav tradition, but that manifested itself only in one, quite personal, facet of his character and was confined to words as when he would curse 'the rotten civilisation of a pretentious bourgeoisie which takes things easily in art as in the other good things of this world'.

Those around him professed an invincible contempt for everything that was Sovietic. He, on the other hand, forced himself to remain neutral in politics and he always paid attention to what might be happening in Russia.

In 1926 and later Diaghilev resumed contact with his own country. This was under the influence of Ehrenburg, Lunacharsky and Krassin, who knew well enough how to attract his attention by informing him about the researches then being made regarding a new form of theatre in the USSR. He asked Prokofiev to write a ballet. Massine was to be the choreographer, and Jakoulov was to come from Moscow to do the scenery. Although there was a certain amount of opposition inside our troupe itself, the ballet was put on and provoked a political scandal and quarrels about the new theory of 'theatrical constructivism' applied for the first time to a ballet—and in Paris before Moscow.

As he wanted to prepare the Parisian public for the appearance of Olga Spessivtzeva in *La Chatte* (by Sauguet and Balanchine, with an architectural décor by Gabo and Pevsner), Diaghilev found another name for her, one that stuck to her. Writing in the *Figaro* he declared:

'Tomorrow at the first performance of the *Ballets Russes*, a new dancer—Olga Spessiva—will be making her début in Paris. It is true that during two seasons there danced at the Opera a ballerina whose name was almost the same, but fate willed it, for some reason or another, that the Spessivtzeva of the Opera was not understood by the most sensitive public in the world—that of Paris.

'I have always believed that in man's lifetime there is a limit to joyful experiences. So, for a whole generation there was only one Taglioni to be admired, there was only one Patti to be heard. When I saw Pavlova in her young days and in mine, I was sure that she was to be the "Taglioni" of my lifetime. My astonishment then was boundless when I met Spessiva, a creature even more rare and more delicate than Pavlova. And that is saying much.

'Our great ballet master, Cecchetti, who formed Nijinsky, Karsavina and so many others, said as lately as last winter during one of his lessons at the Scala in Milan: "An apple was born into the world, and it was cut in two. One half became Anna Pavlova, and the other Spessiva. I would add that, for me, Spessiva was the side that was exposed to the sun."

'Perhaps I may be allowed to speak thus after twenty years of work in the atmosphere of theatres. I am happy to think that, after such a long lapse of time, during which hundreds of *danseuses* have passed before my eyes, I can still present in Paris such artists as Massine, Balanchine, Woitzikowsky, Idzikowsky and Danilova, Techernicheva and Sokolova.

'My joy is still greater when, after having begun twenty years ago with Pavlova and Nijinsky, I come to Spessiva and Lifar. The two first have become legendary while the latter, very different from their predecessors, are with us and are awaiting in their turn the time when they too will become legendary, and part of that splendid legend, too flattering for us, of the fame of the *Ballets Russes*.'

Pavlova never forgave Diaghilev for this article.

It appeared in the *Figaro* on 26th May and on that same day Olga fractured one of her legs. No more unfortunate beginning for a ballet season could be imagined, for it was the twentieth anniversary of the *Ballets Russes*. But a substitute was found for her and the performance was not cancelled.

After *La Chatte* I saw Diaghilev come up to me one day looking very happy indeed.

'My congratulations, Serge, Stravinsky has said to me some remarkable things about you. He is so enthusiastic about your dancing that although he has a commission from America he wants to write a ballet specially for you.'

There is no need to say how delighted and proud I was . . . it was to be *Apollon Musagète* that was created in 1928, the following year.

By 1927 Diaghilev had begun to lose interest in the ballet and this indifference was to go on increasing. To speak frankly, the *Ballets Russes* had been only an incident in a versatile existence that was actuated by a spirit with many aspects. This episode had been unduly prolonged for more than twenty years and it was just that which bored Diaghilev. Circumstances had combined to turn what had been at first a pleasurable enterprise into a burden. Sergei Pavlovitch, moreover, was subject so whims, to sudden infatuations. First of all it had been a mania for phonographs and records. Boris Kochno had bought a phonograph which he turned on from time to time . . . and that became a passion with Diaghilev. Almost every day we met after luncheon so as to listen to records for two or three hours on end. Then he wanted to make a collection of records. But this enthusiasm, however, was only the forerunner of another much more serious for the *Ballets Russes* and it, also, began by chance. Diaghilev had gathered together a whole gallery of models of décors, first for Massine and then for me. Sometimes also he bought books for Kochno, who had rather a fine library. One day he purchased a little volume that interested him— and so began a new passion. First of all we joked readily enough about this fresh mania. But I foresaw early on that one day, because of this new interest, the *Ballets Russes* would no longer exist. And indeed this new activity, little by little, absorbed him entirely. His life was organised around it. He no longer travelled to see a dancer or a *danseuse* but to find a rare book and the budget of the Ballet was heavily burdened.

The 1929 tour was badly organised and was, as a consequence, a financial setback. The only event of the season was the creation in Paris of *Apollon Musagète*. The *Tout Paris* interested in the arts was present at the first performance when I experienced instants of supreme happiness and my joy was especially great when I received a dedicated photograph from Stravinsky. But still the most profound emotion I felt was when I saw that Diaghilev had recovered his old enthusiasm.

'Remember this day, Seriozha, remember it all your life.'

After the performance he made me a present of a lyre in gold which I handed to my 'godmother' Coco Chanel, who that evening gave a ball, as she did after all the first performances.

Then came the holidays.

I saw clearly enough, and with great distress, that Diaghilev was moving farther and farther away from the ballet. He cherished plans for the complete change of his activities. Then he dreamed of having an apartment of his own in Paris, and after that a whole building, and in fact he had begun to look for one before he left. There he would have his library and would devote himself to the only friends whose loyalty was unquestionable— his books . . . and the *Ballets Russes*? A great reform, if not a suppression, awaited them. Sergei Pavlovitch wanted to divide his troupe into two parts. One group of about ten artists, under my direction, would devote itself entirely to research and would undertake, so to speak, pure laboratory work. To this end he wanted to build for me a theatre at Venice, on the Lido.

The other group, that is to say the major portion of the company, was to live on our ideas and to provide maintenance for all of us—including the library. The headquarters were to be in Monte Carlo and tours were to be undertaken in all parts of the world, especially in the United States. It was obvious to me that the *Ballets Russes* were doomed to an early end.

Diaghilev's health also began to fail. None of the above plans was ever to be carried out.

At the end of the year we went to London, Birmingham, Glasgow, Edinburgh and Liverpool. With *Les Dieux mendiants* (Handel's music) we had a triumphal success, but Diaghilev's temper got worse and worse. He quarrelled with each one of us in turn. He was filled with bitterness at the departure of many of his collaborators, musicians, painters and dancers attracted by Ida Rubinstein's money. He was especially angry with Stravinsky, whom he had called his 'son of genius' and to whom he henceforth referred to in these words: 'Alas our Igor, he is very fond of the good God and small change.'

His brief period of balletomania had come to an end, for ever, it appeared to me. The year 1929 was to begin in an atmosphere of sombre foreboding.

7

THE PRODIGAL SON

On 4th February 1929 I noted in my diary: 'I predict that this season will be the last of Diaghilev's *Ballets Russes*. Sergei Pavlovitch is exhausted. His interest in the ballet gets all the time less and less. The Dance is something that is becoming alien to him. The discovery of an ancient book means much more to him than the creation of a new ballet. Our family is breaking up.'

Diaghilev had led a feverishly active life. Now when he had arrived at the age of fifty-seven he felt fatigued, lonely, isolated like a King Lear, and like Lear also—many of whose traits he shared—he isolated himself more and more. He who had never been able to live without a crowd of friends around him, now abruptly severed most of his old friendships. There remained to him no one except Walter Nouvel, Misia Sert and Picasso, but unfortunately Olga, Picasso's wife, was dangerously ill and Diaghilev could see his old friend only occasionally.

So he had but his family—the Karamazov family—Pavka (the 'uncle' Koriboute), Valetchka (Walter Nouvel), Boris Kochno and myself. 'Pavka and Valetchka are charming,' he would say, 'but if one took their advice one might as well get driven to the cemetery at once.' P. Koriboute, who was exceptionally kind-hearted, could not, in any case, rank as an artistic director. But Diaghilev was very fond of him and looked upon him as a sort of confidant. Walter Nouvel was also an old friend of Diaghilev and had once, at the beginning, been his artistic adviser, but had by now lost all authority in Sergei Pavlovitch's eyes. Diaghilev reproached Nouvel with not having understood two works he considered as the two supreme musical compositions of our time—*L'Oiseau de Feu* and the *Sacre du Printemps*.

Maybe also this isolation in which Diaghilev henceforth took refuge can be explained by the fact that he did not dare to be honest with himself and recognise the errors, or rather the one great error, of his life, in the course of which he had respected nothing except himself.

Finally there was myself. But he no longer had confidence in me. I realised with sadness how we were drifting apart. Unfortunately each one of us was so absorbed in his own occupations that neither confided in the other. At this beginning of 1929 Diaghilev was suffering from physical and moral lassitude, even apathy, with regard to the details of life. However, in a sudden spurt of instinct that was stronger than his lassitude, he would sometimes make discoveries. This time the object was a young man who was still at school when he was recognised as the new genius. His name was Igor Markévitch.

But also, as so often happens in such phases of a man's life, he liked to hark back to the fountain-head of recollection. I can recall our visit to Nijinsky in 1929. The great dancer who had been insane since 1917 dragged out a miserable life in the recesses of a flat in Passy. I think that Diaghilev hoped to excite some spark of consciousness in the unfortunate Vaslav. He came to an agreement with Nijinsky's sister-in-law (his wife Romola Nijinska was in America) and she arranged our visit.

I had never been lucky enough to see Nijinsky on the stage. I had never even met him before his mind became clouded and darkened. Maybe, nevertheless, I was the man who knew him best, since I had been tireless in my efforts to know him, to understand him, to pierce the mystery of his genius.

Nijinsky's fame had been unparalleled. He had been a veritable revelation in London, in Paris, in New York and Buenos Aires. Nijinsky in fact displayed not only an absolute mastery but also a gift for rising in the air (*élévation*) that one might call superhuman. From Nijinsky's example the dancing masters suddenly realised that a man's dancing in a ballet could be as sublime and captivating as that of the most graceful woman dancer, the most ariel, the most ethereal. The dancer's solo became thenceforth one of the essential elements of every choreographic work.

The crowning creation of Nijinsky was undoubtedly the
Spectre de la Rose. This little ballet, in appearance insignificant,
was directed by Fokine at Monte Carlo in 1911 before the opening of the Paris season. The music was Weber's *Invitation à la
Valse*. Suddenly the Nijinsky myth was created. In this ballet,
and perhaps only in this ballet, Nijinsky's *élévation* was alone
enough to create an incomparable masterpiece. Indeed the opportunity was offered to the celebrated dancer for indulging in
his famous 'vertical ascensions' which Levinson said embodied
the sublime ideal of the dance. Nijinsky's leap was a real flight.
His pose in the air seemed devoid of the slightest effort. He
was flying, it might be said, with the lightness of a being born
to fly.

However, and one cannot forget it, Nijinsky's fame was due
to one single, fantastic leap in the *Spectre de la Rose*. For, apart
from this ballet, Nijinsky in fact never performed any other
aerial miracle. But he had become a 'great man', a myth, and the
public was happy to acclaim him as such.

His own creative imagination, however, did not lead him
beyond search for new 'earth-bound' steps which should be
different from the old ones. His later ballets included neither
élévation nor leaps. No doubt here lay Nijinsky's poignant
tragedy that cut his wings so prematurely.

Nijinsky performed his last 'leap' before me in 1939 at the
Swiss nursing-home where he was then living. I was to see him
again in London three days before his death in 1950. In 1953
I led a procession to the Montmartre cemetery where we paid
homage, as from Paris and the Dance, to our God of the Dance
who lies buried near his illustrious predecessor, Auguste Vestris.

But in 1929 when we entered his apartment one was struck
at once by the hospital atmosphere that reigned. There was a
smell of chemicals, attendants dressed all in white . . . silence.
Madame Pulska, his sister-in-law, was not there. A servant went
to 'announce' us to Nijinsky, but it was obvious what he was
really doing was to make sure the unfortunate man was in a fit
state to see us. A door opened. The door of Nijinsky's room. It
was like a dungeon. There was a man lying half-naked on a
low divan. A dressing-gown was open over his bare chest and
he was resting with his legs stretched out and crossed. This
attitude he maintained all the time. His nervousness showed
only by the movements of his hands. At one moment he would

scratch them until they bled while at another moment he would
make affected gestures with them.

The servant went over to him and said that friends had called
to visit him.

'Bring them in,' I heard him say in the voice of a man apparently quite sane. We went in. I approached him and touched his
hand with my lips. It was burning hot. He gave me a furtive
look, that of a hunted beast. Then, all at once, he smiled at me,
so frankly, so childlike, that I fell immediately under the spell
of his charm. During the whole time we were there he alternated
between smiles, grunts and stupid, painful bursts of laughter. At
first he did not seem to notice Diaghilev but then little by little
he appeared to recognise him and at moments listened to him
with attention and even with some sign of good sense. Diaghilev
spoke to him about me, said I was a dancer and therefore I
liked him, Nijinsky, the great dancer.

'He likes me?' he asked brusquely. Those were the only
words he spoke in Russian. After that he broke into unintel-
ligible French.

'Yes, Vatza, he loves you and so do I, we all love you.'

Nijinsky began to laugh.

'That's adorable.'

Diaghilev spoke to him about dancing, about what in former
pays he had liked beyond all else, hoping by such references
to bring him back to consciousness. Nijinsky listened with
apparent indifference but his brain was obviously working since
he began to look at me fixedly and with astonishment, with a
sort of apprehension even, as though he were asking himself who
I could be. Diaghilev told him again that I was Lifar, a dancer,
and that I had come to greet him. The muscles of his face
contracted as they used to in former days when he was watching
comrades dancing who he felt might eclipse him. It was not
jealousy that moved him then but a desire to do better still, to
be unique.

'He jumps?' he called out suddenly. Then his face relaxed
and he broke out into clear, juvenile laughter which made me
for an instant forget how pitiable was his state. Diaghilev had
gone pale. Had this sudden outburst of Nijinsky's frightened
him? A Nijinsky of former times? Sergei Pavlovitch seemed much
moved.

'Yes, yes, Vatza, he can leap, he leaps very well, you'll see.'

Then it was he got the idea of taking Vaslav to the Opera. As it happened that evening *Pétrouchka* was on the programme, one of Nijinsky's favourite roles . . . Karsavina, his former partner, would be there. Diaghilev told me only that he wanted to have Nijinsky photographed with the artists of the ballet, but I could see from Sergei Pavlovitch's sparkling eyes that what he was really hoping for was something better than that. The great Nijinsky at the Opera . . . in surroundings where he had passed his life, which had been all his life . . . might he not recover his reason?

He told his idea to Vaslav's sister-in-law who had just got home. She seized on the suggestion—with the energy of despair. She also had read hope in Diaghilev's eyes.

From the way Nijinsky was looking at Sergei Pavlovitch it was obvious he had recognised him. He was evidently pleased we were there. During the two years his wife had been away in America no one had come to pay him a visit. He remained alone—deserted.

They began to get him dressed. I asked him to rise, which he did very willingly. I was struck by his small stature. He got out of bed in a strange fashion. First of all he went on all-fours from his divan, then crawled round the room and only then stood upright. I noted that, in a general way, he seemed to be attracted by the floor, to feel a need to be as low down as possible (his divan in fact was almost on a level with the floor) and to grab hold of something. As he walked he leaned forward and felt at his ease only when lying down. Diaghilev measured us. Vaslav was half a head shorter than me. The calves of his legs were dreadful to see, enormous, rounded, but so flabby that it was astonishing he could stand at all. He was induced to have a bath. I looked after him as one might a baby and forced him to obey me by tensing my own will. While I was shaving him he sat patiently, though from time to time he made a grimace and then smiled sweetly at me. He was obviously frightened of the servants and this was most plain when the man began to cut his hair.

When we came back that evening to take him to the Opera, Nijinsky was already dressed and was sitting in a relaxed attitude, but his face had a vague look and he was staring upwards. I held his arm to help him walk downstairs. He was silent. Then suddenly he said to me:

'Be careful.'

I did not hear another word from him. He had withdrawn into his shell and was oblivious of the outside world. We got into a car. He was calm and speechless the whole time.

A nervous thrill shot through me as I got him across the Opera stage. Diaghilev and Rouché came to meet us and they led us to our box. The first ballet had already started (I myself danced only in the last one)—Nijinsky looked around the theatre and the stage but clearly he was not with us. What was he thinking about?

The rumour soon ran around that Nijinsky was in the theatre. Some of the audience, old friends and admirers, came to see him, tried to talk to him. But he did not reply. He just sat and smiled.

During the second interval and before *Pétrouchka*, he was led onto the stage to be photographed with us, Karsavina (The Dancer), myself (The Moor), Diaghilev, Benois, Grigorieff and Keremeniev. When he saw the camera Nijinsky smiled as he used to in the days of his triumphs.

He was taken back into the theatre and Diaghilev told me later on that during *Pétrouchka* Nijinsky's face flushed, that he 'smelt powder'. After the performance, when it was suggested he should go home, he declared abruptly:

'I don't want to.'

He had to be carried off.

I remember all these details so well because they concerned the great Nijinsky, 'The God of the Dance' whose mastery of his art had long seemed to me to be inimitable—but also because the incident fitted well enough into the atmosphere of anguish in which I lived for those months, with the presentiment of death that I felt was hovering darkly over our 'family'.

Some time after that, in 1929, Massine's Spanish professor was suddenly to become mad. When he got to London, after the company that was to dance *Le Tricorne* (by Falla and Picasso) whose choreography he had arranged, he was stupefied to see that his name did not appear on the playbills either as dancer or choreographer. He left the Coliseum and rushed off to Trafalgar Square, where, on seeing a red light in a church window, he thought, perhaps, that he was outside some cabaret in his own country, for he smashed a window and clambered into the church, where he was discovered quite mad and dancing on the altar.

Later I went with Diaghilev to see him in hospital and Sergei Pavlovitch remarked to me:

'There you are, the dramas and passions of the *Ballets Russes,* and it's all my fault.'

As far as I was concerned I was soon to experience great joy mingled with bitterness. One day in Paris, Diaghilev, Walter Nouvel and I were meeting to decide on the programme for the spring season.

'We have two creations,' said Diaghilev, '*La Bal* by Rietti with Chirico's décor, and *Le Fils Prodigue* by Prokofiev with Rouault's décor, but we must have a third.'

A pause, then Sergei Pavlovitch went on but addressing me this time:

'After all, Serge, perhaps you could try to make a ballet?'

He flipped through his note-book slowly, indolently, looking for a ballet that could be revived.

'Ah, here we are, Stravinsky's *Renard* . . . we can put on *Renard* again . . . well, Lifar, will you do that ballet or not? Will you try your hand at it?'

I would have been better pleased if he had shown more enthusiasm. I remembered how, earlier on, he had asked me to take charge of the choreography for *Zéphyr et Flore*. But I knew the state he was in and I forced myself not to reveal my emotion when I replied with the same apparent and assumed indifference:

'All right, I am quite prepared to try if you want me to and if the thing still interests you.'

I set to work completely alone in a studio belonging to the Salle Pleyel. After several attempts I had got ready the first sketches for the dance of the Cock and the Fox. When Diaghilev came to the Salle Pleyel he approved of my sketches though without much enthusiasm. The next day he returned and followed what I was doing; this time he was paying much attention. Then he said that I should shortly be 'judged'. All at once I was in a completely new world made up of feelings and thoughts unknown up to then. I was seized by a sort of perpetual frenzied excitement and I was frightened that I might die before I finished *Renard*. My idea was to mingle acrobats with the *danseuses*.

On the day of the 'judgment' I went, with no hope of success, to the studio. The 'judges' were Diaghilev, Michel Larionov, the decorator of the ballet and Boris Kochno. The rehearsal took place amid an icy silence. Accompanied by a piano I sketched out the variations of *Le Coq et le Renard.* Not a sign. Not a word.

During a pause, I heard Diaghilev—I was near the cloak-room —reply in a loud voice to a man who had been saying something disparaging, '. . . since *Le Sacre du Printemps,* absolutely smashing. . . .'

Now I was in full form for the rest of the ballet.

In the taxi, on the way back, Diaghilev said:

'I'll put you on the playbill, I'll give you our best artists and you'll have a free hand. The sketches you have made are splendid and very significant. Through the dance you make common cause with Cubism.'

We went off to Monte Carlo. The pleasures of creation had made me forget, for a time, my anxiety and through this work I acquired a sort of self-confidence which was quite new to me. Sergei Pavlovitch commuted between Monto Carlo and Paris. Sometimes he came to my rehearsals but he never stayed long, he just approved. It was as though he wanted to avoid any long conversations, any confidential talks. He paid a good deal of attention to my ballet, but this hardly affected that drifting apart which I had realised. I did not know its exact cause. I attributed it rather to the change in his tastes than to the illness which gripped him unknown to me. I was unhappy about all this especially as he had, although I was responsible for the ballet, engaged Dolin without even telling me.

Then we all left for Paris. Our season was to begin with two creations and a revival—*Le Fils Prodigue* and *Le Bal* with Balanchine choreography and *Le Renard* with mine. Diaghilev alternated between enthusiasm and the most complete depression. It was with obvious disapproval that he watched the rehearsals of *Le Fils Prodigue.* The ballet moved slowly in a general atmosphere of listlessness. I myself was so absorbed in my own creative work that I did little more, in fact, than be present at the rehearsals. Sergei Pavlovitch was, indeed, totally disappointed with *Le Fils Prodigue* and tried on several occasions to talk to me about it.

All in all this ballet brought us misfortune after misfortune. Prokofiev was dissatisfied with it and his relations with Balanchine and Kochno, the librettist, became more and more strained.

Diaghilev, too, was displeased with his ballet-master, who, he said, was secretly directing ballets for Pavlova and was in negotiation with Balieff of the *Chauve-Souris*. So Sergei Pavlovitch had decided not to renew his contract and to have only one ballet-master—Lifar.

On the morning of the general rehearsal Diaghilev came to see me.

'Seriozha. I beg of you to save my twenty-first season in Paris. Up to now I've never had a fiasco, but I will this time if you don't help me. I'm relying on you.' Such almost supplicating remarks were something new from Diaghilev. That evening I got a telephone call from him. He was being kept at the theatre to decide technical details and the lighting arrangements for the evening's performance. He would not get back before it started and asked me to go to the theatre with Koriboute and to get Kochno to send him his dress-clothes. This sort of thing had never happened before. Generally his departure for the theatre on an opening night was the occasion for a good deal of ceremony. He went off as though he was starting for a long journey.

Sergei Pavlovitch made me sit down and was silent for a minute. After that he just blessed me, made the sign of the cross over me and embraced me.

I was seized by a kind of terror that transformed me. I did not want to go to the theatre. *Le Fils Prodigue* made no impression on me. I feared a flop and said so to Koriboute, who was in a state of panic and lay stretched out on a divan.

Eight o'clock, five minutes past, ten minutes past . . . Koriboute gazed at me. He was mute, supplicating and looked like a man condemned to death. There flashed through my mind the film of my life, the loving care of Sergei Pavlovitch had made me an artist—all I was proud to be. A great pity for him swept over me. There he was exhausted, ageing . . . even if it was to be for the last time, even if thenceforth I must fly with my own wings, I had to dance that evening.

I leapt up from the couch.

'Off to the theatre, I'm going to create "my" *Fils Prodigue*.' Koriboute sobbed.

I danced *L'Après-Midi d'un Faune*. I could not see Diaghilev. He was neither in the wings nor in his box. *Renard* was a triumph . . . applause . . . cheers . . . but I refused, despite Stravinsky's urging, to go and take any curtain-calls. After the interval came *Le Fils Prodigue*. Still there was no Diaghilev to be seen.

I danced *Le Fils Prodigue* and improvised as it were in a nightmare. The hero I was personifying was myself, tortured by a presentiment that this was the end of something, the end of a dying world . . . it was I with my feelings of renunciation, with my need to renounce, to renounce a protection that threatened to become restrictive, oppressive . . . It was I that was harrowed . . . what I was acting was my own life.

When the curtain went down the audience burst out into thunderous applause. Some people were weeping. The public had been touched—but could not know why . . . only one could know . . . but in fact—the thought of him as a judge haunted me—what would he say about it? All I had done that evening— playing very 'dramatically'—employing 'touching' effects—was opposed to his ideas on art. Yes, from that evening I became the prodigal son—I had introduced realism into art.

But he remained invisible. Walter Nouvel came into my dressing-room and embraced me affectionately:

'Bravo, Lifar, you were magnificent, splendid. . . .'

I was surrounded by people cheering and making much of me. Still he did not appear. Then, all of a sudden, I saw him in a corner. I had never seen him look like that before. He did not move. Tears were streaming down his cheeks. He was far from me. I was appalled and thought, 'If Diaghilev is remaining in that way, silent, it is because he is reproaching me for having sacrificed art to personal triumph, for being a ham actor, for having employed "anti-artistic" methods.'

A little later on while I was resting after having removed my make-up, Walter Nouvel came and told me that Diaghilev had gone to have supper at *Les Capucines* on the boulevards and that he was expecting me. Should I go and perhaps risk a public humiliation?

I went all the same and when I entered the restaurant I was given a wonderful reception by my friends who were there. Diaghilev had kept the place of honour for me, facing him and between Misia Sert and Coco Chanel. Near us were Picasso, Rouault, Stravinsky, Prokofiev, Cocteau and Boris Kochno. I raised my glass and addressed Diaghilev:

'I drink to you and your twenty-first season. I drink also to *your* triumph.'

Diaghilev thereupon got to his feet, looked at me for a long moment, almost as though he were in pain, his eyes veiled in tears:

'Yes, Lifar, thank you. You are a great artist, a real artist, and I have nothing more to teach you.'

After Paris came a German tour—Berlin, Cologne—it was a great success. Sergei Pavlovitch was making his last triumphal progress with Prokofiev's *Le Lac des Cygnes* danced by Olga Spessiva, who had come back to the *Ballets Russes,* and Stravinsky's *Le Sacre du Printemps.* As for my *Renard,* it definitely established me as a choreographer.

In July we all met in London. After the brilliant revelation of *Le Fils Prodigue,* which the English at last appreciated, Diaghilev once more concerned himself with Igor Markévitch, then aged sixteen. The distance that separated me from Diaghilev increased daily. I became more occupied with myself and more dejected also. Nevertheless he still had need of me. The holidays had scattered us. He went back to Germany in company with Igor Markévitch against the categorical advice of his physician—he was then suffering from an attack of large boils, the consequence of his diabetes.

At Vichy, where I finished the ballet season, I got this letter from him. It was dated 2nd August:

'My very dear Seriozha,

'Your telegram allayed my anxiety, all the same, I have not had a single letter from you. Why have you not written? Can you have forgotten me? Did you get my letter from Paris?

'The Hindemiths are charming but he has not produced anything yet.[1] He is full of hope and good intentions. His cantata is curious but one can see that it was composed hastily and the show that goes with it is poor. I have met here many Paris friends among others Madame de Polignac, Madame Dubost etc. I am nourished here on Mozart and Wagner. Both are geniuses and they are marvellously well played. Today at *Tristan* I wept salt tears The books also are all right. Thank

---

[1] Diaghilev had asked Hindemith for a score for which I was to compose a choreography that I was to dance myself, the book was to be by Boris Kochno and the décors by Bérard.

Boris [Kochno] for his first letter. It seemed anxious but judging from the telegram everything has been arranged.

'Don't forget that the cat embraces you and blesses you.' Instead of a signature he had drawn a big cat.

This was the last letter I was ever to get from him. After that came only telegrams.

On 7th August we both left for Venice, he from Salzburg and I from Vichy.

❦ 8 ❦

THE TWILIGHT OF THE GODS

On 9th August I arrived in Venice. My heart was torn between
two emotions. There was the joy I felt at seeing Sergei Pavlovich
once more in those beautiful surroundings where I had been so
happy in his company and under his guidance; then again there
was my anxiety about the decision I had taken, or rather which
I feel inclined to say had formed itself deep down within me.
This decision I had not as yet ever spoken of. Perhaps from a
sense of decency in view of Diaghilev's approaching death.
Today I can mention that my mind was already made up. I
had come to tell the master of my youth that I was going to
leave the *Ballets Russes*. I felt that I must, that I owed it to
myself to do so. In any case I foresaw that the *Ballets* were going
to die or at least lose their character. I had learned with them
all I could learn. Diaghilev had given me everything, that was
true enough. We had both realised this on the evening of the
Fils Prodigue first performance. Now I must fly with my own
wings and become myself responsible for my art and my soul.
I had no idea of how Diaghilev would receive the news. Possibly
quite well. But despite my firm resolution I was sad, sad as
from a fading youth, from a farewell to a kind of happiness
which had fled for ever.

When I got out of the train I looked for Diaghilev on the
platform. But he was not there. At once the thought struck me
that he was now no longer as punctual as he used to be, that
his memory was failing. I went off to the Grand Hotel des Bains
on the Lido and I was already slightly anxious. Then Sergei
Pavlovitch was not on the hotel steps to welcome me as was his

habit in former times. I looked up and there he was at a window.
He was slowly waving a handkerchief and he seemed aged,
exhausted. At a first glance I hardly recognised him, so much had
he changed in only two weeks. He was old, unkempt, his face was
pale, of a wax-like pallor. My heart was heavy and I forgot all
else but him as I ran up to his room. As he embraced me there
were tears in his eyes.

'What's the matter, Sergei Pavlovitch, you're not ill are
you?'

'Yes, I don't feel very well, the journey must have tired me.
I am very weak and fatigued, everything fatigues me. All my
trip to Germany did was to exhaust me. At Munich I felt for
the first time this dreadful pain in my back—and it has lasted
for six days. I can't sleep, or get about or eat. My stomach will
not digest anything. My God, how tired I am. I wanted to go
and meet you but I could not manage it. My knees gave way.
My legs won't carry me any more. The German doctors said
it was rheumatism, but I'm afraid it's something much more
serious . . . and you, how are you?'

I did not know what to answer. All I had meant to tell him
faded from my mind, had become inane. I was filled only with
sorrowful pity for this stricken old man. But mingled with this
feeling there was, I must confess, a slight repulsion, a physical
repulsion against a body already occupied by an alien presence,
the presence of annihilation and death. I changed my clothes
quickly and took Diaghilev to see his doctor, who, after examin-
ing him, tried to reassure him. This physician too talked about
rheumatism, the result of boils and overwork. He prescribed
massage and rest. The doctor's remarks seemed somewhat to
appease Diaghilev's fears—but not mine.

When we got back to the hotel Sergei Pavlovitch took a huge
room with two beds and asked me to stay with him. He had a
panic fear of being alone and thought that if no one was
with him he would surely die, but that if someone was with
him then the other's presence would be enough to ward off
death.

That night was the first of a series of sleepless ones for me. I
did not get any more sleep until 20th August. The following
days were grey, oppressive, stifling. I was his real nurse. I
spent hours massaging his legs, making him swallow his various
medicines, dressing him and helping him to get up, for he could

no longer do that by himself. His strength ebbed away from day to day.

Did he realise, during those last few days, how alone he was, how tragically alone? Only I remained and even I had moved away from him, no longer really belonged to him. Now there began to revive within me that resolution I had come to talk to him about. Sometimes, and especially during the nights, he would talk at length about memories of his youth. He was homesick for his country that he would never see again. He spoke with emotion about his first journeys abroad—Italy and his visits to Venice and Rome. He recounted his first season when, with Pavlova in *Cléopatra* and Chaliapin in *Boris Godunov*, he had had all Paris at his feet.

On 12th August he took to his bed and never got up again. From that moment he began to burn, to be consumed. Fever seized him and his temperature rose from day to day, from hour to hour. On the 17th it was 39·5 (103 F.), on the 18th 40·5 (105 F.) and during the night of the 19th 41·1 (106 F.). The doctors who were treating him—Professor Vitoli and Dr Vidali—practically never left his side, but they could neither explain nor arrest the organism's combustion. Several times his blood was analysed but the examinations revealed nothing.

Boris Kochno, whom I had sent for, arrived at last from Toulon. He had had his whole head shaved. Sergei Pavlovitch could hardly recognise him. During the night of 16th August Sergei Pavlovitch burst out into a loud fit of weeping and cried out to be removed from his bed and given mine. There was a belief in my family that if a sick man is moved into the bed of someone near to him it was a sign that death was approaching. Diaghilev, a profoundly superstitious man, knew this, so his request filled me with terror.

The next day while I was downstairs with Boris Kochno a groom brought me a message scribbled by Diaghilev's trembling hand ... 'Tell the doctor my pulse is dreadfully irregular and ask him if he can come and see me for a minute after luncheon.'

We rushed upstairs and there a horrible sight met our eyes. Sergei Pavlovitch, breathing with great difficulty, was trying to drag himself on all fours to my bed, but he could not raise himself to clamber into it. He had wanted to ring for a servant but could not find the bell, had lost his balance, fallen at the foot of his bed and then endeavoured to drag himself to mine.

Then it was that I realised there was no more hope. Sergei
Pavlovitch was going to meet his end. From that instant we
did not leave him alone for a minute.

Coco Chanel and Misia Sert had come to Venice on the Duke
of Westminster's yacht, they visited Diaghilev and spent almost
an hour with him. Then they went off to continue their cruise.
But they were so alarmed that they came back again on 18th
August. They were appalled by the difference two days had made
in him. On their first visit there was still some hope he might
recover. They had at once sent for the German doctors who were
on the yacht, but they also understood nothing about Diaghilev's
condition. Perhaps it was acute rheumatism, or typhoid fever—
the high temperatures seemed to suggest the latter. However,
towards the end of the afternoon he was still able to say a
few amiable words to his visitors. During the night of the 18th
to the 19th we sent for Father Irenaeus of the Orthodox Greek
Church, but Diaghilev was in a coma and was unaware of anything happening about him. At two o'clock in the morning the
fever rose to 41 (106 F.). Sergei Pavlovitch was stifling. It was the
death-agony.

I sat close to the bed and supported the dying man on one
side while Boris Kochno was on the other side. Misia Sert was
watching at the foot of the bed. The doctor and the female
nurse stood near the window. So the night wore away.

At dawn on 19th August, about five o'clock, his respiration
all at once became very rapid—five or six breaths a second—
but the air could no longer find its way into his lungs. At 5.45
his breathing ceased quietly, peacefully. I shook him a little.
He was still panting.

The doctor tiptoed over and said in a low voice:
'It is the end.'

At that moment the first rays of the rising sun shone over the
horizon and illuminated the dead man's face, down which large
tears were trickling. He was only fifty-seven years old.

Kochno and I jealously discussed what each of us should do
for this divine being.[1]

At first I did not fully realise what this death meant. I
did not realise he had left us for ever. I moved about like a
robot. But the first thing I did was to call in the sculptors and

[1] In my book *Sept ans aux Ballets Russes* I have recounted this scene at
length.

the photographers to make the death-mask. It was horrible when the sculptors to remove the mask struck a heavy blow on Diaghilev's head.

Boris Kochno, Misia Sert, Coco Chanel and the Baronne d'Erlanger made the arrangements for the funeral. I shut myself up alone with the dead man and allowed no one to enter the room until I had finished preparing the body for burial. I shaved him, I trimmed his moustache to the shape he always had it—in the fashion of Peter the Great. I bound his jaws together with a napkin. I dressed his hair. I put on a tie and cuffs with the cuff-links he had given me in Italy. I folded his arms together over his breast and put a camellia in his button-hole. The people who then came into the bedroom were struck with his appearance, so youthful, so handsome. One might have thought that there he lay still alive and that those terrible nights had never existed.

Koriboute then arrived and he, Boris Kochno and I watched over the body all night. Suddenly a terrific storm broke. Fierce winds howled. The lightning-streaked sky lit up the face of the dead man in strange fashion.

At dawn they brought a coffin. He was placed in it together with a little crucifix which Misia Sert had put in his hand as soon as he expired. We all gave him one last kiss on his forehead.

The coffin covered with wreaths was embarked on a dark funerary gondola. Thus was accomplished the prediction. Diaghilev had died on the water, on an island . . . the long, black gondola glided slowly away towards Venice. . . .

A few days later everything was calm once more, all was serene on the little island of San Michele where Serge de Diaghilev reposes for ever.

But all was tempest and tumult in my heart.

I must admit that on the day of the funeral, after days and nights of fearful nervous tension, my nerves had given way. Some of those who at one time called themselves my friends have described my collapse in terms they intended to humiliate me. For long I was embarrassed and much put out by this, but today when life has swept by I can only pity such people.

I will just recount what my real position was. At twenty-four years of age I was once more alone in the world. Seven years before, when I was seventeen. I had arrived in France with no friends, no relations. I had passed through experiences that were most trying for a sensitive youth. There I was in a country of which I knew nothing, not even the language. Serge de Diaghilev looked after me, had literally adopted me, had been at one and the same time the fostering father, the guide to my moral and mental education, the master of my work and my art. I had lived through seven years of intense and practically unceasing labour. This devotion to my task had isolated me. I owed everything to him. Why, then, one may ask, was I preparing to quit this man who had done so much for me? The paradox is only an apparent one. My labour had, of course, borne its fruits and I was beginning to be conscious of my own personality and, at last, to gain some self-confidence. But, as I have just said, this work to which I owed everything had also isolated me. And that great animator Diaghilev, who had given me so much, was now tending to brake the impetus he had aroused.

Indeed, during the last few years before his death, I had become gradually aware—or thought I had become aware, for it is a fact that I did think so—that Diaghilev did not have a real, sincere respect for the personalities of others and what they may possess in the way of irrepressible independence, but he had rather an aesthetic taste for domination—in the manner of a Pygmalion—and it was this 'moral' aestheticism which now shocked me. And it shocked me to the extent of making me believe that, for Sergei Pavlovitch, everything had just been a game, an attitude, an expression of selfishness, and that he had never felt for me—or indeed for anyone else—any sincere sentiments of affection. And everyone realised this.

But all this I felt and experienced *while he was alive*. Once he was dead, there I was plunged into hopeless solitude once more. And in dismay I felt an urge to draw near to everything which evoked the memory of Diaghilev. It was from this time that dated my real friendship with Paul Koriboute, whom, it is true, I had up to then respected (as did all the company) but in whom I now discovered a marvellous being both sensitive and benevolent. Later on, he himself lived as a hermit at Monte Carlo where he died in 1940. Each year I would go to see the man I called my 'uncle'. In his presence I would enjoy the charm of his soothing serenity and I was very happy to be able to contribute to his support.

There is something which is less explicable. It can only be

understood if one takes into account both the perturbation
afflicting me and also the weird Karamazov-like atmosphere
which surrounded Sergei Pavlovitch. I conceived a liking for
Boris Kochno. Up to this time I had felt nothing but aversion
for him—and he did not like me much. He had, for the rest,
always been very close to Diaghilev to whom he was devotedly
attached. And this was strange enough and can be explained
only by the taste the creator of the *Ballets Russes* had for the
ugly as much as for the beautiful, for a certain 'black aspect' of
the world which he recognised in a man he often treated in a
harsh manner I could not approve of. I will never forget the
painful scene that took place in the presence of Diaghilev's dead
body which everyone seemed to want to keep for himself.

It was then in a confused state of mind that I went back to
Paris. It had been decided to carry on Diaghilev's work and a
directing committee had been set up. It was composed of M.
Ratkov-Roijnov, a near relation of Sergei Pavlovitch and his
legatee, S. Grigorieff, the former director of the *Ballets Russes*,
Walter Nouvelle, Boris Kochno and myself as leading dancer and
ballet-master. In September a meeting of impresarios was held at
the Grand Hotel. The main business concerned the renewal of
the contracts Diaghilev had made in England and Spain. I
agreed to this being done but during this same meeting I
became convinced that as a matter of fact it would be quite impossible to carry on Diaghilev's work, at least in the spirit that
he conceived it. Far too much depended on his artistic personality. In these circumstances it would be far better to give up
the whole idea. And I there and then made up my mind that
this would be the right solution. The *Ballets Russes* must come to
an end and leave only a memory indissolubly linked with that of
Diaghilev himself. And I myself must go away, go anywhere,
perhaps even back to the Soviet Union—for this idea flashed
through my mind for a moment!

However, I countersigned the contracts. The members of the
company were getting impatient and each day would turn up
to get information at the Hôtel des Arcades where I was staying.
I know that by refusal to give an opinion I was signing the death
warrant of the *Ballets Russes* where I ought to have had responsibilities far greater than those of a leading dancer. But it
was the thought of this which induced me more than anything
else to renounce. I was not capable of stepping into Diaghilev's

shoes and carrying on his work. I decided to announce definitely that I refused the glorious inheritance.

Later on, all the artists who had been born, so to speak, in the *Ballets Russes* seemed to do all they could to obliterate the memory of this connection as though it lowered them in some way—so true is it that often nearly everyone wants to be born of nothing and no one. But it is also true that right through his whole career as an animator, Diaghilev had been careful to provoke emulation by opposing creative artists to one another —Fokine to Nijinsky, Stravinsky to Prokofiev, Bakst to Benois, Matisse to Picasso, Kschessinska to Pavlova. With him no artist ever reigned alone. This fruitful 'game', although it may have resulted in each one giving of his best, also wounded the sensitiveness of more than one. And this is why the memoirs of Stravinsky, of Romola Nijinska, of Fokine and even of Benois are always bitter and sour.

On the contrary, as far as I was concerned, I assumed the inheritance—spiritual this time—and the celebration of Serge de Diaghilev's genius as a debt I would have to pay and which became for me a sort of little intimate and lay religion. In 1964 I managed to induce the Paris Municipal Council to give to the square behind the Opera the name of Serge de Diaghilev. He was indeed the greatest knight-errant of the arts and it was I who placed the wreath upon his head.

So the company of the *Ballets Russes* was broken up.

In order to free ourselves from the contracts Walter Nouvel had a brilliant idea. What he had thought up was this. In order to refloat such a huge undertaking, it was indispensable that Diaghilev's heirs should put up a million francs—quite a considerable sum in those days. Of course they could not do this and so by force of circumstances the artists were freed from the obligation of carrying out the contracts. Princesse Edmond de Polignac,[1] who was the patroness of the *Ballets Russes*, agreed with my way of thinking. So the matter was settled. A letter from Massine—then in America—reached us much later on. He begged us to continue the *Ballets Russes* and offered to help. Kochno, at my urgent request, handed me a statement declaring that he, for his part, gave up all thought of carrying on Diaghilev's ballets.

[1] née Singer, the widow of Prince Edmond de Polignac (died 1901), a great patron of the arts and especially of music.

As soon as all this business was settled I went off to Les Sablettes near Toulon. There was no question of taking a vacation or of amusing myself. I needed solitude for meditation and searching introspection. Although I did not, it is true, quite succeed in my aims, this sojourn in the South did help me. I became aware of two realities which I had hitherto, luckily or unluckily, been unaware of—fortune and fame. I had had no money and had never felt the need for it. I had a name but I did not know what it was worth.

Up to then I had never known what money was. I had never had any either in Soviet Russia (where at the time of my escape money had, anyway, practically ceased to be tender, for instance one swapped a grand piano for a few pounds of butter) or in France from 1923 to 1929. During this time, it was true, I was supposed to receive a salary, which, however, I never saw, to such an extent indeed that I did not know what it was. Diaghilev paid all my expenses and when I wanted pocket-money I simply took what I needed.

Now I noticed I had no money, not enough to pay my hotel bill. I sent a telegram to Walter Nouvel, who had become for me a sort of tutor-secretary, and the matter was quickly settled. But I had to tackle this problem of money especially as I am by nature rather indifferent to it—I suppose that this is a characteristic that will remain with me for the rest of my life.

My other discovery concerned fame. I had a name without knowing it. Diaghilev—and this was typical of him—had jealously hidden from me any laudatory press notices concerning myself. It was also his habit to keep from the Press information about his stars. He would insist upon the high quality of the *Ballets Russes* as a *whole*. So, I did not suspect how well I was known. However, a few days after my arrival in the South of France I got a telegram from Walter Nouvel telling me that Jacques Rouché, the director of the Paris Opera, wanted to see me without delay. Then came a telegram from Cochran in London, and a third from Anna Pavlova offering me a contract to dance in her troupe. Finally came a still more pressing telegram, this time from Jacques Rouché himself. I hardly paid any attention to it. I was still suffering from the shock of Sergei Pavlovitch's death. But little by little this idea of fame attached to an artist's name began to take definite shape in my mind.

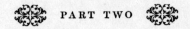

PART TWO

THE RISE

One day I got another telegram from Nouvel. The apartment Diaghilev had taken in Paris, boulevard Garibaldi, only a few months before his death had had seals put on it.[1] Here were all his belongings, his art collection and his library. That same day I took the train. Some of his friends had decided to save all Diaghilev's property, which otherwise would be put up for sale. When we arrived at the flat it was indeed sealed up and we could not get in. But after a thorough search we managed to discover a tradesman's entrance. From that moment began the 'pillage'. As a matter of fact, it appeared later on that I was really robbing myself.

We operated with the full connivance of Diaghilev's heirs, who, moreover, scarcely knew him and were not only ignorant of his essential genius but were also unaware of his dearest tastes and closest friendships, that is to say of everything that was his soul and life. Koriboute, Nouvel, Kochno and I would go in by the small entrance and emerge twice as bulky as we entered, for we hid our booty under our overcoats. These manœuvres lasted for more than a week. To gain time for our goings and comings we stowed everything away in a room Kochno had taken in his own name at a nearby hotel. We only had to dodge in and out. It was very convenient. When the operation was completed Kochno had only to shut his door and declare that everything in the room was his. We thus saved a remarkable collection of autographs, manuscripts, rare books, scores,

[1] It is normal French official procedure for seals to be placed on the doors of a dwelling after a death. To break or remove these is a serious offence.

and inestimably valuable documents of all sorts including the files Diaghilev kept concerning his literary and musical publications.

I have said that, in my confused state of mind, I had for a moment the idea of going back to my country, to Soviet Russia, but the idea soon left me.

The Soviet embassy (diplomatic relations had been resumed between France and the USSR), thinking no doubt that Diaghilev had no direct heirs in France, put forward a claim to his property which, they said, should be given back to Russia. Thus it was that one day I was summoned to the rue de Grenelle 'for an affair concerning the estate of Serge de Diaghilev'. Now, at this time the most terrifying rumours were current among Russian refugees as to what went on behind the high walls of the embassy in the rue de Grenelle. It had been transformed, so the story went, into a well-guarded branch of the Cheka. So the summons I had received alarmed my friends and we got together in a council of war and took the following decision. While I was in the embassy one of our people would walk up and down before the building with the red flag. The others would wait in my room. If by midday I had not reappeared they would inform the police.

At eight o'clock in the morning, then, I presented myself at the embassy. I rang at the door of the Soviet consulate (one had to get into the embassy through the consulate). The door at once opened and then slammed shut again. All retreat was cut off. Before me was standing a giant of a man with a revolver in his hand.

'Hands up!'

I was terrified and replied in Russian. The formidable Cerberus seemed only to understand French, so I explained I had been summoned to the embassy and I showed him the letter fixing an appointment. He snatched it from me.

'Pass on.'

I walked into a small drawing-room with walls covered in red stuff. The warder here left me alone but as he went out he was careful to bolt the door. I waited. Time passed. Ten minutes. A quarter of an hour. An hour. I got impatient and at the same time felt alarmed. I was also suffocating in this small room adorned with a portrait of Lenin. Two hours went by. I was overcome with a kind of apathy. I imagined I had been locked

in a gas-chamber, but I was indifferent to everything. I was
ready to die.

Finally the door did open and there came in a much more
distinguished-looking official. He asked me to follow him. We
walked across a courtyard covered with gravel that scrunched
under our feet. We entered a building to our right. I was now
quite convinced that I was about to be shut up in a cellar. I made
as though to go down the stairs.

'No, sir, we are going up to the first floor.'

That made me feel a good deal more reassured. I was introduced into the office of the first secretary of the embassy. He
received me very amiably, spoke about Diaghilev, whose brother,
a general, had just been discovered as a prisoner in Siberia.
He also talked about Sergei Pavlovitch's collections. He congratulated me as well. He had seen me dance in *Le Fils Prodigue*
and was enthusiastic about my dramatic acting and my high
leaps. We chatted, in this way, for a good half hour, after
which my host accompanied me to the main entrance of the
embassy.

Here there was a surprise indeed. The police and a crowd of
inquisitive idlers were mobbing the embassy. Of course. I
could understand it all. I was the cause of the excitement.
Walter Nouvel had got tired of waiting for me and had called
on the police. But, no, I soon realised my mistake. The huge
headlines in *Paris-Midi* explained everything. The night before
Bessedovski, the *chargé d'affaires*, had chosen liberty by clam-
bering over the embassy walls and landing up in the Italian
embassy garden! . . . my visit cured me of any desire to go back
to the Soviet Union.

The interview with Jacques Rouché, the big chief of the Paris
Opera, was the starting-point of years of contact which were of
decisive import for all my career, all my life as an artist. It is
true that I had already met Rouché who was a close friend of
Diaghilev and a good friend of the *Ballets Russes*. I knew him
as a man of much shrewdness, a remarkable critic and an excellent
connoisseur of the arts. But from this interview dated our close
relations which led to a collaboration lasting fifteen years.
During this time I got to know him better and better and to
appreciate him ever more highly. Jacques Rouché was not only
the head of the Opera (which was not yet nationalised but only
subventioned by the State) in which he sank much of his personal

fortune, but in his conception of art his spirit was always bold and youthful.

Perhaps it was because there was nothing of the narrow-minded party man about him, maybe it was because of his unfailing tact, but the very real and profound reforms he carried out shocked no one; they had indeed none of the appearance of revolutions, yet they were more thorough—and long-lasting—than a number of the spectacular and much-boosted enterprises of certain 'modernists'.

I found him at his desk, the little man, who, I knew, liked to declare, 'I'm one of Diaghilev's disciples', and I also knew that he sometimes added: 'I will carry on his work. . . .'

'Lifar, I'd very much like to see you on the stage of the Opera. What would you say if I suggested you should produce a ballet and dance in it? Say, for instance, the *Prométhée* of Beethoven . . . as far as the business arrangements are concerned I can offer you 5000 francs a performance and twice as much as that for the choreography.'

'That's not the problem, sir. In my opinion it is such an honour to appear at the National Academy of Dance that I would willingly do it for nothing. But there is one thing that disturbs me. I have not danced for some little time, I could not make my *rentrée* without having gone into training for some months. And it remains to be seen if I could ever get back my old form—and I could not accept to appear at the Opera unless I was in top condition.'

'Well, Lifar, there's no question of starting dancing tomorrow. Count two full months for the choreography and the rehearsals. From now to then you will certainly have been able to get back your old form.'

'Very well, then, I'll try. Engage a choreographer, I'll learn the part and try to dance it.'

'A choreographer! But I'm counting on you; the author of *Renard*. The subject I propose is thrilling, don't you agree?'

'Most certainly, but it's a task beyond me and I would not like to take it on. It's one thing to direct *Renard* for the *Ballets Russes* and it's quite another to produce *Prométhée* on the largest stage in Europe. Down there I had comrades always ready to help and in addition I did not have to worry about the *corps de ballet* whereas here I should be entering a new world, and the capacity of your *corps de ballet* appears to me really feeble.'

'That's just why I am asking for your collaboration. In any case, you must dance the role of *Prométhée*. I'm most anxious you should give me your definite promise to do that.'

I turned things over in my mind for a moment. When I went to see Jacques Rouché I was decided to refuse all the propositions he might make me. But now all at once I had a crazy urge to dance at the Opera.

'I will make a definite promise and will do the best I can so that you'll not regret having asked me . . . but all this is on one condition only, that Olga Spessivtzeva should be my partner. . . .'

'I don't doubt for a single instant that you'll be a success. But since you won't take on the choreography tell me to whom you'd like me to apply. Staats?'

'To speak quite frankly, I would rather some other choreographer.'

'Would you like me to engage Mme Nijinska?'

'Since you agree giving *Prométhée* a choreographer from the *Ballets Russes*, I would rather suggest Balanchine.'

'All right, Lifar, where is he? Get him to come here.'

When I told my friends that Jacques Rouché had asked me to do the choreography for *Prométhée* but that I had refused, they all agreed I had done right, but their approval was for reasons which I confess I had not thought about. *Prométhée* they explained was the bedevilled ballet of the whole repertory. Vigano had had an appalling flop with *Prométhée*, Karsavina had injured her heel while dancing in it, etc. . . . I must say that as though to live up to its bad reputation *Prométhée* did cause a series of misfortunes. After the first rehearsal Balanchine fell gravely ill. Blondeau, who was the first-rate general manager of the Opera, died a few days before the first performance. A year later at Saint-Nazaire I was to baptise a submarine by the name of *Prométhée* but I could not go on board for the first high-seas trial since I had a heavy cold. Something went wrong. The submarine did not surface and of the two hundred men on board only one was saved—Commander Dumesnil. It was Jacques Rouché who, as the messenger of fate, prevented me at the last moment from taking part in the launching. My photograph which I, as the 'godfather' of the ship, had sent to Saint-Nazaire, lies among the crew at the bottom of the ocean.

M.V.—G

A few days after my interview with Jacques Rouché, I met Cochran. We had a very commonplace business conversation about my appearing in his London review. I was to be paid £200 a week (in those days that was a large sum) in addition to my rights in the choreography of a short ballet I agreed to direct. It was called *La Nuit* and I advised him to ask Sauguet for the music, Bérard (one of Diaghilev's last discoveries) for the décors and Kochno for the book. My contract with Cochran bound me for ten months in 1930.

And to crown all, I got word from the legendary Anna Pavlova asking me to call and see her at the Hôtel Plaza where she was staying. It was not without a good deal of emotion that I accepted the invitation of the great 'goddess of the Dance'.

When she received me she was stretched out, like Madame Recamier, on a divan. She was capricious, playful like a coquettish woman accustomed to having her slightest behests obeyed.

'My dear Lifar, I must tell you how much I admire you. Of all Diaghilev's dancers you are the only one I ever thought of engaging in my troupe. I hope you will not refuse to be Anna Pavlova's partner?'

'I would be overjoyed and honoured. All the same I would very much like to know what I would dance. What would the repertory be?'

Anna Pavlova pretended not to have heard the last part of my remark and she cut me short:

'Strictly between ourselves, I'm not a little tired of Vladimirov and would be glad to replace him with a young—and very talented—partner—you for instance.'

That made it clear to me what she meant by the word 'partner'; the fact was that it was 'carrier' she meant. This cooled me off not a little. All the same I should very much have liked to dance with her.

'Would you not consider enriching your repertory with some new creations?'

'And for what reason, my God? Do you think my repertory so bad as all that? It draws full houses The public is accustomed to seeing me in certain roles and asks for nothing more. Why change anything at all?'

Then suddenly, I do not know why, I broke out into a vehement discourse.

'Anna Pavlova, I consider you are the greatest genius of

the Dance—of all time—past and present. So maybe the profound admiration I feel for you will allow me to tell you the whole truth. It makes me sad to see that you do not give the public the revelation it awaits from you, and that you spoil your genius when each evening you repeat yourself, thus destroying yourself, your lovely legend, your myth.'

'It's possible, Lifar, that you're not altogether wrong, but in your opinion what ought I to do?'

'Appear not very frequently in public and always in new roles ... re-create your myth each time ... you should, like the gods or princes ...'

I broke off on seeing Dandré, Pavlova's husband, come in. She repeated the gist of our conversation to him. He interrupted harshly:

'Idle fancies, illusions, chimeras, and moreover, Monsieur Lifar, it seems to me that you came here not to make proposals but to listen to those made to you.'

He turned to me:

'Well, Monsieur Lifar, do you accept the offer to be Anna Pavlova's partner?'

He annoyed me. I replied curtly:

'No, monsieur, I refuse.'

'You refuse. Well and good, then we've nothing more to say to each other.'

So, obviously, all I had to do was to take leave. However, Anna Pavlova kept me.

'Wait, Lifar, I want to speak to you about another project. The idea is to organise an evening at the Opera, a performance to the memory of Diaghilev and as brilliant as possible. I know that Rouché has already approached you. He likes you very much and he liked Diaghilev ... he will not, I think, refuse to arrange such an evening at the Opera.'

Dandré disappeared as abruptly as he had come and we were able to discuss in detail the programme of our gala. Of our galas, in fact, since there were now to be two. The first dedicated to the memory of Diaghilev. Pavlova was to appear in *Les Sylphides* (the first piece she danced in with the *Ballets Russes* in 1909) and in *Le Lac des Cygnes* ... she said again that she would be happy to appear with me and that she thought I was the best dancer in the world. We left each other on very friendly terms and I almost forgot the disagreeable impression made by

Dandré's intrusion. The very next day I went to see Jacques
Rouché and asked to arrange for two galas with Anna Pavlova.
He at once agreed. So I was to have the honour of becoming the
partner of the divine Pavlova, of working with her, of some-
times being her teacher—at her request—as I was of Olga
Spessiva.

Two weeks later, after a rehearsal, Jacques Rouché asked me
to go up and see him in his office.

'Listen, my dear fellow, you're making a lot of unnecessary
trouble for me. You ask me to organise two galas with you and
Pavlova when as a matter of fact you've no intention of taking
Part in them.'

'What do you mean?'

'Just this. Here you are, here's the programme Pavlova has
sent me from England, and here's her letter—read them.'

Although I searched very carefully I could not find my name
mentioned—nor that of Diaghilev—Anna Pavlova (that is to
say really Dandré) had decided to forgo my collaboration in
the two galas. I said this to Rouché. With one stroke of the pen
he annulled the programme.

'Let's talk no more about it.'

And Anna Pavlova did not dance at the Opera at all.

Jacques Rouché introduced me to the troupe. He said that
he hoped that according to their custom the French artists
would extend a kind welcome to a newcomer who was leading
dancer and choreographer of the *Ballets Russes*. There was silence
and certainly there could have been no other reply. I got an
impression of a cold, even inimical, atmosphere. But I must say
that it changed quite quickly. As the rehearsal went on I made
more and more friends among the younger people. As for the
others, well, there things were very different. However, from
the first day I was *maître* and for a quarter of a century I was
greeted by the words 'Good day, *maître*' from all, from the
'little rats' to the stars. I was a sort of happy shepherd.

At the first rehearsal of *Prométhée* Balanchine seemed to be
in a very bad state of health. Things started off unfavourably.
All the time I kept saying to myself . . . 'Now, I would have done
it in a quite different way.' There was no second rehearsal.
Balanchine went down with a congestion of the lungs and had

to take to his bed. And he would be out of action for a month. It was Rouché himself who told me this and he added:

'Upon my word, Lifar, it is clearly fated that you must take on the choreography of *Prométhée*. You cannot refuse any more.' And I had not the slightest wish to refuse since the whole ballet was already sketched out in my mind. So I set to work without delay. My idea was that the central personage should be Prometheus himself and not any of his creatures. I arranged three groups, first Prometheus, then his creatures (that is the mythological characters such as Death, Love and so forth), and lastly the chorus as a setting for the movements of the protagonists —a sort of living back-drop in fact.

My plastic conception of Prometheus's role was influenced by the Diaghilev ballet traditions—lines sharply broken and sometimes abrupt gestures. All the same, I felt I was already obeying the promptings of my free inspiration, of my identification—as a dancer—with the personage. I arranged these dances for myself, for me alone . . . and so I was liberated from all rules. I let myself go. I just noted the plastic images that came to me spontaneously, causing me great creative joy.

But things did not go so well with the *corps de ballet*. As I was new to an institution proud of its century-old traditions, I did not at once dare to modernise the ensemble. Sometimes it happened that I moved away from the usual groupings, but this I did prudently, I would even say timidly. However, I did make the dancers lie on the floor to perform their *jeu de jambes* in that position. But I proceeded gently with what was a sort of revolution.

From the plastic point of view, the other personages came half-way between the *corps de ballet* and Prometheus. For their dances I resolutely rejected tradition and my creation was on two planes, the one real and the other imaginary. Of the two creatures the partner interested me the more. I saw her as a Galatea incarnated by Spessivtzeva. Luckily she now belonged to the Opera. Jacques Rouché had engaged her.

For the role of Death I found a marvellous interpreter in the person of a young *première danseuse*, Suzanne Lorcia. The part of Love was offered to Camille Bos but she refused it and I had to ask Mlle Lamballe to take it.

Work progressed rapidly. I was then staying at the Grand Hôtel and from my windows, while I was myself cutting out

Prometheus's leather tunic, I could see the statue of Apollo that decorates the façade of the Opera. I shall visualise it all my life long. At the end of each rehearsal the troupe displayed increased esteem for my work. I had finished by obtaining perfect discipline. Olga Spessivtzeva gave me precious help. Her docility was an example to the others and not on one single occasion did I hear her raise any objections or make the slightest criticism.

I can remember one amusing incident during a rehearsal.

I had executed two *tours* in the air and instead of ending up standing or with one knee on the floor, I fell sideways. Everyone rushed to the rescue—Jacques Rouché, the musicians, the *corps de ballet*. They thought I had made a mistake and had hurt myself. I got up quite calmly—for this *pas* figured in my choreography—and said in an indifferent tone of voice:

'Well now, what's happening?—let's carry on.'

But soon trouble started.

As I was a Russian I had been engaged only for a single ballet—*Prométhée*—and for one performance, and Rouché had arranged that at all the first rehearsals there should be present Staats, the ballet-master, and two leading dancers, Ricaux and Aveline. The first, in my absence, was to assure that the choreography should be rightly carried on, and one of the two dancers was to take my place in the role of Prometheus. But both refused to accept declaring that in no case did they want to be associated with such a 'horror'.

Another row, more serious this time, nearly broke out between us and the two authors who had reworked the libretto of *Prométhée*. One of them, M. Chantavoine, the general secretary of the National Academy of Music, after having been present at a rehearsal, just demanded that *Prométhée* should be dropped from the programme. According to him, I had so blatantly misinterpreted the intentions of the librettists and of Vigano (the creator in the 19th century) and had so thoroughly transformed *Les créatures de Prométhée* into *Prométhée et ses créatures*, that there could be no question of accepting my choreography. Jacques Rouché refused point-blank to take this advice. On hearing this and above all on realising that *Prométhée* would be put on and would play to full houses, the two gentlemen in question insisted that their names should not appear on the play-bills. At the same time they wrote a letter to the Society of Authors stating that they were the 'anonymous' librettists and claiming that royalties should be regularly paid to them. The situation indeed became rather comic. On the one hand they insisted their names should be taken off the programmes, and on the other hand, having refused to give their approval to *my* work, they claimed money for their work.

All this I explained to Jacques Rouché, who, however, found himself in a delicate position. He did not wish to quarrel with the 'authors', though he had to admit that I was right. He decided, then, to extricate himself in this way. He would pay my fees from his own pocket while inducing me to accept that on the programme it should be stated 'the argument by MM. X and X'. And he put an end to the interview by pulling out his cheque-book.

Of course I refused to accept any royalties but I could not make any protest against anonymous collaborators. And that is the whole story about the curious wording of the *Créatures de Prométhée* programme which still surprises a good many people.

But this was not the last of the incidents. During the dress rehearsal there was such a row that I was on the point of leaving the Opera before the performance of my first ballet. The man who caused the commotion was J. E. Szyfer, charming and agreeable in ordinary circumstances and who was to become one of my best friends.

The story of how he entered the Opera is worth telling. As a young composer of Polish origin he had written the music for *La Croisière jaune*, a film whose first showing was to be at the Opera. Therefore the music had to be rehearsed and so Szyfer was, on several occasions, summoned to the Palais Garnier. He liked it there—and he stayed on.

In those days conductors considered the Dance with hardly concealed contempt and avoided conducting a choreographic score. The only ones who did so were Henri Busser—quite willingly—and François Ruhlmann who also deigned to wield the baton provided it was not too often. There was, then, a desk to be occupied and Szyfer occupied it with easy mastery especially after the triumph of *Prométhée*. Later on others imitated him, among them Philippe Gaubert who composed first one ballet and then another which he himself conducted.

But to return to the violent quarrel between Szyfer and me. We were rehearsing. In the second *tableau* the orchestra played a variation twice as slowly as usual. After a few beats, I made a sign to stop and asked for the music to start over again. There could only be a mistake I thought. Szyfer did as asked and without a word . . . but in the same tempo, too slow, impossible to dance to . . . I got angry and called a little sharply for the tempo as adopted during preceding rehearsals. Szyfer paid no attention. I stopped the orchestra and the conductor and I began a lively discussion. Szyfer explained to me that he must obey Beethoven's indications and not mine, that he refused to compromise his reputation as a musician by exposing himself to perfectly justified criticism. I replied that I cared nothing for the critics or for his reputation and insisted that the music should be played as at all the rehearsals, that is to say as my dancers knew it— and according to my instructions.

'Let's begin again. . . .'

Same story. Same discussions. At the fifth attempt Szyfer said arrogantly:

'I can't play it any other way. This is a very celebrated piece of music.'

I was greatly enraged and roared at him:

'And I too am very celebrated. . . .'

One can imagine the tumult this sally caused in the orchestra. Under a hail of insults and whistling, I picked up my briefcase and went off into the wings. I saw Rouché get up and run towards me.

'Sure enough,' I said to myself, 'after such a scandal, he is going to throw me out on the spot . . .' and I hastened on towards my dressing-room so as not to meet him . . . and never come back to the Opera.

Rouché caught up with me . . . 'Calm down, Lifar . . .' so instead of turning me out he was talking to me in a friendly way. He said he quite realised that the tempo was not danceable, that he would talk to Szyfer and asked me to make it up with him. That evening at the Café de Paris in the presence of our director, Szyfer and I sealed our pact. I got all the necessary concessions.

Then came the 31st December. I danced the prologue of *Prométhée*. All the 'choreographic world' of Paris was there and ready to pass judgment . . . condemned? acquitted? congratulated? In the third row of the stalls I noticed Kschessinska, Egorova, Nemchinova, Preobrajenska—in fact all the representatives of the Dance. The first two rows were reserved for season-ticket holders. . . . I got a clear impression—and an artist knows after a few minutes—that the public was 'hooked' . . . in spite of some reserve here and there—which disappeared as soon as I did my great variation in the prologue. Each of my *tours* with the sideways drop provoked applause. My *grands jetés* roused the whole audience . . . my own fever had communicated itself to the public. When the curtain fell it was a real triumph.

Total victory. My dressing-room was full. I did not know where I was. I could not hear what was said to me. For the first time—but not for the last—Jacques Rouché went into an artist's dressing-room. He was very moved and he was there, with Olga Spessivtzeva, waiting for me and there was the champagne he had ordered. He embraced me:

'Lifar, I am going to put into your hands the future of the National Ballet and of the Dance at the Opera. . . . Henceforth this is your home . . . stay here! . . .'

❀ 2 ❀

PROFESSIONAL FREEDOM

1930

As I look back on it the year 1930 seems to me to have been quite a peculiar one—it resembled none of those that had gone before nor any of those which came after. It was a year apart; an intercalated year, so to speak. Yet I say to myself today that it had its proper place in my life, which I was then beginning to realise more and more clearly was to be one of upsurging destiny. The idea of death and that of fame through work had never left me and they now formed the two poles of my existence. Diaghilev's death had shaken me to the core and I was only just emerging from a state of dismay. Rouché had just given me a splendid token of his esteem. I was to direct the Dance at the Paris Opera for the next twelve months. I guessed that my real and creative career would begin then. Between death and creation I had a whole year poised as it were in the void. It would be a time suitable for meditation and dissipation. I made up my mind to burn it up in style.

The dominating, indeed the only, element in my life had been work. But during 1930 I did nothing. I just let myself live and thought only about minor achievements. I did not worry about anything.

I had never been rich. Principally because I had never thought about money, which had gone as it had come, without my knowing how. In 1930 I was rich for good. The dancer had earned a very great deal of money. He was the best paid in the world.

I had never bothered about smart clothes. More than one person in Paris used to laugh at my beret and my down-at-heel shoes. But in London in 1930 I became a regular dandy. I bought a magnificent outfit, the choice of which I left to one of my secretaries, a former Russian general, and he dressed me just like a fashion-plate, Prince of Wales style.

During that year I wasted my time most methodically.

In the mornings I rode in Hyde Park, then came luncheons, teas, parties, automobile drives, fittings at my tailors'. What with balls and exhibitions, I had not a minute to remain alone, to commune with myself.

A few days after the triumph of *Prométhée* Lorcia was promoted to the rank of star and I took a plane for London, but I had to commute between the two capitals, which got me used, once and for all, to travelling by air.

Then I left for a long stay in London. I was accompanied to the airport by the whole Picasso family.

Before taking off we had to wait a long time at the airport. General Kutiepov had been kidnapped that day and cordons of police were engaged in undertaking a thorough examination of passengers. At last I got off, hailed as a hero by the Picasso family, for whom getting into a plane was a veritable defiance of death.

When I got to London I settled in at 13 Bruton Street, which was the house of the charming Madame Ancel and where the Grand-Duchess Maria Pavlovna used to stay. There was, I think, no one else in the house except Lord Alington—that incarnation of Oscar Wilde revised and corrected in 20th century taste—and myself.

I had gone to England to work, not to amuse myself, but all the same I had practically nothing to do. At Lord Rothermere's request some choreographic turns, mounted with unheard-of luxury, were introduced into Cochran's review. I had myself directed an unpretentious work called *La Nuit*. It was thoroughly well booed except for the episode where I appeared carrying on my shoulders a six-year-old child. Besides that I danced in *Frix* with music by Lord Berners, décor by Wood and Balanchine's choreography. Finally I took part in a most commonplace Scottish ballet which was considerably applauded every evening. No sooner did I appear in a short kilt than the audience shouted and pranced for joy.

I was the star of the review and became a darling of London.

The success I met with was outstanding although my artistic activity was pretty well reduced. In a fit of enthusiasm I directed for Alanova a *Diane* with music by Hindemith in which

I was able to realise a choreographic idea I had cherished since
1924 when with *Zéphyr et Flore* I had almost become a choreographer. I had already used new positions for women's dances.
This was my first 'order'—others followed, less interesting no
doubt but singularly lucrative. Sometimes I refused. Thus the
Rothschilds asked me one day to appear at one of their private
concerts in Paris. The fee was high, 25,000 francs, a very large
sum at that time. And several well-known artists were going to
take part. I declined, while stating that I would willingly come
as a guest. Thereupon I took a plane, arrived in Paris and appeared among the guests.

I often danced but I was not very satisfied. More and more
often I experienced a real 'spiritual hunger'. No doubt I would
have left London, and western Europe, had there not been a
beacon before my eyes—the Opera.

The celebrated Moise persuaded me to give up the ballet and to
act in dramas with him. Certainly I did not want to desert my
art, but the proposition attracted me, for the dramatic stage had
always tempted me.

Stokowski asked me to go and direct ballets at the Metropolitan in New York and no doubt I should have accepted his offer
had it not been for the Paris Opera.

However, the most interesting proposal came to me from
Russia.

I was on excellent terms with the French and German ambassadors. J. Truelles of the French embassy had obtained for
me a diplomatic passport very useful because of my frequent
travelling. But I knew no one at the Soviet embassy, though I
had indeed met Sokolnikov, the ambassador, at an evening party
given by Lady Fitzgerald. She was a friend of the British ambassador who had just been appointed to Moscow and through
him she had met Sokolnikov and decided to introduce me to
him. During the party we exchanged commonplace remarks and
things looked like stopping at that.

No invitation, but all at once I became aware of a certain
Minsky among those around me. His real name was Vilenkine
and he was an old man of distinguished appearance, though on his
lips and in the lines of his mouth there was something difficult
to define but disagreeably sensual. In former days he had been
a poet and a philosopher highly appreciated in certain literary
circles. He belonged to the Russian emigration, which, however,

had a tendency to be suspicious of him. At the same time, indeed, he got some money from the Soviet embassy for slight services rendered—very small sums, since the Soviets also were not very sure of him. I do not know how it came about that he was in London, for his usual headquarters were in Berlin, where he collaborated with one of the most pleasant of the Soviet commercial representatives, Grunberg, and wrote articles in *Veillée*, a sort of link it was sought to establish between the Soviets and 'repentant refugees'.

Minsky would often come to see me. He would speak very intelligently about art and about Diaghilev in his younger days, those of the *Monde Artistique*. Then he would question me about the last period of the *Ballets Russes*, about which he himself had very jumbled-up information. Little by little these conversations veered towards politics. He would expatiate upon the excellencies of life in the USSR, upon the spirit of collectivism, the protection accorded by the State to letters, science and art. Finally, one fine day, he handed me as from Gorki—who indeed did all he could for the defence of art and artists—an invitation to meet Sokolnikov at the Russian embassy.

I went there with Minsky, who moreover was present at the whole interview. After a few usual and commonplace remarks Sokolnikov broached openly the matter that interested him. At Gorki's suggestion Stalin had invited me to go to the USSR and there take charge of what he called the 'choreographic front'. The idea took my breath away so I decided to joke a little.

'Mr Ambassador, I cannot thank you enough for the honour done to me . . . but I am so surprised that I do not know what to reply. I do not quite understand how you can invite me, call on my services, when you know well enough that I am a White Russian—and thus an odious individual—that I have a Nansen passport and belong to that class against which the dictatorship of the proletariat has declared war to the knife.'

'What importance has all that for us? I ask only one thing of you: that you behave loyally towards the Soviet government. Since you have often declared that the only thing which interests you is the Dance, I am sure that you would be loyal and consequently would have nothing to fear. As far as the purely artistic domain is concerned your talents would develop and express themselves in complete liberty. We want art to flourish in the most progressive country in Europe. We are trying to create a proletarian art, but we are not losing sight of artistic culture and its traditions. Our aim is that the most humble worker may enjoy the fruits of great, universal art, that art which, when all is said and done, is not the art of any particular class. Nowadays the works of Pushkin are printed in millions of copies and Tchaikovsky's operas can be heard in places where only a few years ago his name was unknown.'

'Did I get your exact meaning, Mr Ambassador? You tell me that a work of art belongs to no particular class. What then do you make of Marx's lessons, which teach, on the contrary, that a creator always bears the mark, the stigma, of the class from which he comes? His work is necessarily, therefore, marked in a similar way. I do not quite see how the Soviet government can conduct propaganda for the works of Pushkin and Tchaikovsky, both of whom were gentlemen, aristocrats. Their works, then, must be aristocratic. They can only harm the people, the poetry of Pushkin especially with its concept of art for art's sake.'

Sokolnikov appeared rather embarrassed. Minsky made a sour face.

'Let's see, perhaps I did not express myself very well. Certainly every work of art belongs to a class and we have the duty to create an authentic proletarian art. But as long as it does not exist, allow us, then, to inspire ourselves with the great examples and take from them what is the best in them . . . but we are getting away from the subject of our conversation. One day, if you like, we will talk at length about art questions in general. For the present, let me go back to the proposal of your possible collaboration with us. Do you want to take part in our constructivism? What do you think the ballet should be in the USSR?'

'First of all, I am wondering quite seriously whether the ballet is necessary at all in the USSR. Our academic art is too much a class art, of royal, aristocratic class, more indeed than any other art. What was the ballet in our country under the old regime? Who made up the audiences? The imperial family and the members of the highest aristocracy, they considered the ballet as a sort of 'dessert' and especially as a nursery for carefully chosen, pretty women. People went to the ballet to choose a mistress. Tell me in all frankness, Mr Ambassador, what has changed since? The classical ballet is dead I admit, but favouritism remains, and the new rulers, like their predecessors, come to the theatre to look for a mistress—I won't mention any names but you know who I mean—from among *danseuses* who maybe do not any longer dance as well, but who remain just as attracted by a pearl necklace.'

Sokolnikov turned pale, but I went on:

'What would I do if I were to accept your proposal? Well, first of all I would break up the existing troupes, those of Leningrad and of Moscow . . . the Dance is a real necessity for the people whose whole life indeed is linked with dancing. Not only would I not destroy the Dance. That would be a deliberate impoverishing of life and a crime, but I would encourage the Dance. I would cultivate it by seeking out among the people the best dancers and the greatest creators. We Russians quite naturally try to express ourselves in dancing. I would advise them, guide them, mould them . . . and who knows? Perhaps in time such dancing coming straight from the people and based on them would produce a new classical school, unique in the world, greater than anything known before . . . perhaps . . . but for the present you are simply living on an inheritance.'

In this 'planetary' utopia Sokolnikov thought he saw a real programme, one carefully thought out, which I was proposing to implement in the USSR.

'I do not want to discuss your plans in detail nor to see what is at the present time practical and what is not. But one thing appears certain to me—your idea is the right one, it is sane and we have need of just such a man as you—one of your worth. Believe me, there is nothing for you in this decadent Europe, where art is rotting. So, come back to our country and you will see for yourself, on the spot, what can be done. We shall easily find a common meeting-ground. You can render great services to Russia. You can take an active part in the creation of Soviet Russia's magnificent art.'

'I am sorry, Mr Ambassador, but for the present I am too fond of the rot. I am afraid that my place is not out there but here amid the putrefaction . . . the fact is that I am too fond of art, and art is not politics.'

And that is how the conversation ended. I never saw Sokolnikov again, but thirty-five years later I was able to write that in the USSR 'there can be seen, there is to be found the nobility of an aristocracy of the people'. Life had proved me right.

I was introduced into London Society by people who had been friends of Diaghilev.

One of my principal 'chaperons' was the Baronne Catherine d'Erlanger who was at Diaghilev's death-bed. She had come to visit him on 18th August, the day before he died. She had brought him a superb bouquet of flowers and Sergei Pavlovitch had welcomed her with these words:

'Oh, Catherine, how beautiful you are and how happy I am to see you. But how ill I am. I am very, very ill.'

I also owed my position in Society to the family of Lord Birkenhead. Lady Eleanor and Lady Pamela Smith were two wonderful friends. I knew also Lady Diana Cooper, Lady Fitzgerald, Lady Juliet Duff, Lady Londonderry, Lady Cunard, the Duchess of Portland, the wife and daughter of Somerset Maugham and the Sitwell family. I was sometimes taken into Buckingham Palace by the Duke of Kent and his friends until King George asked us to go and indulge in our gaiety elsewhere. We then from time to time went over to the Prince of Wales's apartments in St James's Palace. Often we met also at the Hungaria restaurant that I made my headquarters. Here in the company of the Prince of Wales, of Dudley Ward and the actress Lia de Putti sometimes, I danced and sang, to the strains of a Tzigane orchestra, until far into the night.

Several times attempts were made to marry me off. First of all there were two young, and ravishingly beautiful, London girls—and then there was a 'Lady'. With her, let us call her 'Lady F.', the adventure was particularly droll. We were good friends, just on the brink of *amitié amoureuse*—especially on her side. The looks she gave me were so eloquent that I avoided being alone with her. I feared indeed that despite all courtesy and refined manners, a careless word might put us both into a compromising position. One day I got from her a note. It was quite simply worded, charming and friendly, inviting me to spend the evening at her house. I foresaw a private conversation and my foresight was not belied. She received me alone but with such cordiality and so kindly that all my apprehensions melted away. We spent a delightful evening, chatting about this, that and the other, sometimes seriously, sometimes jokingly, but without any allusion to sentimental matters. We took leave of each other as two good friends. However, a few days later I

Bronislava Nijinska, the first woman choreographer and Lifar's first and most demanding teacher (Coll. Lifar)

Lifar as Borée in *Zéphyr et Flore* (Doukelsky-Massine) (Photo Riess)

1929 Karsavina, Diaghilev and Lifar with the unfortunate
Nijinsky on the Opéra stage (Photo Lipnitzki)

1929 Venice with the
beautiful Nathalie Paley
(*New York Times*)

Higher, ever higher!
(Coll. Lifar)

La Nuit (Sauguet-Berard) Lifar's second choreography, created in
London in 1930 (Photo Sasha)

The 'divine' Spessivtzeva (Photo Lipnitzki)

Left   Lifar in *Le Spectre de la Rose* (Weber-Fokine) (Coll. Lifar)
Right   1932 Lifar in *L'Oiseau Bleu* when he had just been appointed 'star dancer'—the first man to be so entitled (Photo Harcourt)

Lifar as Prince Albrecht in *Giselle* (1932) (Photo Teddy Piaz)

In *L'Oiseau Bleu*. Lifar after much difficulty succeeded in introducing Tchaikovsky into the Opéra repertoire (Photo Harcourt)

1931 *Bacchus et Ariane*, music by Roussel, décor by Chirico
(Photo Condé-Nast-Hoyningen-Huene)

was asked to call on a famous London lawyer in the City. You can imagine how astounded I was when he said:

'I have ventured to ask you to come here so that we can make definite arrangements about your marriage settlement.'

'My marriage settlement? but I have no intention of getting married.'

Had he got me mixed up with someone else? What was going on?

'Lady F. wants to marry you. She has instructed me to go over with you the clauses of the settlement. What are your terms? My client proposes to build a theatre for you, to make over to you a block of flats in London, three manors in the country and a palace in Venice. She realises that an artist must be independent, she gives you complete liberty to travel and live where you like. You can go off to your own place of residence on the day of the marriage.'

I let the lawyer talk on. What he had to say was not only interesting but amusing.

'You say Lady F. wants to become my wife, but what part do you play in all this?'

'Lady F. has asked me to speak to you about the possible clauses of the . . .'

I interrupted him.

'In that case I don't think I need discuss the matter any longer with you. Such matters are discussed and settled between two persons and not three . . . furthermore, I am not up for sale.'

There was never any mention of this meeting between Lady F. and myself and, curiously enough, this 'incident' did not in any way change our relations with each other. We remained excellent friends, went on seeing each other and going out together to the theatre or to concerts.

With Lady F. and some other friends I was present, for the last time, at a performance given by Anna Pavlova at Golders Green.

Pavlova danced. Her whole body vibrated. Her arabesques were divine. Her success, however, was relatively slight compared with the triumph of her partners whom the public forced to repeat their Russian dances. I was, perhaps, the only person to applaud like a madman. And finally I threw her a rose. She caught it and bowed to me.

After the performance I took my friends to her dressing-room

M.V.—H

and introduced them to the great Pavlova. Then I let them go off and we remained only three of us—Anna Pavlova, her dresser and I.

'Annoushka, what's the use of all that? What's the use of these performances that have nothing true about them?'

Half-lying down, musing and coquettish, she replied in a sing-song voice:

'I love to scatter beauty . . . distribute to the people. We must distribute beauty and accord those smiles to people.'

'But, Annoushka, they don't understand you.'

Silence.

'Is it true what the papers say that this is your last season?'

'That's a silly hoax . . . tell me, my dear Lifar, when are we going to dance together? I've not given up that idea yet, and I'm ready to dance with you, though you don't deserve it.'

'You know well enough, Anna Pavlova, that that would be my greatest joy. You know that I adore your genius when I recognise it in your most divine moments . . . I venerate so much not yourself but what is in you, that sometimes I feel I would like to kill you, so that you should dance no more, so that the sublime vision should be the last, so that you should not spoil yourself, not besmirch your genius.'

Pavlova got pale. I thought she was going to turn me out of the house. But instead of that she put her arms round my head, clasped me very tightly. I kissed the foot of the 'Dying Swan'. Pavlova was much moved.

'And now go, leave me alone . . . I must be alone . . .'

'Please give me something as a souvenir of this evening.'

'All right, all right. I will send you something . . . now go . . . go.'

I withdrew. I never saw her again. I got no souvenir from her. But the one I have is the most precious, it is the memory of that last sight of her.

The holiday season arrived. I took advantage of it to go to Venice. Only a year had passed since those terrible days . . . but I had changed so much in that year. I had regained my spiritual poise, and because of this my memory of Diaghilev, my cult for him, had become more serene, had deepened.

That year the snobs of the whole world had made the Lido

their capital and the season there was especially brilliant. I
knew almost everybody and went about particularly with Volpi,
the Grand Master of Venice, with his daughters Marina and
Anna-Maria as well as the Visconti sisters. I had in mind a
plan that was dear to Diaghilev, that of organising at Venice a
summer theatre, and I was in negotiations with Volpi for buying
the Casa Casati when news arrived from London that I had
been ruined in a financial crash. I will not, of course, go so far
as to say that I was pleased, but, speaking frankly, I did not
think of it as a catastrophe and the news in no way clouded my
stay in Venice. But I soon had to face the problem of Diaghilev's
estate.

Indeed, hardly had I got to Paris than I had to busy myself
with the library and archives of Sergei Pavlovitch. All the property, as I have said, was put under seal and was to be sold at
auction in the Hôtel Drouot in order to cover the debts he had
left. The most rare volumes (including the first books published
in Russia during the 16th century), precious manuscripts
(among others unpublished letters from Pushkin to his fiancée),
were thus to be dispersed, that is to say, to all intents and purposes, destroyed. That must be prevented at all costs. Very
luckily the responsible judiciary authorities had realised the
position and had decided to endeavour to find a purchaser
for the whole collection before putting it up for sale by auction.

The three outstanding possible buyers were the Soviet embassy, a well-known Paris Pushkinist, and lastly myself, to
whom a right of priority had been accorded. Naturally enough,
for me, there was no question as to whether I was or I was not
going to buy Diaghilev's property. It must be bought at whatever
cost, and I had to lay hands at once on the hundred thousand
francs necessary. Although I had been ruined by the London
crash, I must say that the officials entrusted with the task of
liquidating the estate were most helpful and allowed me a year
to complete the purchase. In this way, without any aid from
anyone, I was able to take possession of the Diaghilev collections,
except for what, as I have already explained, remained in the
possession of Boris Kochno.

It was during this stay in Venice that I was to meet someone I
can never forget. One fine morning, after having bathed, I had
fallen asleep under the Baronne d'Erlanger's parasol. I woke
up. In front of me stood Mme d'Erlanger and a young woman

whom I did not at once recognise (as a matter of fact I had been introduced to her as far back as 1927, she was the daughter of the Grand-Duke Paul) . . . I jumped up.

'Dear Madame, let me present our great friend Serge Lifar . . . Lifar, you are looking at the most beautiful and the most interesting of women—Princess Nathalie Paley.'

The 'most beautiful of women' dazzled me less by her beauty than by her charm, an indefinable charm that sang in her voice: 'Do you speak Russian?'

I was tongue-tied, bemused, unable to utter a single word. The Baronne turned to Nathalie:

'You can see he's still half-asleep, we won't worry him. Let's move on. Serge, when you wake up come and join us.'

They walked away.

I stretched on the sand and soon fell asleep again. In my dreams I was crazy, I saw myself with Nathalie and I was telling her a thousand tender nothings. The imaginings of my early days, Kiev, then Paris, all was suddenly fused into one, crystallised. She could not be a woman like others, she was a goddess, the most perfect creature that ever trod the earth.

I woke up and bounded off to the beach. The Baronne d'Erlanger and her companion were no longer there. I had to wait for the evening before seeing Nathalie and then we agreed to go the next day to Diaghilev's tomb on the San Michele isle.

All my last week in Venice was spent in conversation with Nathalie. Sometimes they were conversations without words, or were quite superficial. The only thing that counted was what each of us guessed lay behind the word. I had to go back to England. It was with inexpressible regret that I left my friend. But I was extremely anxious to finish with Cochran's review and get back to Paris again where would be awaiting me the Opera, 'my' Nathalie and what I felt was to be my real creative work.[1]

---

[1] Princess Nathalie Paley (born in Paris in 1905) was the second of the two daughters of the Grand-Duke Paul by his morganatic marriage (in 1902) with Olga Valerianova (née Karnovitch) Mme Pistohlkors who was created in 1904 Gräfin von Hohenfelsen (by the Regent of Bavaria) and in September 1915 Princess (Knyaginya) Paley by the Emperor of Russia.

AT THE SOURCE OF CLASSICAL DANCING

Once I was back in Paris I was alone again. Not so much alone among people, since henceforth I was assured of the loyal support of Jacques Rouché (he was the second man in my life who had had complete belief in me though on a different plane) and I had begun to know what fame is. But I was alone in face of the task to be accomplished, alone, that is, with nothing before me, since, and I would like to make this quite clear, when I took over the direction of the National Opera Ballet I found precisely nothing, no troupe, no audience, no living tradition, not even any realisation of the situation or desire to remedy it.

At the Paris Opera in those days the Dance was regarded as an agreeable amusement, a display of effortless grace where pretty girls assumed poses and were accompanied by male dancers whose role was to show off the ladies. Since a performance of this sort does not demand any very close attention from the audience, it had become a tradition for the chandeliers to be left lighted in the theatre. In this way people could recognise one another, the subscribers could exchange greetings and pay visits from box to box before going off to the sacrosanct *foyer de la danse* where old gentlemen met and made much of charming young women. And for a great many people such opportunities as these constituted the most obvious reason for having ballet performances at all.

This conception of the Opera as a drawing-room—rather Italian or maybe Stendhalian—was no doubt quite attractive in a highly policed society which secretes its own pleasures. But it had nothing to do with the idea of art which I intended to foster.

Although I did not know how long I should remain at the head of the National Ballet, I had that sure faith in my destiny which has never left me and I was fortified by the feeling that I enjoyed Jacques Rouché's entire confidence. So I resolved to get down to work at once and make a series of sweeping reforms so that the Dance should become again an art worthy of the name—which in my heart of hearts I regarded as almost a kind of religion.

There was everything to be done. I started off energetically and the first thing I did was to give orders for the chandeliers to be put out during performances. In this way the attention of the audience would be directed towards what was happening on the stage. There were many other urgent reforms to be undertaken. I demanded from every performer an artistic make-up, for the art of make-up was totally unknown in the Opera ballet corps. At first I had to be myself the teacher. I forbade the wearing on the stage of all jewellery not forming an integral part of the costumes or absolutely necessary for the roles. I had real wigs made to replace the lumps of tow which up to then used to be stuck on dancers' heads. I did away with the trunk-hose worn over tights and the elastic on dancing-shoes. I made all the male dancers shave off their moustaches and forbade these to be worn on the stage. The hardest thing of all was to get the *danseuses* to dance on the tips of their toes and not half-tiptoe.

But all these measures were just the first sweep of the broom. I had to deal with the Dance itself; that is to say I had to train male and female dancers who would be able henceforth to display not only their physical efforts and their technique but also grace.

The Opera dancing-school which normally should be a real forcing-house for future talents was under the control of Carlotta Zambelli, who had been a great dancer in the old manner and was to all intents and purposes a fixture. So I decided to proceed in another manner. I soon picked out the most promising pupils and sent them away from the Opera into the dancing-schools which some of the outstanding Russian *danseuses* who had either been forced by the Russian Revolution to settle in Paris or who had on the dispersal of Diaghilev's ballets been obliged to open. Of these was the one the 'great' Mathilda Kschessinska had created in Paris in 1929. There were also the schools of Egorova, of Préobrajenska, of Trefilova, of Volinine and of

Balachova, all brilliant stars of the Théâtre Marie in St Petersburg and of the Grand Theatre in Moscow. From these teachers the young men and women dancers of Paris had everything to learn. It was their good luck—and mine—that Fate helped in the choreographic reform which I had made it my aim to accomplish in France. Out of these Russian schools in Paris came such dancers as Baronova, Toumanova, Markova, Darsonval, Schwarz, Chauviré, Vyroubova, Daydé, Lafon, Vaussard, Bessy, Techerina, Charrat, Sombert, Skorik and others.

But while waiting for this new generation, which would not be long before coming forward, there was much to be done. First of all there was a working atmosphere to be created. The final blow to the old order was struck when subscribers were excluded from the *Foyer de la danse*. Everyone knew that these gentlemen regarded it as their own domain where they intended to make their own ideas prevail.

So, of course, I could not make a frontal attack on positions rooted in 'tradition' and powerfully defended. I could not from one day to the next shut the doors of the *Foyer* in their faces. So, in this matter also I decided to proceed more subtly. I arranged for rehearsals to be held at the times the subscribers had the habit of arriving in order to turn the *Foyer* into a club. No sooner did I perceive a *danseuse* in close conversation with one of these 'balletomaniacs' than I would call out:

'Mademoiselle, your variation . . . quick . . .'

Again, in order to re-establish a tradition of work and of artistic sincerity, I did away with the protection up to then enjoyed by the girl-friends of the subscribers. This innovation had the effect of considerably improving the output of the *corps de ballet*, moreover it gave new courage to the artists. Henceforth everything would depend upon ability and training and not upon a few words whispered by such or such an influential personage. When the young pupils realised that what I demanded of them was rewarded with just and suitable promotion and that their chances of becoming stars were determined by their efforts and their natural ability, the dancing-school of the new generation came right over to my side.

But all these necessary reforms did not take place without arousing reactions—sometimes highly venomous—from the old guard whose natural allies were the subscribers excluded from their hitherto sacrosanct domain. So the subscribers declared

war to the knife on me. In order to understand how great their
influence was, it should be borne in mind that the Paris Opera, in
those days, was merely subventioned by the State. The subscribers regarded themselves as the masters of an institution
to whose upkeep they contributed. They therefore complained
to Jacques Rouché. They did not reveal the real reason for
their feud but accused me of destroying French choreographic
tradition and said that the young 'barbarian' was a serious
danger for the French ballet! Now, in those days, Jacques Rouché
was devoting part of his personal fortune in order to infuse new
life into the Opera to which he had devoted his existence. He
therefore looked very much askance at intrigues menacing free
and unfettered creation which, moveover, was rendered possible,
in part, by his own generosity. But since he could not risk at
that moment a head-on collision with the subscribers he tem-
porised and skilfully used me as a bugbear:

'Certainly, my dear fellow, of course, of course, but this Lifar
is an impossible man to deal with and I wouldn't like to seem
to be poking my nose into his professional activities . . .'

But on the other hand he would say to me while, as was his
wont, fingering his little white goatee, 'Don't pay any attention
to what anyone says, carry on.'

But the subscribers were shouting for Lifar to be thrown out.
Rouché would answer 'Only be patient, he'll leave of his own
accord.'

I remained for twenty-seven years!

But Rouché was obstinate and courageous. The subscribers
lost out. Moreover, not long afterwards the subscriptions were
abolished in exchange for an increased subvention from the
State.

If I managed to clean out these Augean stables the credit must
go very largely to Jacques Rouché, who supported me, with the
utmost loyalty, all the time. Such conduct, so rare, must be
considered as one of his titles to fame.

The basis for a real artistic effort had been laid down. The
achievement of a new artistic expression was, naturally enough,
to take much longer. The triumphal welcome accorded on
20th December 1929 to *Prométhée*—and which had been the
cause of my entering the Opera—had deceived me somewhat.

On that memorable evening both the 'Diaghilevians' and the Opera public were united in one outburst of enthusiasm. The latter, however, were essentially conservative and quite alien to the daring innovations of the late creator of the *Ballets Russes*. I had thought that this manifestation of enthusiasm meant that Diaghilev's inheritance had been transported to the Paris Opera and accepted there. But things were not as simple as all that—as I was to discover for my own good.

I was filled with the idea of organising a veritable homage to Diaghilev's memory. Not some work in the manner of Massine, Nijinska or Balanchine, but an entirely original ballet so as to perpetuate, in my own way, the aesthetic tradition of the *Ballets Russes*, and this was *Bacchus et Ariane*. I had conceived it on a very large scale. In order to remain faithful to Diaghilev's instructions I had to have everything new, the décor, the costumes, even the curtain. Giorgio de Chirico undertook the task. The book was written by Abel Hermant and the music by Albert Roussel. If one adds that I was responsible for the choreography, it would be difficult to imagine a whole that was more original, more 'new' for the Paris Opera.

Olga Spessivtzeva was Ariadne and I was Bacchus while Serge Peretti was Thésée.

The performance provoked a real storm among the audience. While some applauded loudly, others just as loudly expressed their indignation. There was an uproar that recalled the scenes aroused by the very first performances of the *Ballets Russes*. As soon as Chirico's curtain was lowered catcalls broke out all over the house. Quite obviously the regular Opera-goers were not yet prepared for this new aesthetic. But the protests of part of the public were not only provoked by Chirico's curtain. These spectators, indeed, found as little to their taste the too sensual *ciseaux* of Ariadne, the gloves worn by Spessivtzeva and the ballet dancers, or the high boots of Bacchus, or the too free interpretation of the ancient myth. They disliked the abandonment of the principles of classicism or romanticism and, above all, they disapproved of my famous leap, a gigantic bound of some eighteen feet high into the wings where I was caught in the arms of the stage-hands, but it did cause the audience to shiver with surprise and utter cries of stupefaction.

André Levinson, the critic, attacked the ballet in these terms: 'It may well be that I have no one to blame but myself if the ballet *Bacchus et Ariane* not only disappointed me but left a bitter taste in my mouth. Nothing, it seems, will cure me of the dangerous tendency to see things on a large scale when the subject demands it. Whose fault is it if on reading the argument I let my imagination run away with me, or if on reading greedily through Abel Hermant's scenario, and especially his marvellous peroration, I had conjured up for myself a preliminary and imaginary vision—but one touching on the sublime—of what this performance would be—"the reverie of a mystical pagan" hidden under the green uniform?'[1] As from the next season I decided, for a good many reasons, not to put on *Bacchus et Ariane* again; the first of these was that immediately after the first performance and without waiting for the end of the season Olga Spessivtzeva went off to South America—she had insistently begged me to go with her and my refusal had hurt her —so I had to replace her with a *danseuse* from the *corps de ballet*. *Bacchus et Ariane* without Spessivtzeva was not at all the same thing . . . then there was the celebrated leap . . . if the stage-hands who had to catch me in the air made the slightest miscalculated movement, all would be over with me—at least as a dancer.

Furthermore, the critics had influenced me and rightly so, I realised perfectly well that if my ballets met with success they owed it to the dancer and not to the choreographer. My choreographic conceptions did not touch the audience enough. I had been brought up in the principles and ideology of the *Ballets Russes* and I began to see that this ideology, although not necessarily false, was, from many points of view, weak and above all never completely solved the problem. What, then, was to be done? Go back frankly to the good old classical ballet? But surely that would mean giving up all thought of new creations. I was at a cross-roads and needed some relaxation— which I was to get in spite of myself a little later on.

At the time—1931—my mind was full of two projects. The first was the ballet that I had commissioned from Prokofiev. It was to be a sort of autobiographical choreography or a choreographical autobiography entitled *Sur le Borysthène* and was to transport to the banks of my Dnieper the passions around me— Olga Spessivtzeva and Nathalie Paley. The second ballet was

[1] 'Green uniform' (*habit vert*)—that is the official dress of members of the French Academy to which Abel Hermant belonged.

L'Envol d'Icare, based solely on *élévation* as the symbol of the eternal impatience of the dance so eager to liberate itself from the law of gravity.

Prokofiev, one of the greatest composers of our time, thought it quite all right to have his score orchestrated by 'ghosts'. It was not a success and we even ran into a law-suit. The music for the *L'Envol d'Icare* had been commissioned from Igor Markévitch. From what had passed at our preliminary interview I had expected to receive a piece of music in perfect accordance with my choreographic poem. But at the audition I was disappointed. Certainly the orchestration was excellent, the sonority fine—sometimes reminiscent of Stravinsky with all the defects which that suggests—but above all it was not very 'danceable' and even in places definitely 'anti-danceable'.

I asked the young composer to introduce some modifications, but this he categorically refused to do, so convinced was he of his infallible ability. The only thing to be done, therefore, was to give up *L'Envol d'Icare* altogether. This was not the first time, nor was it to be the last, that I found myself at loggerheads with a composer, and the fault did not lie in my incomprehension of music. As a matter of fact I was then in a singularly musical phase of my life and sometimes would spend whole days with Nathalie at the Hôtel Majestic listening to Horovitz play; he is a pianist I consider unique.

The financial problems at the Opera were never solved and Jacques Rouché himself could not pay for everything. Nevertheless, I must not complain. It was indeed possibly these very difficulties which helped me to find my way. The holiday season of 1931 was approaching. I went to see Jacques Rouché so as to find out from him what his plans were for the next season. Our director received me with his usual cordiality but this time it was, I thought, a cordiality tinged with regret.

'Lifar, I've got bad news for you. The government is trying at this moment to carry out a drastic economy programme and to cut down expenditure in all branches of the administration. Now, but you know it of course, during the season that's just ended we have incurred a great deal of expense for certain creations, therefore I am not justified in undertaking any new ones. All this is very sad but there is nothing we can do. We have to look forward to a very poor season for 1931–2.'

I felt that Jacques Rouché was telling the truth—though not

the whole truth. There was need for economies, certainly, but he thought that some expenditure had been incurred inconsiderately and he was rather doubtful about my new ballets. Furthermore—and this was a secret for no one—the old subscribers were demanding that I should leave the Opera 'so as to prevent me from dealing a death-blow to the French ballet'. Maybe they were counting on my disappointment and thought I would send in my resignation spontaneously when I learned there were to be no new creations during the forthcoming season.

I was so taken by surprise that I did not know what to answer to Jacques Rouché, so I asked him if I were not the one too many at the Opera. This question cut him to the quick.

'What nonsense, Lifar, I thought I could speak frankly to you so that we could put our heads together and find out what must be done. If needs be, I would not absolutely reject the idea of a new creation, but all I ask of you is that it should not cost too much. I count on you. Olga Spessivtzeva will be at your disposal. See what you can do and then come and tell me your plans.'

'Give me at least a day to think things over.'

'All right, I'll expect you tomorrow at the same time.'

I thought matters over and realised almost at once that it would be necessary to cut out—at least provisionally—the 'modern' ballets except for that of Prokofiev, for which I had myself signed a contract. What was then to be done? Of one thing only was I certain: I would not in any case walk in Staats's footsteps and be satisfied with putting on short ballets as a compliment to old-time dances and the choreographic schools. Two solutions came into my mind: the purely classical, that is to say the great masterpieces of the repertory, or, again, the 'modern', personal, daring, provocative . . . I had not yet hit upon the third solution, the best, the only practical one.

By the next morning my mind was made up.

'Well, Lifar, what have you got to suggest?'

'Sir, I will put aside all creations and propose the revival of four remarkable ballets, four ethereal ballets—*Suite de Danses* by Khlustine, *Le Spectre de la Rose* by Fokine, *Giselle* and finally a *Divertissement* taken from *La Belle au Bois Dormant* by Petipa. The expense will be very small. The fact that Spessivtzeva will dance is a guarantee of success. She is the best Giselle that can be imagined—and I say that with all due respect to the

Parisian public which did not appreciate her at her real value when she danced this ballet at the Opera before. This time things will be different and I am certain she will have a real triumph.'

Rouché gave me a satisfied smile.

'Lifar, I was quite sure you would have some ideas but I did not think they would be quite so excellent. Bravo! I share your views entirely. You can go ahead.'

The revival of *Suite de Danses* charmed the public. The first performance of *Le Spectre de la Rose* took place on New Year's eve. For this ballet, always so closely linked with the Nijinsky legend, I got Fokine's permission to use Bakst's décors as revised and supervised by his son. The author of the book, Louis Vaudoyer, was present at our rehearsals. The success was really phenomenal and the ballet was given several times during that winter season—that is to say until the spring of 1932—and the house was invariably sold out. This was our second triumph with Olga Spessiva at the Opera . . . and *Giselle* was yet to come.

Owing to an accident I had during rehearsal, the first performance of *Giselle* had to be put off and the ballet was not given until February 1932. That evening all the choreographic notabilities of Paris turned up—I might say on a war footing. This was to be the most searching test of any I had undergone and one that would determine, maybe decisively, all my career. I must say that I had taken the greatest possible care in the preparation of that ballet. I changed the colour of the costume—violet instead of white—and I added a romantic cape. With his complete agreement, I also modified entirely Benois's stage-setting. So as to lend more dramatic relief to Albert-Hamlet,[1] in the second act I put a great bunch of flowers in his arms so that he might, with melancholy, pose them on the tomb of his beloved. I insisted that these flowers, arums and lilies, must be real, because as living things they seemed to me to add, as it were, a human presence to this romantic drama which, for my part, I wanted to see transformed into a Shakespearian tragedy.

This success of *Giselle* made ballet history. Spessivtzeva's interpretation of the part of Giselle was, in my opinion, the absolute perfection of choreographic art. In this role she was the greatest, the most sublime, dancer of the 20th century. I myself endeavoured in this ballet, which I danced over a

[1] Albrecht/Loys in the British versions.

period of twenty-five years all over the world, to ennoble the role of Prince Albert by enhancing it with an ideal of which death through love is the symbol.

Levinson wrote: 'I will go so far as to say that the 1932 version equals—and in some moments surpasses—that given by the *Ballets Russes* in 1911[1] on this same stage, and that the admirably assorted pair Spessivtzeva-Lifar need fear no comparison with the couple Karsavina-Nijinsky.'

The equals of Karsavina and Nijinsky! Can one imagine what these words meant for us? And the public too greeted *Giselle* with immense enthusiasm. The applause went on and on. Finally, tired out, I was able to get back to my dressing-room, where a crowd awaited me—all my friends of the Diaghilev epoch who happened to be in Paris, my comrades, the dancers, the Russian *danseuses* who had opened schools in Paris, and Chaliapin, the great Chaliapin, came to see me. He pressed me in his arms and embraced me:

'It's magnificent, bless you. . . .'

[1] It was in 1910 and not in 1911 as Levinson wrote.

❦ 4 ❦

ARTIST ON THE STAGE, ACTOR IN REAL LIFE

When I glance back along the road I have trodden, I think I
might be proud of the work accomplished in conquering my art
—and myself. *Giselle* had revealed to me spiritual liberation
through the Dance, and a new horizon, a fresh path which I
was beginning to realise was the one I should follow for my later
creations. 'Diaghilevism', strictly speaking, had been left behind.
The task now was to achieve a new classicism which would
benefit by experiences undergone and lessons learned. And through
this return to the sources I was already beginning to lose that
excess of self-centredness which, maybe, is a characteristic
of youth, but which by many had been regarded as a fault in
my earliest ballets where the choreography, so it was said,
concentrated too much attention on the dancer and seemed to
have been composed solely for him. *Divertissement* by Petipa
obliged me to arrange numerous variations for the *danseuses*
and entries for the *corps de ballet*, since, out of respect for the
great French master, I wanted to direct this ballet in his manner.

Before I speak about the battle for the Dance I would like
to say something about my life at this time and the part that
Spessivtzeva played in it.

I have already mentioned that Olga in 1926 rejoined the
troupe of the *Ballets Russes* for the third time and that Diaghilev,
who had great affection for her, presented her enthusiastically
to the Parisian public, found a new name for her—Spessiva,
more easily pronounced for the French—and did everything

he could to draw attention to her natural genius for the Dance.

Diaghilev always used to say to me, 'Your *danseuse* must be Spessivtzeva!' and I wanted, at all costs, for her to be definitely engaged at the Paris Opera as soon as I myself was firmly entrenched there. In fact the engagement of Olga Spessivtzeva was one of the conditions I laid down before I agreed to join the Opera myself. Jacques Rouché accepted—unfortunately however only at the very modest salary of 7000 francs a month, whereas I was earning 30,000—and we began to set to work with much keenness and energy. We were always in complete 'choreographic harmony' with each other and a sincere friendship sprang up between us despite her trying character, which was to get more and more so as time went on. During the years we worked together I endeavoured to get to know her and I was to realise all the complexity, all the failings and also the depths of her tormented soul. She was tireless in her exercises, she was an ideal partner on the stage, but she showed herself full of contradictions in her formidable outbursts. She was irritable, sometimes abrupt, even violent. When tuberculosis declared itself and the slightest fatigue distressed her, she became nagging and shrewish.

But it was at the very first ballet I had to direct with Spessivtzeva's participation (it was *Prométhée*) that I at once noticed the extraordinary spirit of discipline she showed in her work. At rehearsals she had always a smile on her face and was ready to repeat endlessly the most difficult steps and attitudes and poses and never made the slightest protest or any remark at all. She showed a real example of professional conscientiousness, all the more noteworthy since she was already very famous.

Like Pavlova she did not possess a musical sense in the conventional acceptance of the term. Her musical sense, and also her sense of rhythm, were peculiar to her. Sometimes the music seemed to hinder her dancing. I noticed this clearly and got to understand it quite well during our exercises in her studio. Some days the music really infuriated her and we had to go through whole dances without any accompaniment. I gazed at her and admired her! The variations, the adagios, were incomparable. Her lines, her arabesques, were perfect. She carried them through without the least faltering. Her supple and harmonious movements created, one might say, a mute melody. Even when she did make a mistake, the error itself had an aesthetic quality which rendered her dance all the more moving. The rhythm, the unbroken flow, wove themselves into a harmonious whole. And then we would give ourselves up, in ecstasy, to the silent beauty of the dance. In such moments of sublime inspiration Olga would suddenly become very sweet. When it was absolutely necessary to keep in touch with the music, I guided her, I protected her, I carried her along, I transported her.

But in all that she did was she conscious? I do not think so. Her genius was unconscious. She created her plastic art, without, so it seemed to me, her ever suspecting the beauty of the artistic images she created. Yes, it was by instinct that Spessivtzeva was inspired.

She was full of odd quirks and whims and I was never able to find out whether they were due to lack of intelligence or whether they were the first symptoms of the malady which was later to overwhelm her. I can remember how one day she flabbergasted me with some strange remarks. We stayed late at a rehearsal and it was after midnight when we left the theatre. We were both thoroughly tired out. I wanted to relax, get into different surroundings after long hours spent at the Opera. I suggested we might go to a café and have some amusing conversation with friends. But to my surprise she replied in a preoccupied tone:

'No, no, please, home for me, I've got work to do.'

'Work,' I shouted, 'at this time of night! What sort of work?'

'I'm working on 'The Demon', Lermontov's poem. I'm translating it into French . . .'

'What? Olga, you . . .'

I was dumbfounded.

'Yes, sure, French . . . French, me . . . Liberty, Equality, Trinity!'

I thought for a moment that she was joking, but her face remaihed quite serious—and, all at once, I felt embarrassed.

Later on, queer scenes like this were often to recur. But the most terrible thing was that she sincerely believed she produced, owing to her 'intellectual' conversation, an impression of being a well-educated and highly cultivated woman. But all the same she was very much a coquette. She had a Madonna-like face and a small head reminding one of Perugino's portraits. Her black hair she kept oiled down and never waved. She loved beautiful clothes and was dressed by Lanvin. While she was getting

M.V.—I

ready to go to a party she would spend a long time in front of her looking-glass. Her mirror was, indeed, her friend. She would gaze at her image while talking to herself in a bewitching, captivating voice. One would have thought she was telling fortunes.

There was a strange atmosphere in the little apartment she occupied at the back of a courtyard in the boulevard Saint-Jacques. The front door opened directly into the studio, a large, bare room containing just a few indispensable furnishings. A narrow staircase led up to the first floor where were her room and that of her mother. The whole house was singularly calm and quiet. Ikons with the traditional little lights before them hung about everywhere in corners. One would have thought one was in the private house of some Moscow merchant.

I spent long hours with Olga after our lessons, our exercises and our performances. Often she would read aloud to me some of her poems, which as usual she wrote at night. Sometimes she would also read to me specimens of her prose. It was quite incomprehensible but she thought it 'profound'. In these writings she endeavoured to express the state of her sick soul and to recount her dreams which were just as morbid.

In this atmosphere of factitious meditation and devotion which filled her dwelling, my enthusiasm died down, only to leap into life again during our rehearsals. I would arrive in the morning to give Olga a lesson or to dance with her. After that we did our exercises in her studio and then she was transformed and became much more normal.

Our friendship in those years from 1929 to 1932 was very close. For Spessivtzeva, however, the friendship sometimes assumed the form of a morbid, almost hysterical attachment which was accompanied by an extreme susceptibility, displays of touchy temper and a jealousy directed towards all and sundry and which gave rise to terrible outbursts of anger. These displays of temper distressed me, and I said so, but that only increased her rage. Olga's mother would try to console me. She was really fond of me and it was her dearest wish—which she did not hide— to see me link my life with that of her daughter.

'You and Olga are made for one another. You must not blame her. She loves only you, you alone! Be indulgent, have pity on her. She must be coddled a little. Marry her, marry her. Now go and work with her!'

I have written at length about this woman who was one of the greatest *danseuses* of the century, my partner and a person whose friendship left its mark upon a whole period of my life. But our relations never went beyond the limits of an artistic friendship, since the sentiments Olga felt for me found no response on my side. At this same time also I was hearing the same story from the Grand-Duchess Marie and the Grand-Duke Dimitri,[1] 'Get Nathalie to divorce, she is so unhappy with Lelong . . .'

I was then madly in love with Nathalie Paley and Olga Spessivtzeva did not fail to guess this. Now, at this same time after the triumph of *Giselle*, I had put into rehearsal *Divertissement* and *Sur le Borysthène* (the ancient name of the Dnieper by whose banks I spent my childhood). The rehearsals began early in 1932 and in the rotunda of the Opera.

The two heroines of this ballet—and maybe it was a little cruel on my part to give them these names—were called Olga and Natacha. But however that may be, the role of Olga was given to Olga Spessivtzeva while the male part was to be played by myself. Natacha was to be interpreted by Suzanne Lorcia. The drama exploded during one of the rehearsals. Spessivtzeva realised with a dreadful shock that in the ballet it was with Natacha that I was to find happiness.

Everything happened with lightning-like rapidity. No sooner had I announced that I would begin with Natacha the *pas-de-deux tendre* of the finale, than Spessivtzeva hurled herself towards the open window. With one bound I also reached the window, but she was already on the other side. I just had time to clutch her by the arms. My pianist Léonide Gontcharov rushed up to join me . . . Olga was hanging from our arms more than thirty feet above the Place Garnier. With enormous effort we managed to drag her in. She struggled, she bit us, she did her best to wriggle away from us. At one moment my eyes met hers and I was appalled. We took her home. She alternated between struggles and delirious ramblings and then complete apathy. The next day she did not turn up at the rehearsal and sent word to Rouché that she was leaving the Opera for ever. So she left me, left our art. For the years she still had to live

[1] The Grand-Duchess Marie and the Grand-Duke Dimitri were the children of the Grand-Duke Paul by his first marriage and were therefore half-sister and half-brother of Nathalie Paley.

before real madness caused her to be shut up in an asylum cannot be counted as years in her artistic life.[1]

I never mixed up my private life with my art. Of course there were plenty of temptations. But I managed to ward off the sirens without hurting their self-esteem. I spared them from humiliation, respected their youthful age and refused their caresses. There were also temptations lying in wait for me outside the theatre. I was sought after by people of both sexes. And, to furnish some explanation for my attitude, gossip had it that I scorned the fair sex. I can, however, look back on fascinating adventures in my youthful days—the lovely Mexican girl with whom I spent a week on the *Ile-de-France* coming back from New York in 1933: my passion for Nathalie Paley that was to die before the period of those heedless pleasures I indulged in during the war when death was all the time at my elbow. I was proud too, of my daughter Rosemonde. But shall I ever see my son Georges who came into the world on the day of the declaration of war in 1939? It is true that, save for these few encounters, love was not the great preoccupation of my life . . . at least love individualised and incarnated, for the dream of love was all my existence, as my existence was only a dream. Reality for me was my work, the stage, my art. But how I could love in my dreams! I possessed the art of love in dreams. Whereas in real life this sentiment appeared to me often as prosaic, even coarse. I adored to love in *Giselle* and in this love I spent all my strength.

The power that I felt develop within me would, I guessed already (and life in this respect has proved me right), be the result only of my own efforts and my victories as a dancer. Each time I appeared on a stage it was my battlefield where I must conquer both myself and the audience. Stage-fright was for me the fast beating of a lover's heart, while as soon as the public was enthralled, when I could feel that it was fully satisfied— as through some mysterious upsurge—then I experienced a plenitude of enjoyment, as necessary as the air itself.

And this is why—I can admit it today—I have always been a poor lover, like one who is a stranger to the sensual pleasures of

[1] In 1942 she was placed in an asylum in the United States, but in 1962, as though by a miracle, she recovered her reason.

the couch. My partners showed themselves rather jealous of this stage pleasure which dominated me more than anything else and which they guessed stole me away surreptitiously from them.

Just as I lent myself to them, so also I lent myself to Society, which had adopted me in London and was now to welcome me in Paris, where I could feel I was the favourite I remained right up to the war. In a way I was happy about this mainly because of my insatiable desire to know, to learn, to discover. And I felt I could satisfy this desire better in Society than elsewhere.

I can say that during these years I met everyone: the Russian refugees around the Grand-Duchess Marie and the Grand-Duke Dimitri, of course, but also Charles and Marie-Laure de Noailles, Lily Pastré, Mimi Pecci-Blunt, the Talleyrands, Alex Mdivani, the Lucinges, Paul-Louis Weiller, Arturo Lopez, Charles de Besteigui, the Marquis d'Arcangues, the Ruspolis, Misia Sert, Catherine d'Erlanger, Lady Deterding, Daisy Fellowes, Madeleine de Chevreul, the Rothschilds, Dolly Radziwill, the La Rochefoucaulds, Florence Gould, Marie-Louise Bousquet and Coco Chanel who has been a friend for life. Plenty of others also welcomed me, and made much of me—such as Etienne de Beaumont and Louise de Vilmorin.

Between Paris, London and Rome smart Society was closely linked up, so that in Paris I was received by people I met again in London, in Rome, at Venice, the capitals of a triumphant Society axis.[1] There was also another attempt to make me enter a state of wedded bliss. During my first trip to America in 1933, the friends of Barbara Hutton (who had taken our tour under her wings) urged me to marry her. I told them I was already wedded to the Dance. I advised my good friend Alec Mdivani to marry Barbara Hutton.

Indeed, to tell the truth, the object of my affections was then Nathalie Paley, with whom I lived through a trying, complex, fiery, and by no means happy, passion, when, as she wrote to

[1] They were the Prince of Wales (future Duke of Windsor), Lord Beaverbrook, Lord Rothermere—whom I had met with Diaghilev—Lord Birkenhead, Chamberlain, Randolph Churchill, Lady Londonderry, Mrs Dudley Ward, Lady Fitzgerald, Lady Milford Haven. At Venice the 'popesses' Principessa di San Faustino, contessa Amorosini, contessa Vendramin, the Viscontis; and the 'doges' Volpi and Brandolini always welcomed me heartily. There was also Elsa Maxwell with her bad taste, her gossip, and her overflowing energy.

me quoting Pushkin, 'happiness was so near and, as it were, within hand's reach'.

Around Nathalie had formed a powerful little group which made and unmade reputations, made them fashionable or ruined them.[1] It was a last incarnation of Society as Proust depicted it, a final echo of the easy life in the inter-war period, and this tribunal of Parisian taste decided by autocratic ukases what was smart and what was not. I was not fooled by all this but in addition to there being a kind of pleasure which can only be denied by those who have never known it, I realised that the approbation of this group was indispensable for the work I had done at the Opera. The group did secure a Society triumph for my performances, and this was necessary to me for a task which I valued much higher.

Society life took up much of my time and energy, that is a fact. But how could I resist the temptation to dissipation, to forgetfulness of one's destiny, which that life offered? Here again it was work that lent me strength. The exercises I forced myself to go through every day, between noon and two o'clock, protected me from the outside world, and made part of myself inaccessible to it. During these hours I was in raptures before liberty, it was a sort of prayer that kept me in good condition, it was a means of returning to myself, to the efforts which had always been my ethics, which gave me such strength as the Earth gave to Antaeus. After that I could go back into Society as my spirit was calmed. In Society I displayed my smile and played the game.

[1] Besides Nathalie and myself, it included Baba Lucinge, Niki Gunsbourg, Charlie de Besteigui, Paul-Louis Weiller, Denise Bourdet, Odette Péreire, Lucien Lelong, Figuie Ralli (so called because he was constantly saying *figure-toi*), Consuelo, Simon and Felix Rollo, Andy Ambericos, Margaret d'Erlanger, Gabriella Robilant and our dear Fulco.

5

THE FLIGHT OF ICARUS

I have already mentioned how the ballets of the 1931–32 season—*La Belle au Bois Dormant, Le Spectre de la Rose* and *Giselle*—helped me to get a clearer idea of what was henceforth to be my career as a creator. At the first rehearsals I noticed that our dancers did not know how to support the *danseuses* in the *pas de deux*. I told Jacques Rouché about this and asked if it would not be possible to institute special studies for the *adage*. He decided at once to set up a class for this and appointed me professor. At the same time he gave me the title of 'Star dancer'. This was the first time such a title had been given at the Opera; up to then men could not rise any higher than 'First dancers' (*premiers danseurs*). I danced with my new rank for for the first time in *L'Oiseau bleu*.

For *Divertissement* I had not the benefit of Olga Spessivtzeva's precious collaboration—she had, as I have said, left the Opera. It was Camille Bos who took her place. In *L'Oiseau bleu*, Lorcia, with her usual ardour, provided a bird that was admirable in modelling, softness and technique. I took the double roles of the Prince and the Bird, for I was at that time practically alone and carried the whole responsibility for a performance that would put the prestige of the Opera to a test and determine whether its great director Jacques Rouché was to win a victory or not.

To introduce Tchaikovsky into the Opera repertory needed an excursion into what might be called 'high politics' . . . the French musicians objected that they had their Massenet and that he was good enough for them. However, I succeeded in my efforts, thanks to the collaboration of Spessiva and of Semenova who had come from Soviet Russia. Today Tchaikovsky is one of the great classics at the Opera.

The season came to an end. As often happens, it was easy for me to judge of the victories we had achieved by considering the rival attempts they had excited. In any case they were so many triumphs for the Dance, which was attracting an interested public throughout the world. New companies were formed. There was the Monte Carlo Ballet which under the direction of René Blum (the brother of Léon Blum the statesman) was to try, with the aid of such choreographers as Massine, Balanchine and Fokine, to carry on the tradition of the *Ballets Russes*.

Again, during my journey in the United States I was able to see for myself the offensive being carried on throughout the world by the Expressionist style employed by the Joos German ballets which had a resounding success exploited by the celebrated American impresario Hurok, who had in his own country the exclusive rights in the publicity for these ballets.

'Diaghilevism' kept as it was could no longer really nourish the Dance and Expressionism could do that still less. I realised that a great aesthetic battle was engaged against this latter, not for my personal reasons or those of the Paris Opera, but for the Dance itself, for its future, for its history, it was essential to fight against Expressionism, which was no doubt rich enough in theatrical qualities, but which, because of the easy solutions that assailed it, was fatal for the essence of choreography.

Thus history repeated itself. At the beginning of the century Isadora Duncan's theories had not been able to resist Diaghilev's genius in developing the budding talents of Pavlova, Nijinsky and Fokine. Thirty years later I must counter Joos's theories and to do that I would be both theoretician and dancer.

A half-failure encountered during preceding years had helped to put me on the road to my discovery of the truth. It is a fact that from the time I had been a dancer in the *Ballets Russes* I had felt that too often I attempted to adapt steps to an undanceable rhythm or to discard the rhythm to create, by the sole privileges of the Dance, illusions which captivated everyone for a passing moment of pleasure. It was, however, this half-failure which made me realise the necessity for a revision of

ideas. As I have mentioned, I commissioned in 1930 the ballet
Sur le Borysthène, from one of the greatest musicians of the Dance,
Serge Prokofiev. When I got the score I was worried. It was, to
all intents and purposes, impossible to transfer on to the plane
of the Dance. André Levinson wrote in this connection: 'A recalcitrant score always opposed to dancing. We must attribute
to an aesthetic error the surprising, disconcerting inconsistency
of M. Serge Prokofiev's score in this work of his mature age.
Instead of a vigorous articulation, a sort of polyrhythmic
agitation causes the music to give way under the dancers' feet
like a quicksand. The texture is constantly torn, the themes
change sharply without sustained development, and without a
continuous music from the wind instruments or the strings,
allowing the ballet master to unfold in harmonious fashion
the logical sequences of movement and rest.'

So the great aesthetic battle was engaged. With *Giselle* I had
only indicated the outline of the battle-front. Now I must go
on farther. But then I was seized with an imperious urge to
go and bathe once more in the eternal springs. I left for Italy,
ever dear to my heart, and I went on to Greece, where my greatest
desire was to make my Prayer on the Acropolis.

It was in Greece I realised that the Dance, Man's flight,
should convey in plastic form his highest aspirations and that
it should suffice to imitate them, to magnify them, that is to
say that the Dance must become once more what it was essentially and originally, an independent art, perhaps the first of all
the arts. To illustrate these truths what better theme could be
found than that of Icarus, if the classical mode of expression
could be rediscovered and if it were adapted to celebrate the
efforts made by the Icaruses of our days and of always, to
know and to discover.

Before I speak about my creation I would like to recount
an 'incident' which happened during the year 1935. It is rather
significant, not only because of the stir it caused, but also because
it shows very clearly how, on the eve of my conception's definite
triumph, the opposition had not yet downed arms and was still
on the watch for the slightest favourable opportunity to begin
the attack once more.

The Colonial Ministry had given me a commission for a ballet

—on the occasion of the centenary of the French West Indies. The ballet was to express the triumph of Man over Nature and the elements as well as Man's victory over his own miseries. It can be seen that conceptions which were beginning to be furiously fashionable were associated with this artistic commission and it is easy to realise what I may call the political importance which the project inevitably assumed.

I set to work at once and was not long before finding what I wanted. It was a composition of Bizet's entitled *Patrie* and I based my ballet on that. The models for the décors and the sketches for the costumes were, by a marvellous piece of good luck, executed by Paul Colin.

During the dress rehearsal the Ministry let it be known that I should receive the cross of the Legion of Honour which, I must say, I think I deserved for all I had done in providing France with successful artistic performances in exchange for the opportunities I had been offered. But on the evening of the official performance there was a dramatic happening. It aroused indeed a world-wide commotion. The ball began at eleven o'clock at night. The orchestra stalls had been removed. President Lebrun made his entry. Members of the diplomatic corps and what is called 'All Paris', about ten thousand people, filled the theatre. But it was not long before the tragedy occurred. At midnight, Pizani, who was the announcer, proclaimed, 'And now we have the chief attraction of the evening, Serge Lifar's new ballet danced by the author and the troupe of the Paris Opera.'

Madame Martinelli's song number was hardly over when I went on the stage while my ballet was being announced. I found myself in a narrow space which was all that had been kept for me . . . 'but at the rehearsals,' I said to myself . . . 'and my décors . . .'

'Where are the décors?' I asked.

I was told there were not any. The programme had been slightly modified. It would have been too complicated to have changed the scenery.

'All you've got to do is to dance in the space provided for you!' I at once realised that a plot had been hatched in an attempt to sabotage my ballet. Who could have given the order for the scene-shifters to remove my décor that was in place behind the curtain? No one could identify the man responsible. I did not care, I wanted my décor and I wanted proper space for dancing.

The managers refused. I was furious. I was dressed as a miner, wore a small beard and held a heavy hammer in my hand. While I protested angrily I walked up and down on the stage. The audience which had been patient enough now began to show signs of irritation. The pause lasted five minutes. My partner Didion and the girls of the *corps de ballet* were in tears at my side. They tried to persuade me to give way. But I was obstinate and all the less inclined to yield since the circumstances seemed to me to be very suspicious and smacking of deceit. I declared that in such conditions I could not present my ballet without prejudice to my art . . . but it was no longer for myself that I was obliged to refuse. In view of the deadlock the unfortunate Pizani was pushed on to the proscenium in front of the curtain that remained lowered. He was met with a tempest of protests, boos and whistles . . . then a great silence and I could hear Pizani's voice:

'Mr President, Ladies and Gentlemen, the organisers of this evening's entertainment are in despair . . . but I am constrained to announce that M. Serge Lifar refuses to appear on the stage and dance, for he does not like the décor which . . .'

The rest of his voice was drowned in one long cry of disgust that rose from the audience. It is impossible to describe what was that mixture of stupor, indignation and disappointment. At one bound I leapt in front of the curtain and faced the public. I was not recognised but with a motion of the hand I appeased the furious crowd. Then I turned towards the presidential box, the first on the right-hand side of the stage. I bowed and then raising my hammer I said in a loud voice:

'It is a lie, Mr President.'

But emotion choked me, my voice was strangled. I could emit only some inarticulate sound like a cock's crowing. The audience exploded. Cries of 'Hang him, hang him' could be heard. The President got up—luckily the orchestra had the good idea of striking up the *Marseillaise* and retired. The crowd, heaving with excitement, rushed for the exits. I was horrified but I had nothing more to do than to get off the stage, where, moreover, I was now alone. I quickly took off my costume and got to the exit. No one to be seen, not a friend, nobody. By the porter's lodge I ran up against Jacques Rouché:

'What have you done, my poor Lifar, what have you done, what a scandal!'

'Forgive me, Monsieur Rouché, and please accept my resignation . . .'

'Calm down, we'll meet tomorrow.'

Perhaps in order to understand what was the setting in which this incident occurred, one should remember the peculiar history of that year 1935.

My brother Léonide and I went to the Café de Paris, where I usually went after a performance. All the customers were discussing the events of the fiasco that evening. I felt very ill at ease. Suddenly I came up against the Minister:

'Oh, there you are, Lifar, how did you dare? . . . your duty . . . it is unpardonable.'

Then the crowd spotted me . . . 'String him up' . . . 'Lousy alien' . . . 'Go and join Gorguloff'.[1]

Chairs came hurtling about. Bits of bread were flung in my face and some of them hit the Minister . . .

'Stop it,' he shouted as he got on a table, for he saw how things were going, and realised that at any moment I might be torn to pieces. A crowd from the outside was bashing in the café's doors. Under a hail of stones the plate-glass windows were being smashed to splinters.

At last the police took matters in hand and dragged me out of that hell while the enraged mob still went on roaring and bellowing, but the police protected me from the human herd and went with me as far as my address in the rue Boissy-d'Anglas.

Police cordons barred the road both at the place de la Concorde end and at that where the faubourg Saint-Honoré cuts across the rue Boissy-d'Anglas. The crowds slowly melted away. During the whole night only one friend kept by my side. Philippe, the son of Francis de Croisset, accompanied by Becq de Fouquières, the Marshal of the Diplomatic Corps at the Elysée.

The next morning the papers carried banner headlines: 'Lifar who dared to insult the President of the Republic must be expelled' . . . 'Where should he be sent, to Hitler or Stalin?' In the Chamber of Deputies a question was asked about what was beginning to be called 'The Lifar Affair'. So as to outflank our adversaries and stifle the scandal, Rouché telephoned and advised me to at once ask for an audience of the President of the

[1] Gorguloff, a Russian by origin, assassinated President Paul Doumer at Paris in 1932.

Republic—before the affair got into the hands of the Minister. At nine o'clock in the morning President Lebrun received me at the Elysée. He said to me immediately, in somewhat surly tones which however revealed a very judicious irony:

'Last night I had to sit through a damned boring show— except for one turn—yours Lifar. Goodbye.'

President Lebrun forgave me and obviously he meant to have the matter hushed up.

At five o'clock in the afternoon I was summoned to meet the Minister of National Education who in those days had charge of artistic matters. When he received me there were several other ministers with him. I at once proffered my resignation. The Minister refused it.

'This business has got to be cleared up, Lifar. Have a cigarette, calm down and let's talk.'

I explained what really had happened and how I had been disgusted by the conspiracy I felt was being got up against me, also how Staats the choreographer and *maître de ballet*, my predecessor, had during the performance in question illegally taken the place of stage manager.

To satisfy public opinion all that was done was to give me a month's suspension from my post at the Opera and advantage was taken of this forced holiday to send me to Henri Corbin, the French ambassador at London who was giving parties at which I danced before the Duke and Duchess of York (afterwards King George VI and Queen Elizabeth)—so this very flattering mission fully compensated for the disagreeable impression left upon me by my temporary exclusion from the Opera. The only thing was that I saw my Legion of Honour fade away into the far distance. The Minister reprimanded Staats and when I met Lebrun at the house of Sousa Dantas, the Brazilian ambassador in France, the President joked freely enough about the whole matter.

In the thirtieth year of my age I was not Villon, I was not troubled by the temptation to write a precocious testament, at the most what preoccupied me was the desire to give a more rigorous form to the artistic certitudes which had matured within me.

It was only in the preceding year, 1934, that I had made a

rather tardy commencement in choreographic journalism and literature. My literary godfathers had been Boissy of *Comoedia*, Maurice Martin du Gard of the *Nouvelles Littéraires* and Brisson of the *Figaro*. They had asked me for articles and it seemed to me that I had something to say. I had moreover the wish to express myself in writing but I must admit that my articles of criticism were badly received. Undoubtedly I was still under Diaghilev's influence which had so deeply marked my life and I had adopted, not altogether consciously, his manner when I made very severe attacks on the art and style of Ida Rubinstein. What was accepted from the ageing Diaghilev was thought to be shocking as coming from the pen of a young man of twenty-nine who had not yet made either the public or his friends share sufficiently his deepest convictions. There was an outcry. Why was I so aggressive? In defence of what? My competence as a critic was questioned.

The problem, however, was no longer the same. Now I wanted to express ideas on my art, the Dance, which went beyond the anecdotal and individual attempts of other dancers who, again, did not hesitate to explain how I had arrived at personal views which far outstripped the influences to which I had formerly been subjected. I was sure that the future of the Dance lay in the direction of the neo-classicism I was engaged in revealing. I wanted to proclaim this loudly and distinctly.

The *Manifeste du chorégraphe* appeared on my thirtieth birthday. My object, while proclaiming a new aesthetic, was to defend the independence of the Dance from music. My principle was defined in a very simple formula. Rhythm forms the link between music and dancing, but everything that is rhythmical is not necessarily danceable. We cannot with our bodies express just any kind of musical measure. But on to rhythm music can be grafted. It is therefore up to the musician to submit. He must compose in collaboration with the choreographer. Thus the work produced in common must gain in homogeneity. In a word I proclaimed in my *Manifeste* that for a ballet the Dance must have the first word and the last.

'The first principle of the new ballet—independent of the other arts its sisters—is the ballet-dance, the ballet must be before anything else danceable and borrow its rhythms from nowhere but find them in its own divine essence. . . .

'The thematic of sound must henceforth yield to a corporal

thematic of gesture and movement which will give rise to an imaginary melody.

'I must then admit the possibility—the legitimacy—of a ballet freed from all musical accompaniment. And to go still farther, any ballet whether musical or not *must arise* from its own origin *and not from music*.'

And I raised the cry:

'In the Beginning there was the Dance!'

Thus was ceremoniously opened the road leading back to the sources, to the only real sources which can vivify the future. The *Manifeste* caused a considerable stir. But at the very moment it appeared I knew well enough that nothing is to be more feared in art (and especially in the art of the theatre) than pure intellectualism and the fine theories which do not match up to realities. Often, in those days, and the situation has not so much changed since, mistakes and failures came from too much mental striving. But the simple and the natural are indispensable on the stage. 'Obey your body, follow it, let yourself go instead of thinking too much', that is the advice I have often the desire to give choreographic tyros. Maybe there still echoes within me the advice of my old master Cecchetti, 'Dance as you can, and as *you yourself* want to!'

It was for these reasons that I made haste to put theory into practice by presenting the ballet *Icare* which was an example of the principle laid down in the *Manifeste*. Icarus had always seemed to me one of the most pure and choreographic of myths. Icarus, the symbol of elevation and of the Dance.

The idea of *Icare* had come to me as early as 1932. I had, indeed, then, in memory of Diaghilev, commissioned the music from Markévitch, but when I listened to it, I quickly perceived that no music could match the sober, austere beauty of the Greek myth and the dance visions it evoked for me. Only silence or the muffled beating of the human heart could respond to the upward flight and then redeeming fall of Icarus. All musical anguish, all sonorous accompaniment would have seemed factitious and have distracted a spectator's attention from the essentials of the drama. It appeared to me that a strident noise rending the silence would have been the best accompaniment to the paroxysms which every melodic or harmonic intrusion would weaken.

So I decided to proceed in another way. My *Icare* would be

produced without music. In this manner it would gain in power of abstraction, and would prove moreover that the Dance is able if not to do without any accompaniment, to at least create for itself the one which suits it. In fact, that was a summary of my *Manifeste*.

Now came the question of putting *Icare* on the stage . . . and there was the music. I had only a rough sketch of a score, of rhythms. I went to see my great friend Arthur Honegger and plunged into a long defence of the Dance without music. Honegger soon agreed with me and accepted to orchestrate the rhythms of *Icare* for an ensemble of percussion instruments.

Arthur Honneger—and I cannot say it too strongly—showed himself in this matter not only the most attentive of friends, but the most understanding, the most enlightened, the most disinterested of artists and the most decided to forge ahead for art itself. And on this occasion concrete music was born. So we worked closely together like two accomplices cheerfully— as is proved by the correspondence we then exchanged and which later on found a place in the National Library at Brussels.

Unfortunately and to my great regret I had to dispense with the décor I had asked Salvador Dali to prepare, for he, carried away by his superabundant imagination, handed to me models which could not possibly be utilised for scenery.

After it had been postponed several times, the first performance of *Icare* finally took place on 9th July, 1935. I had myself made my wings and I had to give my arms a special training since the weight upset my balance.

Once again that year I visited my beloved Italy.

Benito Mussolini, the image of a Roman statue whom the Italians proudly called *Duce*, received me in his Chigi Palace. I was introduced by Franco Lecchio a few days before Hitler's official visit in honour of which the city was illuminated as in Nero's time. I was much impressed by the spectacle. During my conversation with Mussolini he told me that he sincerely believed in Anastasia's miraculous escape from the massacre of the imperial family. He also said, 'The highest tree in the world has never reached the sky.'

The next day I danced *L'Après-Midi d'un Faune* at the Villa Medici during an evening reception given by the students in the absence of Jacques Ibert, then the director. The *Marseillaise*

sung by us all ended the performance—despite the hostility
of official personages and the police.

If I try to recollect all my Italian memories I cannot on any
account forget the festivities given in honour of H.R.H. Prince
Umberto, whose youth and good looks won all hearts. I can also
visualise that great friend of France, Gabriele d'Annunzio,
noble and proud as a strutting old cock, glittering with decorations. He still enjoyed no doubt a high reputation among young
women and he cordially hated Mussolini and his flashy fame.
Against the Duce, however, his greatest grudge was for having
usurped his 'legitimate' place and nowadays one must visit
d'Annunzio's museum, Vittoriale, on the shores of Lake Garda,
in order to realise the theatrical pomp in which the poet of the
Martyrdom of St Sebastian lived. He was indeed a great magician
whom Cocteau, in his younger days, imitated.

I can also visualise the great, the immortal Toscanini who
did me the honour one evening of playing *L'Après-Midi d'un
Faune* on the piano as he hummed the melody. That was a real
proof of friendship.

A few days later I was present at a rehearsal in La Scala
of Beethoven's *Symphonies*, when abruptly, in the middle of
the Ninth, Toscanini stopped the orchestra and shouted to the
second violin, 'G natural.' The musician went livid and held out
his score to the maestro. And Toscanini, despite his poor sight,
had to admit there was a mistake in printing. The honour of
music was saved to the great relief of all.

In Paris, during a concert at the Théâtre des Champs-Elysées,
Toscanini conducted *La Mer* and *Boléro*. It was a magnificent
triumph. I was with Maurice Ravel in the wings when Toscanini
came towards us. He was smiling and his hand was outstretched.
Ravel merely pulled an imposing old-fashioned watch out of
his pocket . . . 'A minute and a half too fast' was all he deigned
to say. Then he turned on his heel and walked with dignity
out of the theatre. Toscanini and Ravel never met again.

The last time I saw Toscanini he spoke to me about a plan
very dear to his heart. He wanted to turn Versailles into a sort
of Bayreuth devoted to the music of Louis XIV's reign. The
French government was much taken with this proposal and I
was sent for to discuss tentative arrangements in Rome, but
at the Hôtel de Russie Toscanini rejected my proposals . . .
'With French musicians impossible . . . those who turn up at my

rehearsals are not always the same ones who play at the concerts
. . . so, one evening in Paris it happened that I could not recognise the first violin . . . the one who for the previous fortnight
had been coming to the rehearsals was clean-shaven while the
one I now had on my left was a smiling man with a fine moustache. When I expressed surprise that his moustache had grown
so well in twenty-four hours, he told me quite frankly that as he
was very busy he made it a practice to send his under-study to
rehearsals!'

One last Italian memory. It was in 1950 during an official
tour of the Opera Ballet and, thanks to Wladimir d'Ormesson
and Jacques Ibert, we were received by His Holiness Pope Pius
XII. This was a great honour for the Dance. Almost all religions
were represented in the *corps de ballet* and to each one, in turn,
the Pope gave his benediction in impeccable French.

Before putting on *Icare* I decided to appear in *Le Spectre de la
Rose*—this would limit the damage, I said to myself in a fit of
pessimism which made me doubtful, not about the value of
my work, but about the sort of reception it might get from a
public in no way prepared for this kind of innovation. I think
that I had never danced better than on that evening.

While the applause rose in waves, I thought to myself, 'Bah!
they are clapping and cheering all the louder because soon they
will be booing and whistling and showing me that they only
understand and like an academic dancer. . . .'

When Szyfer, who was conducting that evening, was getting
ready to begin, he lowered his head and stole a timid glance
behind him as though he feared to be at once assailed by a rain
of various kinds of missiles. The first sound effect—one of those
strident noises I had wanted to have ripping through the silence
—provoked no protests. Nor did the very classical décor by
Larthe, nor the ballet itself. I danced in a whirl of enthusiasm and
felt my partners were supporting me with great warmth and
sympathy—for they also believed in my ballet.

The Fall of Icarus . . . I got up and danced the death . . . the
final arabesque. The curtain fell. Not a sound. A crushing
silence throbbing with anguish . . . then suddenly one great
wave of enthusiasm . . . the audience rose to its feet. When the
curtain went up again it was one deep surge that broke from
the topmost gallery to the orchestra. Sixteen curtain-calls. An
unprecedented event in the history of the Opera. The first

to come and congratulate me in my dressing-room were my dear friends Mermoz and Saint-Exupéry who had recognised that my ballet was a symbol of an approaching era.[1] From the very next day discussions began in the artistic world which had been aroused by an intuition that a capital aesthetic revolution had taken place. The newspaper *Comoedia* began a large-scale enquiry under the title 'Can the ballet exist without music?' A number of very eminent persons gave their opinions—which were often rather wide of the mark. The matter was discussed in Society, especially at Marie-Louise Bousquet's house. Gide, Valéry, Giraudoux, Claudel and Mauriac became definitely my friends. Cocteau, Picasso and Braque were so already—and I mention only a few.

[1] In the following year Mermoz, before his last crossing, confided to me . . . 'You know this will be my last flight.' Later, in 1943, I dedicated *Icare* to him, as I did in 1962 to Gagarin and Glenn, the first cosmonauts.

6

HERE AND THERE

In the name of the Dance I had won a victory. Now I had to consolidate its effects in a practical mannner. And this meant facing up to the old problem: how to obtain recognition, in effect, of the Dance's autonomy as an art. To secure this I had been carrying on a campaign since the preceding year. Was I not right when I had gone to Rouché and suggested to him performances solely devoted to dancing? I had said I thought that henceforth we might consider evenings devoted entirely to dancing instead of presenting ballets as the poor relations of lyrical works. I assured him that such a new programme would definitely establish the ballet and at the same time the Opera would gain a public of ballet-lovers which I was sure would increase in numbers each season.

But I must confess that, contrary to my expectations, our director hardly seemed to share my opinion. For a long while he ran his fingers through his beard while at the same time looking at me with his usual quizzical expression which, however, on this occasion, seemed to me to be really embarrassed:

'Personally, my dear Lifar, I ask for nothing better. Still, the public does not like ballet evenings at the Opera. They do not interest them. Take only one example. In July 1921 Fokine and I tried to organise a season of ballet. It was a disaster. Our subscribers will never want to accept it!'

'But my dear Director,' I begged, 'do have a try.'

'All right, I will consult the subscribers, but I think I know in advance what they are going to say.'

Jacques Rouché had guessed right. And I also might well

have guessed right. I have said how the subscribers disliked me. If the *corps de ballet* really had to work and appear on the scene in important creations, then these gentlemen would find their pleasures considerably curtailed, for they would no longer be able to keep their old customs or play the role they had in former times. Out of two hundred subscribers six only were in favour of evenings wholly devoted to ballet—and one of the six was Mapov who knew Russia and had been an admirer of the Imperial Ballet. But I would not say that such practical unanimity (the reasons for which were quite clear) did not secretly stimulate the spirit of competition, the smiling challenge and the taste for a good tussle which were characteristic of that admirable man Jacques Rouché. At any rate, I for one would not admit defeat in spite of everything. In a determined manner I said to him:

'Let me try the experiment. If it fails I will leave the Opera.'

The chief's eye told me I had hit the mark. He smiled in his beard: 'All right. Try.' I had won my point.

At our first evening ballet performance the house was sold out. The first was followed by others—always with the same result. So much so in fact that from 1940 onwards ballet 'Wednesdays' were established and it became necessary to organise a season—'a month of the Dance' to which foreigners flocked much as they do to Beyreuth. This 'Ballet Month' became so much of a tradition that one cannot imagine the Paris Opera being able to do without it.

The art of the Dance had won its place in France. Now what must be done was to spread this French message to the rest of the world.

It is true that I had already undertaken some long tours but my travels in the years 1936, 1937, 1938 and 1939 now assumed the appearance of official tours devoted to the glory of an art which France had had the privilege of restoring in its splendour.

I had already been in the United States in 1933. Despite the opposition of an American impresario who was the enemy of my independence and who had already done his best to prevent me from obtaining a footing in the USA, I met with great success in New York and Chicago as well as in Montreal. Metro-Goldwyn-Mayer had offered me contracts in Hollywood. Rockefeller pro-

posed to help me get together a troupe for tours all over the
American continent. But I had already realised that it was my
destiny to be the instrument not of anyone, not myself, but of
an art, that in order to be productive the life of a dancer needs a
centre of creation where he can be faced with himself. I wanted
to have nothing to do with the wandering—and indeed miserable
—existence of 'touring artists'—even if they are applauded every
evening. I knew that I needed the Paris Opera for it was only
there I could really create. I knew that I owed it all the fame
I had brought it, since I was sure that the crowds did not dis-
tinguish between the Opera and me when they applauded—
rather more thoughtfully now.

I chose to live rather for the history of art than for the passing
day.

In 1934 I went off to South America. A whole group of friends
accompanied me to Villefranche where I embarked on the
Augustus. It was, of course, the dancer they were making much
of, but also this time something else than the dancer. The Russian
refugees in France had got up a Pushkin Committee with the
object of celebrating as brilliantly as possible, a little later on in
1937, the centenary of that creative genius's death. My life-
long admiration for the admirable author of *Eugene Onyegin*,
the memory of my ideal love for Tatiana, the fact that I had acquired Pushkin manuscripts, had aroused my enthusiasm, my
devotion to this project, and I left France recognised in some
measure as the power behind the throne of the international
committee and charged with the task of setting up throughout
the world branch associations. They were soon to rise to the
number of a hundred and sixty-six. Moreover, I had decided to
make use of the calm and quiet of the crossing to set down on
paper the thoughts about my beloved author which crowded into
my head and heart. I also wished to write a preface to a collection
of his unpublished letters which I wanted to get issued as a book.
I knew all I wanted to express. All I had to do was to write it
down, and to do that I would peacefully await the perfect quiet
of the high seas. So I took leave of my friends. I was already an
author!

When the suitable time came, I got out my paper and my
inks. I arranged them all with loving care and then, one fine

morning, I dipped into the ink-well my green goose-quill pen
ornamented with a little ruby. Then I dipped it in again . . .
and after a few minutes I dipped in it once more. I felt I was an
actor playing the part of a writer. I began to feel hot. What
should I say? Where should I begin? Where was that enthusiasm
which I thought ought to dictate everything to me? I was
sweating profusely and I felt cold. I tried once more. Nothing.
I had nothing to say. My heart was empty, hypocritical. I
had thought all too readily that I was gifted for everything, and
there I was plunged into the depths of the most horrible literary
helplessness .For all my life long I shall never forget that crisis. For
the first time I was experiencing impotence, and this impotence
was I thought total, universal, permanent. Now, in the only
field where I wanted to make my mark, I was powerless. My
world was plunged into darkness.

All my stay in Brazil was affected by this . . . although we
had a successful season. The troupe was received by President
Vargas, then newly elected. At the head of the municipal ballet I
directed the preparation of *Jurupary*, a work by the great
national composer Villa-Lobos. But I did not enjoy any meeting,
any triumph. My soul was empty, bitter, and without contact
with the outside world.

But on the evening of the last performance when I put on
Villa-Lobos' ballet I felt that the joy of creation had visited me
once more. I had only one desire, to get away from the festivities
that followed, so I ran off and shut myself up in my room at the
Hôtel Gloria. My impotence had been overcome, my paralysis had
disappeared. I rushed to my table and wrote and wrote . . .
when the night was over I had finished my article on Pushkin.

The problem of what I would call 'the revolution of genera-
tions', of the younger people whom I was winning over to the Dance
as both a new art and an eternal one, as against the old 'positions due to favouritism', this problem I was to encounter often
in the course of my travels when my appearance would arouse
conflicts like those I had been able to settle in France.

Thus in 1935 I was officially invited by the Polish government
in whose country I was to carry on researches into Polish folklore
together with the famous composer Karol Szymanowski. At

his request I agreed to appear at the Warsaw Opera at a gala performance given by President Pilsudski in honour of the International Red Cross. What could I have done to offend influential personages? After having drawn up the programme and chosen my partners from the *corps de ballet* by paying attention only to merit and not to the official grading, I went off to Zakopane and returned to Warsaw only in time for the dress rehearsal which took place on the same day as the performance itself. The lady who was the director of the theatre, together with the ballet-master, then collected all the troupe in the foyer for mutual presentations. The *corps de ballet* welcomed me with applause. Then it was that the ballet-master came up and slapped my face . . . general consternation.

'Madame, if you want me to take part in tonight's performance I must ask you to at once dismiss this individual,' I said, and giving her my address at the Hotel de l' Europe I left the theatre.

At six o'clock the Minister of Fine Arts called on me and presented his excuses. In the evening I took part in the gala. But at the moment I was preparing to make my leap in *Le Spectre de la Rose* I had time to notice a sword hidden among the flowers that decorated the window . . . I avoided the blade. To induce him to think up so cruel a vengeance the ballet-master must indeed have been furious at my choice of young *danseuses* for my partners instead of fat *ballerinas* who had 'got there'.

After I had been received by President Pilsudski at the Belvedere Palace I left Warsaw. All the artistic world of the Polish capital and the dancers of the Parnell Ballet accompanied me to the station. When I got to the German frontier I sent the following telegram to the Minister: 'I pardon the vulgar outburst of the ballet-master. If you see fit give him back his position.'

In this train I travelled with Karakhan the Soviet ambassador in Turkey. I dined with him in his compartment and we had a long conversation. I was to meet him again. In that same year, under Rouché's auspices, took place the first cultural exchanges between France and the USSR, exchanges which I had recommended in the hope they would allow me to find a partner skilled enough to tackle *Giselle* which had not as yet been put on at the Paris Opera. It was with a good deal of emotion that we awaited the arrival in Paris of the first of the Sovietic *danseuses*. She was Semenova, who gave six performances. Now Semenova was the wife of the ambassador Karakhan. And this is how an unpleasant incident occurred.

In the first act of *Giselle*, which I danced with her in the mad scene, she was carried away by her acting; she was, moreover, used to unsophisticated audiences. So, obeying the doctrine that preached realistic art, she cried out 'Mama, mama!' Someone in the audience shouted 'And your papa?' . . . Loud laughter from the public.

But she was, all the same, a marvellous dancer, although *Giselle* was not the part for her. She was heartily applauded. Both of us, to answer the calls, ran forward towards the footlights, but all at once Semenova rudely pushed aside the hand I held out to her and rushed on alone. I walked off the stage and an indescribable uproar broke out . . . whistling, boos, a general hubbub . . . 'Lifar, Lifar,' they shouted, but I refused to appear again. Jean Zay, the Minister of Education, Karakhan, Potemkin, the Soviet ambassador at Paris and Jacques Rouché came to seek me out and try to induce me to come on the stage and quiet the row in the theatre. Each time Semenova appeared alone and the outraged audience got more and more indignant. At last I did decide to go on the stage and was loudly cheered. In the second act came my greatest triumph—such were the reactions of the public. I had to repeat three times my variation of Albert . . . I had danced six performances with Semenova and she left Paris without saying goodbye to me. Yet, it was on my invitation that she had come to the Opera. The ambassador Karakhan said to me as a sort of excuse:

'Don't forget how young she is.'

'And my youth,' I replied, 'doesn't that count for anything?'

I was never to see Karakhan again. Two years later he was, on Stalin's order, shot in the USSR.

Possibly it was this incident which induced Potemkin, out of revenge, to do me a bad turn in 1937. I have told how it was our intention to make that year, the centenary of Pushkin's death, the occasion for a great manifestation to the memory of the marvellous Russian poet, and how enthusiastic I was about the scheme.

Thus a great exhibition devoted to Pushkin had been organised by my efforts. A committee of honour had been formed and

M. Julien Cain had given me permission to hold the exhibition at the Bibliothèque Nationale, of which he was then the head. When he got wind of the preparations for the Pushkin Centenary, Potemkin, the ambassador, sent a note to the French government and demanded that the artistic celebration should be called off if it did not have at its head a Soviet representative. Jean Zay, the Minister of Education, summoned me to his office and informed me that His Excellency the Ambassador Potemkin himself wished to preside over the committee. Zay added that he was, as honorary president, ready to invite the ambassador. And he gave me to understand pretty bluntly that a little complaisance on my part would greatly further my chances of seeing in the near future a red ribbon in my buttonhole.

I was fuming with rage at this fashion of treating the Russian emigrants and of truckling under to the Soviet demands. I refused the bargain. Zay made Julien Cain countermand the permission to hold the exhibition at the Bibliothèque Nationale. I rented the Salle Pleyel. The official celebrations were abandoned. However, President Lebrun intervened and the exhibition was indeed opened in the presence of all the Diplomatic Corps . . . only my Legion of Honour once more faded away before my eyes!

From 1937 differences of opinion, which became more and more marked as time went on, arose between the two directors of the troupe known as the 'Monte Carlo Russian Ballets'—René Blum (the brother of Léon Blum) and Colonel de Basil. A rupture between them was not long in occurring and it became definite in the spring of 1938 when René Blum with the collaboration of Massine and myself, as artistic directors, decided to found the *Ballets de Monte Carlo* in association with Denham. We undertook then to get together a troupe so as to visit London and then North America. But the American theatres had laid down as an indispensable condition for the engagement of the company that I should take part in the performances. It was on this matter that Massine came to see me and to make an appeal 'to his brother, his friend, his companion in arms, the great artist'. He invoked the memory of Diaghilev, so dear to both of us, so as to persuade me to put my signature at the foot of a contract. This I did with all the greater pleasure since I knew I was meeting the wishes of that discerning and shrewd man René Blum. So I went to see Jacques Rouché and he raised no objection at all to my taking several months' leave of

1938

absence. He gave me at once permission to appear on stages other than that of the Paris Opera.

The business questions were settled without difficulty since as far as I was concerned I had no thought in my mind except that of helping in the artistic success of the venture. The problem of my official position with the *Ballets de Monte Carlo* was a more tricky one. After long discussions we ended by agreeing that I was to be leading star-dancer of the troupe. Massine was to be first ballet-master and I the second. It was expressly understood that several of my choreographies would be included in the company's repertory—including (by contract) *Icare* and my Paris Opera version of *Giselle*. To this end, I selected while I was still in Paris several interpreters for the role of Giselle— Alicia Markova for London, Tamara Toumanova and Mia Slavienska for New York—and Alexandra Danilova for the role of Reine de Wilis. On 26th July I appeared with Markova in *Giselle* at the Drury Lane Theatre in London. The performance was a brilliant success. The next day but one we were to put on *Icare*, but Massine came to see me and said that this ballet must not be given but that we could easily substitute for it one of his own ballets. I would not yield. *Icare* was danced. There was the same reaction as at the first performance in Paris. Not a clap, not a sound during the ballet, but when the curtain came down a mad ovation, a rain of flowers.

After Drury Lane, our company moved to Covent Garden. Before finishing the season, René Blum, so delighted with our success in London, asked me to go ahead of the others and take the *Ile-de-France* so as to make all arrangements for the arrival of the company. He went back to Paris. On board ship the atmosphere was especially tense as it was the time of Munich.

After arriving I was not long before discovering a number of facts which seemed to me of bad augury for my relations with my artistic colleague. When I got to New York, indeed, and saw the play-bills and programmes of the Monte Carlo Ballets, I noticed that my name was carefully hidden away, drowned in a mass. Moreover, *Icare* was announced for one performance only and that at the beginning of a singularly feeble programme. I therefore complained to our impresario Hurok, who was unfortunately taking charge of our tour in the United States. His attitude was unhelpful.

'Let's wait for Massine, he'll fix matters up with you, since it was from him I got the information that enabled me to prepare the play-bills.'

At our first American performance I danced *Giselle* with great success but the next day when I met Massine in the manager's office he declared:

'Lifar, I've got bad news for you. Your *Icare* cannot be given in New York. We haven't got time to rehearse, we have not got the necessary orchestra, and finally it's too modern a ballet and has not a chance of pleasing the Americans.'

'Excuse me,' I answered, 'you have bound yourself by contract to put on my *Icare* and you will have it performed. I have the right to demand this both from the legal and the moral point of view. I have brought you my name, my work and I have helped you to get your company going.'

'I'm sorry, but we can't do otherwise, but we can, if you wish, without any notice, separate.'

'That's just what I am going to do, but only after I have danced *Icare*.'

Then came the complete flop of Massine's *Bogatyri*, specially created in America. A few days afterwards the stage-manager told me that Massine and Hurok had together decided to take my ballet off the programme. That same evening, after having danced *Le Lac des Cygnes*, I called two of my fellow-dancers to my dressing-room and said to them:

'Massine and Hurok refuse to keep their contract. I regard this as being a moral matter much more than a legal one, and most of all it is a matter of artistic decorum. I could appeal to the courts but you know how law-suits drag on and are often muddled up. I can see only one way out and that is to call Massine to account for his conduct. If he refuses, let him choose his weapons. It is with the agreement of M. Denham, our director, that I ask you to be my seconds and present my demands to this gentleman:

(1) *Icare* will be danced as arranged.

(2) After the performance I will leave New York. The *Ballets de Monte Carlo* will hand over to me a first-class ticket for the *Champlain* which sails to France the day after tomorrow.

(3) Our contract shall be annulled 'by common consent' and both parties will renounce all claims against the other.

If M. Massine does not accept this formal demand, I ask you to choose the weapons, the time and the place of our meeting.'

I had the pleasure of seeing them not only understand my reasons for acting thus, but also, in case of need, being prepared to defend my action.

I led my seconds into Massine's dressing-room, told him that what I demanded was merely the strict observance of engagements undertaken.

'Here are my seconds, now choose yours.'

'Serge, Serge, look here . . .' he stammered.

'There's no Serge about it, this is an affair between two men, two artists, Massine and Lifar . . . I will expect your answer within two hours at the most. Good day, sir.'

The duel did not take place. In fact two hours later I saw my seconds arrive beaming.

'Bravo! The dress rehearsal of *Icare* will take place tomorrow afternoon, the first performance tomorrow evening, as the main attraction. The day after tomorrow you will be able to go on board the *Champlain*.'

Icare was a triumph. The next morning Hurok offered me a huge fee to go to Montreal. I refused curtly. But *Icare* went on being danced after my departure.

When I was leaving America a number of journalists came to ask me what reasons I had for going away after a triumphant success. Out of consideration for my partners I replied that it was for 'reasons of an artistic nature'. My partners, however, did not display the same scruples and went so far as to invent a story that I had insulted an American dancer and that Massine and Hurok had to come to his defence.

So I went on board the ship that was to take me back to France.

No doubt the United States, where I had all the same had a great artistic success, did not bring me any luck from the material point of view. In 1933 I had already been fooled by impresarios who had not kept their promises. My dear friend Barbara Hutton, who had sponsored my journey and was present, let me down. So I had been obliged to hire an orchestra at my own expense and pay the salaries of all the dancers.

To meet these expenses I had to sell to the Hartford Museum a whole collection of modern pictures that I had obtained with the Diaghilev estate and which were at that moment on exhibition in New York. This time again I got home without having been in the slightest degree compensated for the efforts I had made and for the triumphs I had obtained with *Giselle* and *Icare*.

Later on, in 1958, I did have to engage in a duel to defend my creations—this time with the Marquis de Cuevas. This great patron of the arts wanted the 'spectacle' of a duel, he was proud to cross swords with the dancer. After his 'victory' we fell into each other's arms.

7

THE END OF A WORLD

The Paris I found seemed to me to have a somewhat changed aspect.

Very soon after I landed I met René Blum who had been already informed of the trouble I had had with the directors of his company. He expressed, very tactfully, his regrets that things had turned out as they had done, while at the same time assuring me of his very sincere friendship. Moreover he gave me an important piece of news. As from 1939 the administration of the national theatres was to be nationalised. The scheme had been initiated and supported by his brother Léon Blum and by Jean Zay, the Minister of National Education, and by Georges Huisman. René Blum himself had examined the plan very carefully. He thought Huisman would be appointed the new director who, he said, counted absolutely on my collaboration. Such were the first symptoms of a new state of things.

Life went on and one had to get down to work again. We created such works as *Oriane et le Prince d'Amour* by Florent Schmitt, the *Cantique des Cantiques*, which, after *David Triomphant*, illustrated the theory I had put forward in *Icare* and in which Honegger clothed my rhythms but only in a more sonorous and powerful fashion owing to the Martenot sound-waves and all the symphonic orchestra. There was also *Enéas* by Albert Roussel. These creations met with great success from a public already trained and prepared for any daring innovation. *Oriane et le Prince d'Amour* was especially applauded. It is a masterpiece but it occasioned very great difficulties for the *corps de ballet*. They, however, overcame in a really remarkable

way the numerous stumbling-blocks in the score. So, for the
first time, through a letter to the Press, I addressed my comrades
telling them how much I admired them and I declared that
since they had been tempered by the test of a work which
forced them to strain their talents to the utmost, they could
henceforth deal with and overcome anything.

Lycette Darsonval was a superb Oriane and since 1936 she
had also been dancing the part of Giselle. This very beautiful
artist's eminent qualities were rewarded by the attribution to
her of the title of *danseuse-étoile*.

In that same year the arts were in mourning for the greatest
singer in the world, the man to whom I had devoted a veneration
as to a very dear friend. Chaliapin died. I had been with him
during his last hours. To the end he remained the actor. One
would have thought he was still playing in *Boris Godunov*—
but it was his last act, he was already dying. I had the honour
and privilege of arranging for his funeral and of paying a tribute to his memory in the name of the Paris Opera. The State
had refused me permission but thanks to M. Marchand, the
chief of the city police, I managed to get the funeral procession
to pass by the Opera on its way to the Batignolles cemetery.

Chaliapin was as famous for his avarice as for his voice. He
always refused to sing for charity. As he would say, 'Only birds
sing for nothing.'

The story went that at his funeral he knocked on his coffin,
I opened it and he asked me to send for his impresario Kachouk
and find out what were the takings. Kachouk replied, 'Full
house.' Chaliapin then enquired how much money had been
taken. 'They've all had free tickets,' answered Kachouk. 'Then
let them bury me quick,' thundered Chaliapin.

When I asked him about Russia he answered tersely, 'It isn't
just a brothel, it's a brothel on fire . . . but I love my people and
my country. And although I was an actor of the people, they've
confiscated my *dacha* in the Crimea.'

When in his apartment in the avenue d'Elyau he recited
Pushkin, that was for me the greatest piece of acting I have ever
seen.

In 1939 there was at last ready the great exhibition which I
had been preparing for a long time. It was devoted to Diaghilev

and the *Ballets Russes*. It was held at the Musée des Arts Décoratifs and was opened by the Minister of National Education.
During the whole of the exhibition records were played of the
works staged by Diaghilev in France and these formed, as it
were, a sonorous background. There were shown also the décors
by Picasso, Derain, Braque, Utrillo, Rouault, Matisse, and of
course also those of Bakst and Benois, and in addition to these
the works of the musical collaborators—Stravinsky, Auric,
Sauguet, Poulenc, Prokofiev, Milhaud, Debussy and Ravel . . .
lectures also were given, notably by Cocteau and Jean-Louis
Vaudoyer.

Before the exhibition closed I wanted to associate with it
our famous elder brother, so I organised a benefit for Nijinsky.

One might often believe that thoughtlessness is a part and
parcel of great catastrophes, or in any case it seems often to
foretell them . . . dancing on a volcano as the saying goes. So
it was in 1939. Never had there been more and more brilliant
festivities, never had Society life been so active.

Receptions, first nights, balls and concerts followed each
other and were heightened in brilliance by the presence in France
of many members of British Society still enthusiastic over the
welcome which the year before had been accorded to King
George VI and his Queen. I was present at most of the parties.
In the reception I received I saw a homage rendered to the Dance
and advantage for my art. Happily I was confident enough to
laugh at my enemies, who, so they said, considered my activities
as just so much personal publicity, especially as Maurice Chevalier, 'The Parisian of Paris', had baptised me 'Prince of Paris'.

Among many other festivities there was in the spring a
magnificent reception given by the Fauchier-Magnans at
Neuilly in their Palladian-style house whose walls were covered
with the paintings of the most famous Venetian masters. It
was at this party that Albert Sarraut, then Minister of the
Interior, obviously gravely preoccupied by current events,
gave us to understand that he feared war was very near. Later
in the evening in a private conversation with me he repeated he
had come to think a conflict inevitable. To Misia Sert, who did
not believe in the danger, he replied, 'I'll have you arrested,
you're a defeatist.'

It was at one of these balls that I made my entry dressed as
Vestris and accompanied by two close and dear friends, out-

standing figures indeed of *Tout-Paris*—Marie-Laure de Noailles
and Minou Bonnardel. It was at this same ball that I met Herr
von Wilczek, the German ambassador. I had often called at his
embassy because his daughters loved dancing—and France. He
told me that evening why the German diplomatic service had
always refused my requests for a visa so that I could accept the
invitations I had often received to go to Salzburg or to the
Olympic Games or even to accept invitations from Richard
Strauss or Furtwängler. The fact was, said Wilczek, that in
Germany I was regarded as a Jew, that this story had been published by certain Frankfurt newspapers and that letters denouncing me and repeating the allegation and emanating from the
troupe of the *Ballets Russes* (then on tour in Germany) arrived
almost daily at the embassy.

The impression I retain of Wilczek is one of a very subtle
diplomatist, very Latin in spirit, a man of wide culture and
whose family connections drew him quite close to France.

As from January 1939 the nationalisation of the Opera and
of the Opéra-Comique was affected, but it was only after long
negotiations that these had definitely become national theatres.

During the month of May it was announced in the Press that
Philippe Gaubert had been appointed director of the Opera and
Henri Busser that of the Opéra-Comique. There was, however, no
question of the nomination of a director-general at the head of
what was henceforth to be called 'The Union of National
Lyric Theatres'.

Furthermore the two appointments announced in the newspapers were in no way official. All enquiries made in high places
met with statements that nothing was known about the whole
matter.

However, as was natural enough, the news given of these
appointments gave rise to messages of congratulation addressed
to the personages 'designated'. They, nevertheless, in the face
of noisy publicity concerning what might, after all, turn out
to be simply false rumours, found themselves in a delicate
position.

One evening, after the performance, I happened to be supping
with my great friend Philippe Gaubert who had always proved
himself in all circumstances a man of the most marked under-

standing. We were in the bar of Werber's, rue Royale, where my
'staff' and I had our usual headquarters. There was present also
charming Madeleine Régnier, Gaubert's wife, whose father was
the all-powerful president of the most powerful Agence Havas.
I put it to Philippe and Madeleine that it seemed to me im-
practicable to leave things as they were, that public opinion
would not understand why what had been announced should
not be confirmed and that furthermore if nothing was done to
confirm it some moral prejudice would be caused. They supported
me in my friendly remonstrances and decided to talk to M.
Régnier. And he that same night had an interview with M
Edouard Daladier, the Prime Minister, who got into touch
with his minister Jean Zay about to leave for the United States.
The next day but one the nomination of M. Jacques Rouché as
head of the Union of National Lyric Theatres was official while
the appointments of Philippe Gaubert and Henri Busser were
also confirmed. I was heartily pleased with myself at this happy
solution whereby three persons of great value were put in their
right places. However, events were not to leave them much
time in which to show what they were capable of as a team.

When the news came through of the signature of the Russo-
German Pact I was in Cannes where I was to dance at the ball of
the *Petits Lits Blancs* under the patronage and in the presence
of the Duke and Duchess of Windsor. By this time the British
authorities were warning their nationals to return home. The
atmosphere had become all at once heavy and menacing. On
Rouché's instructions I motored back to Paris and at once went
to the Opera. I was to take the place of my comrade Paul
Goubé in *Le Spectre de la Rose*, since he had been called up.
On 2nd September, general mobilisation.

On 3rd September it was war.

Men went to the war not as though to heroic exploits to be
accomplished with joy, but they went like condemned criminals
doomed to eternal and inevitable tortures that would deprive
them for ever of their nice, quiet, little bourgeois life, they went
like men headed for a life-sentence of hard labour.

It seemed to me that in the social circles where I moved, it
was myself—treated only lately as a dirty foreigner—who took
the phony war most seriously, sometimes also tragically. And
this was not only because I found myself for the first time, if
not exactly poor, at least hard-up. But it was a fact. The

national theatres shut their doors as from the month of September. I was practically without resources. During all the autumn of 1939 I received, as a salary, only 3000 francs a month. So my life was henceforth quite changed. The worst trial for me was learning to do without taxis. I had to get accustomed to travelling in the Métro which up to that time I had taken only very rarely.

But, in spite of everything, I went on living at the Hôtel Vouillement which I found very expensive and I had a hard job to make both ends meet. But all this was nothing compared with the moral anguish that afflicted me.

What tormented me most was the enforced idleness for I was accustomed to leading an intense, even a feverish life.

I was continuously harassed by the thought that the Paris Opera might stay shut for a long time and that this forced stoppage might mean the end of the French Ballet, for it is a dancing law that a long interruption is the same as a death sentence. So, before I had reached the age of thirty-five I saw threatened both the work of my life and the ballet I had managed to resurrect for France my second country.

I wanted to serve France in another field and to thus escape from inactivity. I went to see the Minister of the Interior, Albert Sarraut, and handed him a letter wherein I had expressed my desire to serve France. This step made those around me smile. They thought I was a little feeble-minded and were sure all my fine resolutions would dissolve in the face of reality. I remember that when I went to see Huisman who was then director-general of Fine Arts, he said:

'What I don't understand, Lifar, is why you stay here. You are a foreigner, you are under no obligation to do anything here. Why do you want to get yourself mixed up in this mess? Life in France is not very pleasant just now, and be sure that it will get much less so. Better to go away abroad while there is still time—like your comrades of René Blum's Ballet. Take the advice of a friend.'

But I did not want to clear out. However, since there was nothing for me to do in France, what I did wish to do was to try to use the French Ballet in the service of French prestige abroad. Then I came up against difficulties. On 15th September we held a meeting at the Continental Hotel. Jean Giraudoux was there and we decided at all costs to save the French Ballet. We wanted to 'mobilise' the Ballet's resources and employ them abroad to serve the cause of French art. Giraudoux, who was Minister of Information and had control over all matters concerning the arts, welcomed my scheme with enthusiasm. I went to see him as soon as he was appointed to his ministry and as a result of this visit it was decided to reopen the Opera despite the fierce opposition of Jean Zay, the Minister of Education, and of Huisman.

It was with Jean Giraudoux, a friend of long standing, that I worked out the programme of the ballets and that I drew up a plan for a tour in Australia. But Eve Curie very nearly managed to upset the whole thing. Eve Curie, the daughter of Pierre and Marie Curie, possessed an occult, vague, but all-powerful influence on what was called 'The Continental', that is the staff of the Ministry of Propaganda housed in that hotel. It was filled with mothers' darlings, young men who had nothing military about them but their uniforms and who were pompously described as being 'detached'. The Continental indeed became the focus of a little myth well suited to the time of the phony war, a myth that aroused smiles and tittle-tattle.

It was common knowledge that nothing could be done at the Continental except through pull. What were her exact reasons or under the influence of what clan she acted I never did find out, but the fact was that Eve Curie did all she could to prevent my journey with a ballet troupe.

I can also say that I had the greatest difficulty in organising this tour and right up to the day we left I had to face all sorts of troubles. In order to help me succeed in the enterprise it needed all the help of Daladier's and General Gamelin's authority. At the first, as a matter of fact, I had not thought particularly about Australia. I just wanted to undertake a propaganda tour abroad. If I did decide on Australia it was because I met Basil who had a contract with the Australians. So we made up our minds to work together and form a Franco-British troupe. And finally we did collect an excellent company. Basil engaged *danseuses* and dancers in England and I in France. On 16th November the *corps de ballet* left for Australia via London. I was to take a plane direct to Australia. I may add that easy as it was to get the women to go I had great difficulty in obtaining permission for the men. However, Lukasiewicz, the Polish ambassador, was most helpful. It is impossible to recount all the visits I had to make, all the persons I had to approach so as to get permission for young, fit, healthy men to leave France.

I had then to get together a troupe and this was no easy task. The Monte Carlo Ballet had been beheaded by the downright desertion of many of the dancers who left for abroad. The Opera *corps de ballet* was crippled by the mobilisation. René Blum realised the situation, deplored it and helped me all he could.

On 16th November the Opera at last opened again with my ballet *Promenade dans Rome* and I had to work at the Palais Garnier for a whole month, so that it was not until 16th December that I took the train for Marseilles.

On my way to Marseilles I took advantage of being in the South to say goodbye to my very dear friend Lili Pastré, then at her country house at Monredon. Her husband commanded the air force in the Mediterranean. I can still remember how nervous people were at the news of the German pocket-battle-ship *Admiral Graf von Spee* arriving in the waters of the River Plate. However, I spent with friends some last happy hours in France. Then I felt I must send a telegram to someone with whom I was linked by ties of affectionate friendship—Diana Varè, the daughter of the Italian ambassador. She was in Rome and I wanted her to know I should be in the sky above her city, so I cabled 'Will fly over Rome in the morning'. The plane was to take off at 8.30 on December 18th. I got to the air-field at the last minute, but hardly were we in the air than we ran into a violent storm. After an hour's flight we had to turn back to Marseilles, with one motor out of action. There we were to be transferred to a hydroplane not due to leave, however, until the next morning.

All that day I killed time wandering about Marseilles with Georges Kessel—Joseph's brother—whom I had met there.

I telephoned to Diana telling her about our false start and mentioned we were being put on a hydroplane that would not take off before the next morning. But when we were settled in the hydroplane we were told our original plane had been re-paired and that, after all, we were to take that.

So we changed over. The two planes took off almost at the same time and I was thinking no more about Diana. But the hydroplane we had just got out of was lost with all hands in the Mediterranean. When Diana heard of the catastrophe she thought I had been among the victims and she became nearly crazy. Clad only in her night-dress, she rushed off to see Ciano, a friend from childhood days . . . 'Serge, Serge must be saved', and for a long time afterwards she still suffered from nervous crises. And I during that time, with nothing on my mind, was flying over immense spaces and eagerly enjoying the new thoughts, the fresh sensations that filled my soul.

In 1938 during the official visit to Paris of the King and Queen of Great Britain, I led off the performance given in their honour. The French government had, for this occasion, ordered from me a *Suite de Danses* by Chopin. The next day a messenger from the British embassy came to see me in order to express the pleasure Their Majesties had felt at my dancing and also to hand over to me, as a proof of their pleasure, a gold cigarette-case engraved with the royal arms and this inscription: 'To Serge Lifar, *maître de ballet* of the Paris Opera, from His Majesty King George VI.' I was so delighted with the present that henceforth I carried it always on me.

Furthermore, I wore for this journey a costume of my own invention which I may say did not lack originality. After all, I said to myself, this is an official propaganda mission for France and French art which has been entrusted to me by the government. So, in these circumstances, an ordinary civilian suit would have seemed to me ill-becoming, even ridiculous. So I devised a kind of fancy uniform which I wore more or less in the English fashion and with a beret. It was only later that my pronounced aversion for mosquitoes, and other stinging insects, induced me to drape over this uniform the tulle veil of Giselle. But to come back to my story.

We were flying towards Karachi when I was seized by a sudden inspiration, due no doubt to the contemplation of the vast blue sky. I said to myself that at the first performance in Australia I must dance nothing else than *L'Oiseau bleu*. So I rushed to the pilot's cabin and asked in a very self-confident tone if I could send to Sydney a message more or less on these lines: 'Company arriving stop reserve *Oiseau bleu* at top.'

The British officer looked me over, noticed the royal arms on the cigarette-case I was fingering, looked me over again and answered 'Yes, sir'—and sent the message—in code. All the Powers, at war or not, intercept and decode such a message.

When our plane touched down at Karachi and I walked down the gangway the sentinels presented arms. I took little notice of this, but when we got to Calcutta there were fresh honours that seemed to me rather out of place. When we took off again we were escorted by British military planes. We met Japanese airplanes on observation flights. Stops at Singapore, Surabaya and Bali. By this time I was wrapped in tulle, still everywhere I was received with a display of ceremony and marks of respect which were rather disconcerting. At Darwin the weather was tropical and I took refuge under three thicknesses of mosquito-net in my little wooden hotel built on piles. Then I heard the loud sirens of the police-cars. Then 'Mr Lifar, Mr Lifar'. They were bringing me an invitation from the Governor —though I had feared I was about to be arrested. Then I crossed all Australia to Sydney. Preceded and surrounded by motor-cyclists I was received at the official residence of the Prime Minister, Mr Menzies, who during my stay often accompanied me himself. I guessed it was feared some attempt might be made on my life. Then, suddenly, at a discreet allusion intended to inform me that one was ready to receive His Majesty's message, the truth flashed upon me. Ever since that telegram I had been taken for *Oiseau bleu,* an extraordinary and secret envoy, bearer of a confidential message from the Court. At the height of the war I was, moreover, to meet once more this *Oiseau bleu.*

Trouble just had to happen. It was caused, in fact, by the self-centred mythomania, almost insane, of Basil. First of all I found when I got to Sydney that the posters announcing our performances were headed 'The Russian Ballets of Colonel de Basil'! So the ballet troupe organised and financed by the French and British propaganda authorities was advertised as 'Russian Ballets'. And this at a time when Soviet Russia was attacking Finland after having swallowed half of Poland and was arousing the indignation of the whole world. I foresaw plenty of trouble and ordered the posters to be suppressed. But it was too late. Paris had been informed and began to send furious telegrams. There was nothing to be done. Soon the French embassy informed me I had been recalled to Paris at once. However, I missed the first plane I was to have taken—it sank off the island of Timor. Once more I had escaped death, which continued to play with me as though I were the victim of a provisional reprieve. So I had time to dance *L'Oiseau bleu* as

well as *Icare* and thus, by the applause they evoked, to save
the whole enterprise.

On the way back I stopped for several days in Bali and was
breathless at the beauty of the mountains and volcanoes.

One day, after I had danced together with the sacred dancers,
I wanted to show them, in my turn, some Western dancing.
First of all I danced *L'Après-Midi d'un Faune* to the music of a
record. Then I wanted to dance *L'Oiseau bleu* accompanied by
their orchestra. But they did not know what we call *danse
d'élévation*. When I leapt and bounded they took me for a demon
and ran after me wanting to kill me. I owed my escape to the
prompt action of a few friends.

I took the last plane to leave before the German invasion of
Holland which was to involve in war the privileged Indonesian
lands. I landed in Naples where Diana Varè, whom attacks of
nerves had made almost unrecognisable, came to meet me. We
drove together into Rome while I kept on saying to myself—
'My God, here's another victim I've made unwittingly.'

I was curious to discover just what was the state of things in
Rome, the capital of a country which although not at war had
certainly for some years past drawn close to Germany. In
1938 I had already had the opportunity of approaching both
Mussolini and Ciano at a meeting arranged by my friend Franco
Lecchio, later Italian ambassador in Spain during the war. Then
again, in August 1939, at the Excelsior in Venice, Ciano had said
to me in a half-jovial, half-aggressive way:

'We'll soon meet in Paris. It won't be long before we get
there. We'll pay for everything in lire.'

'Over my dead body then!' I had answered, but I was, all the
same, bewildered. I wanted to know what his attitude would
be now the real struggle had just begun.

As it was I found Ciano on the Pincio at the horse-show with
Mussolini presiding. I was the guest of M. François-Poncet, the
French ambassador at Rome. But the Duce's son-in-law appeared to me this time to be a much changed man. We exchanged
a few words but he seemed anxious, much less inclined to joke.
One of his remarks was: 'Take care, the German armoured
divisions are extremely strong, I've seen them on manœuvres
and they are not, as people say in your country, furnished with
cardboard tanks just for show. You can say this. Cry it out aloud.'

I was so impressed by what Ciano had said, as well as by the change in the man, that I described the whole scene to M. François-Poncet, who, however, cut me short with the words:

'No, no, not at all, Hitler is just bluff.'

I found the Paris of 1940 with no lights at night but by day bathed in brilliant sunshine. I had come back from such a great distance that I did not realise very well where I was. This springtime seemed absurd as a setting for the first pangs of anguish which were provoked by the news from the front. But I had work to do. I put on at the Opera *Entre deux Rondes*, a charming piece by Samuel Rousseau, and also *Médée* by Milhaud. Furthermore, on my return from Australia, I had been officially mobilised and appointed by Major Bianchini (who received me at the Ecole Militaire) to propaganda missions under cover of an alibi-job—that of observer on the Eiffel Tower (with prohibition to use the lift!).

I can well remember the astonishment of all the officers when I passed my medical examination at the Town Hall, place de la République. I was stark naked and pretty well embarrassed: 'How's this, you, Lifar? haven't you got any pull?'

And I, standing to attention, and hiding a certain amount of wry humour, replied:

'I haven't tried to use any, I'm doing my duty like everyone else.'

It was only then that they congratulated me. Their first impression had been one of incredulous amazement. It was my turn to be incredulous when I learned that foreigners could neither receive nor even buy the gas-masks which all the French were obliged to carry about with them. Some of the foreigners had only the privilege of dying at the front.

At the request of Marshal Pétain, the ambassador in Spain, the French government had arranged in that country a tour of the Opera Ballet as propaganda for French art. The Marshal had asked that I should be placed in charge of the troupe. However, we left for Spain on the same day that Pétain returned to France. He had been recalled by the government which was beginning to panic at the most serious news from the front.

It was a curious tour. We were triumphantly received while the great tempest of panic and disaster was sweeping on. At Barcelona we were acclaimed. But we were able to see some of the first rich families arriving from France to seek shelter. In that neutral country the Press published the communiqués of all the belligerents. The German reports were only too eloquent: the French front smashed, armour was pouring through the breaches, assault planes were in action. Defeatism was filtering into our troupe. I would find dancers in tears after reading the reports. I did all I could to make sure the girls' letters to their homes in France did not disclose what the opinion was in Spain, where the defeat of France was regarded as a foregone conclusion. In Madrid the situation got steadily worse. Some overexcited Falangists wanted to sabotage our French enterprise. General Franco's daughter was present at a reception given in her honour at the Hotel Plaza. Nevertheless, the building was surrounded by Falangists obviously intent on creating a disturbance. I was decided at all costs to avoid a scandal and it seemed to me the only man in Madrid who could get a grip on the crowd was the celebrated matador Belmonte whom I knew quite well, so I rushed off to the café where he was generally to be found and by good luck there he was. I explained the situation. He understood at once and his friendship for France made him get into action immediately. He seized his cape and hat. We jumped into a car. When we arrived the mob around the hotel had got denser and was shouting hostile cries.

Belmonte, like a bull, faced up to the crowd: 'Stop it!' he roared. 'I order you to stop it!' His immense popularity carried the day and the mob burst into cheers and quite forgot all bellicose intentions.

The performance was at the Zarzuela Theatre and was a great success. As I came forward to take the curtain I saw in the first box to the right the German ambassador in uniform adorned with swastikas. He clapped vigorously, as did all the people in the audience.

Our next performance was in Bilbao, but by this time the situation in France was deteriorating very rapidly. Everyone realised the end was near. So it was with heavy hearts that we headed for home. At the frontier we were subjected to vexatious treatment by the suspicious Spanish police. The artists—even those such as a ballerina who had been the mistress of the former Spanish ambassador in France, and Lycette Darsonval—were thoroughly searched. At last on 8th June 1940 we got to Hendaye amid a scene of total disorder. The issue was in no doubt

whatever. I rushed at once to the telephone and asked for
General Jouard at the B.C.M.C. to tell him what I could not
say from abroad. I put it to him that as disaster was so near, it
would be better to save the Opera *corps de ballet* and put it in a
safe place, by sending it to make a tour in Morocco for instance.
Or, at least, allow it to await in Toulouse the events which must
inevitably occur.

All the reply I got was, 'No defeatism, everyone back to Paris.'
I could not believe my ears. I called Sarraut, who had become
Minister of National Education. I pleaded again, I explained.
Finally I was interrupted, 'You must obey. It is an order.
Come back at once.' I went back dumbfounded to the troupe
and told them the news.

With the ninety persons of the company, the scenery, the
costumes and the accessories from the Opera, we occupied
a special train now hurrying towards Paris. And the exodus
unfolded itself before our eyes. We saw a whole country in flight.
We were in the only train headed for Paris.

On 9th June we arrived in the capital and learned that the
government had on the previous day (the same day that I
had received orders to return) left Paris. There was chaos
at the Austerlitz station. A black cloud from the petrol dumps
on fire hung over the city. There were no taxis. The *danseuses*
burst into tears. We all dispersed into a milling swirl like a flea-
market. I felt I was seeing before my eyes the dissolution of
the troupe it had cost me ten years to form and to which I had
devoted so much of my heart. It was a family I loved dearly.

I went off on foot to the Opera, where I wanted to be before
going anywhere else. When I got there all I saw was a poster
announcing a matinée performance of *Zauberflöte*. I ran up to
Rouché who was in his box watching the performance.

'Bravo, Lifar, so you're back.'

'But what a catastrophe. It's the end.'

'What are you saying? Everything's going on quite well.
Now you'll see that everything will be all right. You're only
tired. Go and get some rest and come to see me tomorrow.'

I looked at the house. There were hardly ten people present
—the theatre was empty, empty like a coffin! Philippe Gaubert,
the new director of the Opera, then came in. We walked away
together. On the top of the flight of steps he ripped off with his
stick the playbill announcing the *Flute*—an enemy work.

The next morning I went back. What was my stupefaction when I saw a placard on the façade 'The Direction of the Opera has retired to Cahors'. I was flabbergasted and ran off to the B.C.M.C. There I found an atmosphere of drama and panic. They were burning the archives. A lorry was being piled up with various fittings. I met Jouard wearing a helmet. He was weeping from his only sound eye—the other was hidden under a black patch. 'Thank you, Lifar,' he said to me, 'it's the end. They've all made off. I'm the last.'

I walked down with him into the courtyard. There he got in his car and rapped out before he drove off: 'Lifar, get out of the mess as best you can!'

I was soon to learn that Mussolini's Italy was dealing us the finishing stroke by declaring war, and was machine-gunning on our roads the refugees and the remnants of the French Army.[1]

Jean Hugo of the B.C.M.C. quickly provided me with an authorisation to leave Paris (I was mobilised) but in the agony of the moment he had forgotten to specify the month in the date! But when I reached home I heard of the order by General Hering, the Military Governor of Paris: 'All citizens in a fit state to fight must remain in Paris.' The next day I met Linore, the secretary-general of the Opera, who said to me, 'We must not leave Paris. You must stay, Lifar.' I went back to my hotel and was told it was to close down. I called at the American embassy. William Bullitt, the ambassador, was raving against the French, 'They don't want to fight, it's shameful.'

I confided my most precious possessions—documents on the history of the Dance, and above all the Pushkin manuscripts —to my friend Felix de Lequerica, the Spanish ambassador, who agreed to keep them in his embassy until the end of the war.

My friend Boulos Ristelheuber put me up, at first, in his house on the boulevard Flandrin. It was with him and Marie-Laure de Noailles—both of them had failed in their attempts to leave Paris—that we were to witness the last acts of the drama. On my advice we then took up our quarters at Marie-Laure's house in the place des Etats-Unis. A gloomy sky covered Paris. The radio kept on repeating 'Paris will be defended'.

[1] It would seem that Hitler was never to approve of the Italian intervention. Nor indeed did Paul Valéry who declared to me later on during the Allied bombardments of the peninsula in 1944, 'Let them smash Italy to bits.'

But Paris became more and more deserted and then to our stupefaction we heard that Paris was an open city.

On the morning of the 14th, as I went out to take a walk through the abandoned streets, I saw the black, white and red flag with the swastika on the Arc de Triomphe . . . and then on the Eiffel Tower and then on the Ministry of Foreign Affairs. A long column of German cavalry was riding through the city instead of mechanised units which were obviously still in action. Groups of machine-guns were posted at cross-roads. A small plane was circling in the sky before landing on the deserted place de la Concorde. Squadrons of planes came hedge-hopping to deafen the few remaining citizens.

I walked all about Paris. Every door and window was open. Even to this day I can see the mounted Republican Guards riding along the quays as though they were overtaken by the end of the world. Where could they have been going? I caught a glimpse of a few disarmed French soldiers wandering about, then some prostitutes and an old Frenchman with the ribbon of the Legion of Honour in his buttonhole. He was on the Champs-Elysées and he was weeping . . . that was all the population of Paris.

Then, all at once, I noticed lying on the ground, where some-one had thrown it, a child's little sabre ornamented with a French flag. I picked up this moving, ridiculous and symbolic piece of flotsam from the immense shipwreck. I have always kept it. I have it still. I treasure it but I do not know why.

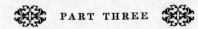

PART THREE

LIFE WAS LIKE THAT

PARIS UNDER OCCUPATION

1

MY MISSION

Paris abandoned in the sunlight. The first days of what is now called Occupation. The capital had already assumed its new mask. Almost everywhere there appeared the black-white-red swastika flags. Wooden palings barred some parts of the pavements in front of requisitioned buildings. For the guidance of the troops which remained in Paris (or of those who were passing through and fanning out southwards—where it was said fighting was still going on) there were notices indicating the chief thoroughfares and the offices of the German authorities. Only very few passers-by were there to glance furtively at the unaccustomed figures in green with short, flared Russian boots. The war had rolled away but not as people had thought it would. Paris was like a huge, deserted theatre, all without significance, where the stagehands were busy shifting the scenery and preparing for the next 'act'.

The Parisians who had remained tried to contact each other by some means (the telephone and the Métro still worked but many people had left their homes) so as to have companionship during these sad, unforgettable hours which no man could say would not become fraught with all sorts of dangers.

On the first evening some German trucks pulled up in front of Marie-Laure de Noailles's mansion. A few officers entered in order to requisition this dwelling so rich in artistic treasures, among which the two Goyas were the most precious ornaments. The Germans spent the night in the house. They knew it well enough since in 1932 they had installed there a private cinema. The next morning I hurried off to the American embassy and

came back with an official paper bearing the words 'This is
American Property'. William Bullitt had been kind enough to
give me this since President Wilson had stayed in the house at
the time of the Versailles Treaty. I fixed the paper to the wall
of the house and the Germans withdrew. Marie-Laure admitted
I had saved her home from a long requisition and maybe from
pillage. However, on 15th July I had to leave when Charles de
Noailles returned from the army. Such was our first contact
with the Occupation authorities.

Curiosity drove me out into the city's streets. I walked about a
great deal, so anxious was I to witness the strange spectacle
of quite a new sort of life. I spent most of the early hours of the
Occupation with William Bullitt and Barnes, American diplomatists, and also with José-Maria Sert, whose contacts with the
Spanish embassy were close. We drove about in a car to check
off what was the 'state of the premises'. These friends had remained in touch with the only French authorities still in the capital
—those of the Hôtel de Ville. It was moreover at the suggestion
of these friends that I was summoned there on 17th June, 1940.
I should have been there at eight o'clock in the morning.

I must admit I was late.

In those days the few of us who had not been able or who had
not wished to leave Paris felt a little responsible for its fate.
We were plunged into a sea of catastrophe and considered we
ought to do something exceptional, something heroic maybe . . .
or anyway we felt we should devote ourselves to some kind of
work. Also we hated being inactive and of just submitting to
the sad fate afflicting us.

I kept wondering why I had been sent for, since I was astonished
that in the midst of disaster the fate of the Opera *corps de ballet*
could preoccupy anyone. As soon as I got to the Hôtel de Ville
I was shown into a huge office. Here were M. Langeron, the
Prefect of Police, with MM. Chiappe, Villette, Darras, Marchand
and others. After they had asked me to sit down they informed
me without any more ado that they had formed themselves into
a kind of secret committee whose objects were to take immediate
measures to save, in any way possible, French property from
requisition and then to maintain French authority in the heart
of the occupied city. To achieve these ends, they explained, it
was essential to resume work wherever possible and where it
was not possible then we should give the appearance of so doing.

Everywhere French control of French property must be strengthened. From time to time I expressed complete agreement.

But, they went on, more was expected of me. They knew of my international prestige and that my reputation was great with the Germans who were especially interested in music and dancing. On the other hand I was not quite French. My Russian origins made me fairly close to Germany's great ally Soviet Russia. In short, I could surely accomplish a great deal with the Occupation authorities. For such reasons they had thought of me and this was the mission they had agreed to confide to me. I was to utilise my prestige—and my origins—to preserve under the tidal wave of Occupation that part of the national patrimony represented by the Opera, its stage, its dancers, its treasures, its archives. Of course I did not hesitate for an instant. With an enthusiasm elicited by the historic times we were living in, I said at once that if I were judged worthy of such a mission I would be happy and proud to serve in its hour of need a country that was mine by adoption, where I had been able to make my career and which in happier days had heaped rewards on me.

The members of the committee, who seemed to be satisfied and touched by the expression of my feelings, added that in order to carry out the mission confided to me, I would have for the duration of the Occupation complete liberty of action— *carte blanche*. I would have to be responsible for my own acts, though when I could I would be answerable only to my chief the interim Minister of National Education, Gustave Roussy, the rector of the University of Paris. They would inform the Germans at once that at the Opera it was Serge Lifar who was responsible just as at the Théâtre Français it was Michel Bourdet.

They also pointed out how serious was the mission and how heavy it would weigh on my shoulders. I would be a French official yet a dancer of Russian origin who was not even naturalised French. The mission was, of course, as I understood, one with an artistic appearance but with a national substance that I accepted in the name of France. They thanked me and congratulated me and we were all much moved.

As soon as I left I was to be received by Gustave Roussy whom in fact I knew quite well. He was in his sumptuous apartment of the Sorbonne at the corner of the rue des Ecoles. First of all he spoke about the seriousness of the situation then added he knew all about the mission and said he was very happy

I had accepted and had shown my devotion to the highest interests of my adoptive country. Then he gave me a written confirmation of my appointment as *maître de ballet* of the Paris Opera. He explained that it was in this capacity only I was to act, as it was one most suitable to reinforce my artistic prestige in the eyes of the Germans and so win their confidence.

Then he lowered his voice and went on that naturally he knew I had already been informed that my mission had other objects which could not be mentioned officially. In any case I would be responsible to him alone and that he would back me up in all circumstances.

Then he got up. Looked into the room next to his office as though to be sure it was unoccupied. Shut the door carefully and came back not to sit behind his desk but next to me. In a very low voice, he went on:

'Of course, as far as the money necessary for carrying out your mission is concerned, don't feel yourself restricted to any fixed budget. Secret funds will be at your disposal and you will always be covered. Draw on these funds for as much as may be necessary to revive and thus protect the Opera. If you succeed the price could not be too high. In this matter also you have complete *carte blanche*.'

I thanked him and said, in effect, that such liberty of action was what would help me most. I then proposed to appoint a Frenchman, Louis Laloy, former general secretary who had not left Paris, as honorary director of the Opera. He would not interfere with my mission. Roussy noted this name. While he saw me out he thanked me again and repeated that he had full confidence in me.

Then, there I was in the streets of Paris and not a little confused. I walked off with my hands in my pockets and in no particular direction. Without paying any attention to them I passed a few batches of German soldiers. They were beginning to visit the capital. I was musing on what had happened to me and I guessed that a page of my life had been turned over. Up to then, by my work, the love of my art and my will to devote myself entirely to the stage I had attained to worldwide celebrity. I stood at the peak of my art. I could heartily thank the masters who had helped me to achieve this position. I felt however that I had repaid my debt to them by honouring their teaching and their example. But now the artistic prestige I had gained had led to something else, had opened up for me new fields, had given me a new role. That day life had become more serious.

So I decided to hurry off to the Opera and there to tackle immediately the tasks that henceforth would be mine. Garnier's monumental edifice showed only a stony face. It was hermetically sealed. So I went to the police-station in the rue Taitbout and asked for the chief superintendent who was there with all his staff.

I told him who I was and showed him the letter confirming me in my new appointment. Then I asked him to open the Opera doors. He first telephoned to the Hôtel de Ville and then came with me. We had with us a locksmith he had sent for. We had to force locks before we could get into—I was going to say my own house . . . but into the house I had left only a few days earlier. The first thing that struck me was the deplorable state of the place. You could have sworn a whirlwind had swept through it. Everywhere signs of hurried departure. The building I had known all ceremoniously decked out in festive attire was now a chaos. Everything in disorder. Papers strewn about. Scenery toppled over. A jumble of costumes, musical scores streaming out of abandoned, half-filled boxes, carpets displaced and now seeming to float down staircases. For a long while I wandered about in surroundings that recalled ten years of joy, of labour, of memories. Then I realised all I should have to do. I must be caretaker, telephonist, dancer, *maître de ballet*, professor, director. So what? I would be all these and sooner than that. I threw the stage-entrance wide open—that was for the time being the only publicity possible. And I prepared to wait in a deserted Opera in the heart of a deserted Paris.

The very next day some members of the Opera staff who had not been able to quit Paris—but who had made up their minds to emerge from their holes into the light of day once more— came to prowl around 'their' house in the hope of getting some news.

So, little by little, I saw arriving machinists, scene-shifters, stage-hands, dancers—and even the fireman called Glouglou (his real name was Jules) because of his resemblance to the figure, well known before the war, which appeared on the advertisements of Nicolas, the wine-merchant. The Opera was coming back to life.

As soon as I saw these first results I made off to the avenue Mozart where Louis Laloy lived and asked him, as I had suggested to Gustav Roussy, if he would agree to become the responsible administrative officer of the Opera. He was delighted and said he would help in every way he could.

Carlotta Zambelli and Mme Mante now came back to reopen the dancing-class. In a short time Aveline followed them. Since I knew the real needs of those who had been abandoned in Paris—after they had been told to remain—I took up my quarters in Rouché's office and began to hand out generously subsidies and moneys from the secret funds on which the rector had given me permission to draw. The money was passed to me by Laloy, who occupied the little office of the secretary-general. All this became known soon enough. Mothers who had at first hesitated sent their 'little rats'.

The classes started up again. The scene-shifters set to work. But the first and most urgent task was cleaning. These were strange days of mingled haste and idleness, feverish activity and the tedium of waiting; we were still anxious but already the stage was coming to life.

The first and most important duty my mission imposed upon me was to see that the Opera escaped the requisition the Germans had decreed for all unoccupied buildings of an official sort. So I ordered that work must begin and that everyone must be present. The stage must be occupied. The place must become animated. We must 'go through the motions', not to arouse faith, which we all had lively enough, but to avoid the worst. We must make the gestures of life so as to recover life. In fact we must practise a sort of artificial respiration so that our famous 'home' might at length recover its spirit and its soul.

Only the orchestra remained absolutely empty. All the musicians had fled. But scenery was put in its right place, the floodlights were operated. The machinery was tested. Inventories were taken.

Then I had a first warning.

Very soon someone I trusted came to tell me: 'Look out, the money you are distributing makes you suspect. It is being said, here and there, that you are a German agent, a fifth columnist.'

This news left me perplexed. No doubt I was ingenuous but still I found it difficult to understand why people were so willing to accept the accursed cash. They took the money readily enough, but I, who distributed it, was the enemy, indeed already 'the Boche'.

However, since the Communists were then playing up the Germano-Russian alliance, I was for them the 'Comrade'. But I guessed rather than knew whence came the support and the help for their organisations. But, rightly or wrongly, I made no comments. I let them gossip and went on carrying out my mission and took my decisions privately with Louis Laloy.

❧ 2 ❧

HITLER AT THE OPERA

On 18th June, the very day that General de Gaulle made his historic appeal from London, we were summoned by the authorities of the Hôtel de Ville to a meeting to be held at the Théâtre Français. The time was fixed for three o'clock. I arrived accompanied by Boulos Ristelhuber, who at this time was my confidential friend. I had not told him the secret of my mission, but he could help me because not only had he been a member of Paul Reynaud's staff, but he spoke German. Moreover he was a prudent man and since his father had been French envoy in Canada, Boulos was acquainted with diplomatic usage which we would henceforth need to employ. I barely had time to recognise and greet Edouard Bourdet's brother—Edouard was my opposite number at the Théâtre Français, when the door opened and in strode a young German officer. As with one accord, all twelve persons present stood up. The officer clicked his heels, thrust out his hand and saluted us with a resounding *Heil Hitler*. Then, with a sweeping gesture, he invited us to be seated. He announced himself as Bernard Radermacher, personal representative of Dr Goebbels. He was, more or less, the director of artistic activities in occupied Paris.

Then he had each one of us presented to him by one of his assistants. He welcomed us, and after a few words of greeting he approached the subject of work. He told us that on Saturday 22nd there was to be at the Comédie-Français a matinée in honour of the Occupation authorities and in which French artists would take part. I listened to all this bemused but only too glad the Paris Opera had been spared the task. I had the impression of having escaped from a shot fired at me.

When Radermacher had finished talking, Bourdet made a sign that he wanted to speak and then, with alarm, I heard him declare, 'But we have no money to put on such a performance.' A feeling of embarrassment, almost of shame, seized me. It seemed to me that, in the person of Bourdet, we were all of us holding out our hands. To make matters worse, the arrogant Radermacher replied in what I thought rather contemptuous terms, 'The Third Reich is rich enough to pay for the performances it orders. You will get all the money you need. Our soldiers also will be able to lend a hand and help you.'

The embarrassment was by no means lessened when the officer turned to me and with a glare rapped out: 'Monsieur Lifar, we are counting on your being good enough to take part in this performance.'

I was taken by surprise and replied it was impossible for me to appear; and then when I recovered my self-assurance I added that I had not danced or rehearsed or had any training for several months, that my partners were absent, that I was quite out of form and that a long time must elapse before I could appear on the stage. Radermacher looked in silence at me for an instant and then said slowly, 'You are making a mistake, Monsieur Lifar, for the Third Reich would give you more possibilities and influence in one day than you could obtain in your whole life!' Then he announced another meeting for the next day at the same time and in the same place. After that he got up, clicked his heels, held out his arm, gave the Hitler salute and withdrew.

The next day at three o'clock there we were all together again in the same room. As each one of us was absorbed in his own thoughts we struck up no conversation. It seemed as though an invisible burden was weighing us all down—what was it? Anxiety, shame, remorse?

Time went by, very slowly. Almost an hour elapsed before we heard footsteps. Radermacher came in. We all stood up. He saluted us as he had on the previous day. Then he walked up to the table but did not sit down. He declared amid a deathly silence:

'Gentlemen, the performance I spoke to you about yesterday has been countermanded. It will not take place.'

An 'Ah!' of relief, a little too marked, shuddered through the assembled company. All turned questioning looks towards

Bourdet, who was, more or less, our spokesman. He made bold
to ask, 'May we know the cause of this decision?' Radermacher
turned towards him and said slowly, 'Armistice negotiations
have begun, we are awaiting the result.'

Then I witnessed a scene that was both very painful and wonderful. There were a dozen middle-aged men wiping tears from
their eyes and embracing each other. I alone, forgotten, remained
apart. Radermacher went to a window and, with his hands
crossed behind his back, pretended to be looking at something
outside while he allowed us a few minutes to regain our com-
posure without being embarrassed. Then he turned round and
we thought he was leaving, but he planted himself before me,
clicked his heels, and in a very brutal voice barked, 'Monsieur
Lifar, may I ask what was the reason for your refusal to dance
yesterday?' Behind him I could see fear reflected in all the faces
looking at us. I guessed that the only way out for me was to
pass to the attack. 'What do you take me for, monsieur? I am
neither a blackguard nor a traitor,' I answered calmly. And in
the presence of all those faces disfigured by dread . . . 'How
can you expect me to betray my second country?' A dead
silence—a fitting phrase indeed—reigned in the room. I guessed
all my 'colleagues' would have paid dearly to have been far
away. Radermacher, still planted before me, looked like the
member of an execution squad. For a second anything was
possible. Then, abruptly, he relaxed, clicked his heels, saluted
and then—shook my hand. 'Excuse us, you are right.' He
withdrew.

Later on, Radermacher was to have a friendly attitude
towards me. He had been an actor and was, I think, some
relation to Dr Goebbels. He knew Paris well, spoke French
admirably and liked France. I will not stress the fact he was
also the lover of a French actress (at that time very popular)
with whom he lived in a requisitioned flat belonging to Bern-
stein, the dramatist. Radermacher was also on friendly terms
with a number of French people such as for instance Cocteau
whom he protected right to the end. It was thanks to Radermacher that a first play of Cocteau's was put on very soon. For
the rest some French people realised quickly enough that he was
not ill-disposed towards them.

On 22nd June at five o'clock I was at the Opera when I got a
telephone call from the Prefecture of Police asking me to go at

once to the *Gross-Paris Kommandantur*, then at the Ritz Hotel, place Vendôme. It was afterwards moved to 2 place de l'Opéra, the premises of the C.N.E.P. An orderly officer would be waiting for me at the hotel entrance. No sooner had I hung up than I was informed that Captain Radermacher wanted to see me. This was the first visit he paid me. I received him in Jacques Rouché's office which I was then using. My visitor seemed very courteous, even amiable. Evidently the last traces of our set-to a few days before had faded away. He came to inform me that the visit of an important personage had been arranged for the following morning. He could not, however, tell me either the exact time fixed for the visit or the name of the visitor. He added, before leaving, he hoped I would be present.

Then I at once set off for the *Kommandantur*. The entrance was guarded by armed soldiers either standing to attention or lying on their bellies near their machine-guns. The place Vendôme was quite empty. It was suffocatingly hot and the heat combined with the complete silence produced an atmosphere of anguish. I found the officer waiting for me. He told me in faultless French that the general officer commanding *Gross-Paris* was expecting me. I still did not know why I had been summoned. In the offices was feverish activity. The place buzzed like an immense hive ... typewriters' clatter ... guttural voices barking orders ... clicking of heels. After a few minutes I was ushered into the office of General von Grote, the first—and temporary—governor of occupied Paris. He gave me the traditional Hitler salute. Then, after asking me to sit down, he said, indeed almost murmured, slowly, and in perfect French: 'We have been informed that you are responsible for the Opera House where you are acting as director. I count, now, on your discretion because of the confidential nature of what I am going to say. The Führer will be in Paris tomorrow and he wants to visit the Opera. I expect confidently that you will be present. The visit will take place under your entire responsibility.'

Then he went on to speak in Russian. He came, he said, originally, from Riga and had served in the Russian Imperial Army. Before the war he had lived at Enghien and had been a regular visitor to the Opera. He hoped to go there again soon, when, as he expected, performances would begin once more. It was of course understood that those under his orders would be at my entire disposal to give me all aid and assistance

—such as according me permissions I might need including one for the use of a car. I answered that I needed nothing but enquired at what time the visit would take place. He said he could give me no details but advised me not to leave the Opera. At these words I took leave and was accompanied by the orderly officer as far as the door of the *Kommandantur* offices.

Once more I was full of dismay. As I made my way quickly back to the Opera I kept on asking myself what was to be done. I was in a painful dilemma. On the one hand was my responsibility regarding the Opera and on the other hand it seemed impossible to ignore the imperative invitation I had just received to be present when Germany's supreme master arrived. As soon as I reached the Opera I tried to get into touch with Gustave Roussy so as to report the situation and ask him for advice. But I managed only to get a servant on the line and he could not tell me where I might find Roussy. That evening I decided to go as usual before the curfew to Marie-Laure's house in the place des Etats-Unis where she was still giving me hospitality. The Hôtel Vouillemont, where I had been staying, had been requisitioned. Before I left the Opera I called for Glouglou the house fireman, handed him all the keys and told him he must sleep that night in the porter's lodge since it was possible some Germans might come early in the morning to visit the Opera. I endeavoured once more to contact Roussy but this time a man's voice answered. I thought I recognised it when I was told that Monsieur was not there. Then I was abruptly cut off. So I went home and spent a sleepless night anxiously mulling over how I should behave 'if he came' and telling myself again and again that the part I had to play was a very delicate one in the absence of Jacques Rouché.

The next day, 23rd June, I got to the Opera at nine o'clock, that is to say as soon as the curfew regulations allowed. There was my faithful Jules. With his thick, sweeping, bristly moustache, his képi on the back of his head, he looked more than ever like Glouglou. He was on the stage holding forth to some scene-shifters who had just arrived. He was in a great state of excitement. With violent gestures he was explaining what 'had happened to him the night before'. I understood at once. At five o'clock in the morning two officers had clambered over the iron railings at the stage entrance, had gone into the porter's lodging where, according to my instructions, Glouglou had shut himself

up while awaiting a visit. No doubt he had taken full advantage
of the company of a good bottle of red wine.

'They woke me up,' recounted Jules, 'told me to open the
doors and iron gates of the Opera façade. As I couldn't find the
keys they forced the locks with tools from the rumble of their
car. And for an hour I waited with these officers on the great
main staircase. I had to turn on the lights, no easy task for me
since it isn't my job. Luckily by fiddling about with all the
switches I managed to find the right ones and everything was
all right. At six o'clock four German High Command cars which
had no windows and only low doors stopped in front of the
Opera and about ten officers got out and began by admiring the
Opera frontage. There was one among them who had rather an
easy-going appearance. He must have been the guide, for at
any rate he was giving explanations the others listened to
with the closest attention.' I asked Jules if there had been any
sort of guard.

'No, not at all, I've just said they were officers, surely actors
in uniform who were delighted to visit our house. The man I
thought was the guide was very gay, very interested and talked
all the time. He said "*Bon jour*" to me in French and put his
hand in a friendly way on my shoulder, then he said some
other words I did not understand but which one of the officers
translated I think when he leaned towards me and said in a
low voice, "It's beautiful, magnificent." I agreed of course and
couldn't help answering, "In Germany, no theatre like this, here
the finest in the world." We went into the Grand Foyer where
they stayed a long time lost in admiration. After that we moved
into the theatre itself, which naturally was plunged in darkness.
After a moment's discussion I saw one of the officers break
away and run off. Soon all the theatre was illuminated and at
the same time the machinery was set in motion and the curtain
rose on a stage bathed in brilliance.

'I must say I was flabbergasted. The guide then went up to
the presidential box, then he moved on to the stage where I
really thought he was going to burst into song. He was so
obviously delighted at imitating an actor striking an attitude
before an imaginary audience while the machinery began to
work all exposed without any scenery around about him.'

I asked Jules if he had gone on the stage with them.

'No, no, as I've said, it was surely a singer who had been in the Opera before since he knew all the whereabouts quite well. After that the party moved into the first box, No. 38, right in the middle where you get the best view of the whole. I think I understood they were astonished to see the presidential box by the side of the stage and not in the middle of the row facing the stage. I heard them say several times, "Magnificent, *wunderbar, sehr schön.*" Then the "singer-guide" shook my hand and said in French "*Merci beaucoup*"; after that they went back to their cars.'

'How long did they stay altogether?'

'An hour. When they left one of the officers wanted to give me a tip as from the "singer-guide". He pulled out a thick bundle of banknotes, but I refused, though I thanked him and they apologised . . . but they might all the same have insisted,' added Jules as though rather regretting his handsome behaviour.

As I have already mentioned, this conversation took place in the presence of about ten stage-hands, who then shouted, 'You're a fool, you ought to have taken the tip, you know money don't stink.'

Finally I asked Jules if he was sure it was a singer.

'Yes, yes, as I've said, he knew the place very well.'

Then I, reckoning on the effect I was going to produce, said abruptly:

'Well, my poor old Jules, your "singer" was Hitler.'

'Hit . . . Hit . . .' he mumbled while I explained how I had been warned and had missed him.

Jules passed out. They had to carry him to the porter's lodge and throw buckets of water on his head until he came to. Jules, whose real name was Pierre Théodore, had a heart attack after his adventure. He had to take his pension in 1941 and died shortly afterwards.

Later on I learned that after leaving the Opera Hitler visited the Madeleine, the Arc de Triomphe, the Trocadéro and the Invalides. The armistice had been signed the day before at Compiègne and Hitler had flown direct from that town to Le Bourget airfield. His passion for architecture had induced him to study the plan of our Opera and thus enabled him to serve as a guide to the officers of his suite. In fact he had added to them a German engineer who in 1936 had taken part as a technician in the installation of an organ at the Opera. I have been told that Hitler passed the night at the Hôtel Saint-Régis.

Immediately after this visit I rushed off to see the rector Roussy, but at his dwelling once again I found no one. I reported also, as I had been asked to do for anything important, to the officials of the Hôtel de Ville who were present in Paris. The dramatic situation in which France was plunged gave, alas, to this visit an exceptional importance. So I also telephoned to a number of my friends telling them of Hitler's presence in Paris and of his visit to the Opera, and it was thus that Paris was at once informed. But I imagine that since it came from me the news was quickly twisted so that it was I who was stated to have been Hitler's guide. As the story passed from mouth to mouth it got more and more altered, either from malicious intent or just from the imagination of those who needed a little drama. The story went that I had behaved like a toady to Hitler and shown him traitorous subservience.

Anyway it is true—the news travelled fast—that in two days' time the B.B.C. announced that I had been condemned to death because of 'the honours I had rendered to the Chanceller Adolf Hitler'. I had not even seen him but this announcement had a great effect on my career. As I had been condemned to death by London (even though for an action I had not committed) I became for this sole reason *persona grata* with the Germans. The Governor of *Gross-Paris* treated me henceforth both as a White Russian (we were then favoured by the forces of Occupation) and as one condemned to death by London, and so as an ally and natural friend of the Germans. Later on I was condemned to death six times—that is a good deal in one life, that is still going on! I saw at once the advantage I could derive from this situation—for the carrying out of my mission. I decided there and then what my role should be. I would play at being ingenuous and easy-going, even rude on occasion. No constraint as between friends. I would not henceforth get up for any of them, not even in the presence of Stülpnagel. I calculated that if I permitted myself to show such arrogance, then they would conclude that I felt very sure of myself. But as a 'friend' of the Germans, I became suspect to French people, even sometimes to the 'moderates' who had stayed on in Paris. So I who was working for France came to be considered her enemy. But I was determined to tell the truth about the role I was playing for the accomplishment of my mission, to tell it to two friends: Maurice Garçon, the famous lawyer, and Bernard

Dessouches, formerly of the Second Bureau and the B.C.M.C.

One piece of encouragement was given me, however, in those hard times. At Marie-Laure de Noailles's house I met Bertrand de Jouvenel who had crossed the demarcation line and had arrived from the other zone, the 'free' zone. A man having performed this exploit was not very easily met with in those days. But better still, Jouvenel had seen Marshal Pétain and his closest collaborators. I questioned him avidly. And I drew up a report to be forwarded to the Marshal. But as it happened he had a message for me from the Marshal, who remembered me quite well, since he had met me at Marshal Lyautey's house and also in the dressing-room of Ganna Walska at one of the Théâtre des Champs-Elysées galas. The message was this, that I should keep on actively in my efforts to safeguard the French patrimony and that he himself would help me in every possible way. This was a first swallow in the moral winter we were enduring. I felt myself once more full of courage. Somewhere or other France was carrying on. I was soon to have need of this assurance.

The reflux to Paris of those who had fled was now beginning. Every day one caught sight of faces that had vanished for a time. Even the buses came back from the Exodus. Little by little Paris became repopulated. But at the same time one could see arising a new version of the quarrel between the Ancients and the Moderns. In some people's eyes the thing to do was to denounce as co-responsible for the defeat all those who had played a part, shown some ability, that is to say, for some simply to have lived, under the Third Republic. It must be said that this attitude was especially useful for creating vacancies which could be occupied by those who up to then had been *nothing at all*. This reasoning was a little weak but useful as a means of getting on—or at least some thought it so.

One day two upstanding, hefty Germans in *Wehrmacht* uniform with the badge of the *Feldgendarmerie* turned up at the Opera and asked for me. They stated they were ordered to hand me a summons to appear before the German police and that they proposed to accompany me right away. I realised it was no use getting into a discussion. This was an order. But I was puzzled to think what could be the matter. I followed the men who escorted me into a car of the army High Command. No windows, low doors. We got very quickly to . . . the rue des Saussaies. I was astonished to find myself once more in the

offices which I had left hardly ten days before when I had visited
the B.C.M.C. Now it was a lair of the German police in uniform
or in civilian clothes. I thought it was all a nightmare. What
was I doing there? But at once I was ushered into an office I
knew well enough. But this time it was a German officer who
received me. He proved however to be quite amiable, even
simple and straightforward. After having asked me to sit down
he said:

'Now, I have rather a delicate task to perform. Naturally
we know you and haven't the slightest doubt about you. But
certain information against you has been received in our offices.
So we are obliged to ask you to be good enough to produce
proof of your Aryanism, since in these denunciations you are
accused of being a Jew.'

I was dumbfounded. This was certainly the last accusation
I had thought of.

'But what can I do?' I asked. 'I am of Orthodox religion, I
have a Nansen passport as a stateless person. To what authority
can I apply? At Kiev maybe where I was born? But you can
ask for that, you can because Russia is the ally of Germany.'

The officer smiled with a mixture of commiseration and irritation which gave me a first hint about the sincerity of that
alliance. But the officer's tone was gloomy when he replied:

'It's your business to work things out for yourself and furnish
us with the proofs we demand.'

I felt bewildered, helpless, and in my confusion I made an
attempt to produce the physical proof of a bodily integrity
which would be appreciated by the German racists. Anxiety
had made me ill and I was dim-witted. When the officer realised
what I was about to do, he flew into a rage:

'You're insulting the German Army,' he bawled out as he
thumped his desk. 'And moreover we know that you are protecting the Bischofsheim[1] house, place des Etats-Unis . . . and
your Jewish ballets *David, Le Cantique des Cantiques* . . . and
your Jewish collaborators, Rieti, Milhaud!'

I excused myself for not knowing what proofs I would have
to produce. He calmed down and just said:

'Will you come back tomorrow and bring proof with you?
Come with your brother, for we know you have a brother.'

He had a *laisser-passer* made out for the next day and then

---

[1] Madame de Noailles's maiden name was Bischofsheim.

let me go. Here then was a danger hanging over me and I had no idea of how to ward it off. I tried in vain to get in touch with the Orthodox ecclesiastical authorities in Paris. I attempted to contact Radermacher and Grote but I could not. Again I passed a sleepless night.

The next day my brother Léonide and I went to the rue des Saussaies. There a young doctor examined our eyes and profiles. Then the officer received us, handed a certificate to my brother and told him he was free, for proof of his Aryanism had been forthcoming. Then turning to me he said:

'As far as you are concerned, we must go into your case more carefully, since your nose does not conform to Aryan standards.'

I was so enraged that I shouted, 'You mean my mother was a whore?'

He cut me short. 'I shall expect you tomorrow with the proofs.'

On my way back I thought about that complicity with death that had always been mine. I reflected that I had always skirted death like a moth going to the light. But this time my mission, even if I saved my own skin, threatened to be jeopardised. By the time I got to the Opera I was ready to say farewell to it. Sadly I walked up to my office, then suddenly I had a flash of inspiration . . . my nose! But in my book on Diaghilev, published before the war, I told how I had undergone a cathetic operation, then rather unusual, and I had photographs of myself taken *before* and *after*. There was the proof. I hurriedly searched for the documents and set off once more for the rue des Saussaies. A quarter of an hour later I came out reassured. But this story goes to show the sort of times we lived in.

Later on other denunciations were, from time to time, made against me. One day the furiously anti-Semitic sheet called *Au Pilori*, admittedly 'collaborationist', discovered that 'Lifar' was only 'Rafil' spelt backwards and that I was a horrible Russian Jew disguised in Paris. It was to such lengths that crazy and provocative over-bidding could lead. But these things did not worry me any longer. I had, once and for all, produced my proofs. One day I was talking to some German officers. They were 'intellectuals', men with whom one could talk readily and freely about the dreadful epidemic of denunciations they received from 'good Frenchmen' and 'good Russians'. 'We would tend,' they said, 'to throw them all in the waste-paper basket. Indeed in some offices they do just that. But we have to pay attention to them and make investigations. Out of a hundred denunciations we receive we find on an average that two have some basis of truth.'

In this same paper *Au Pilori*, in which I was insulted and attributed mysterious origins, on one and the same day there appeared attacks on Jean Zay, Bernard Lacache, Jacques Rouché and . . . General de Gaulle. This was the first time I had ever heard mention of the general. Under the heading 'We pillory Charles de Gaulle, England's commercial traveller in oil' I read such lines as these: 'He threw himself into the battle at Churchill's side and learned from him the art of clothing lies in artistic dress. He agreed to betray his own country that was murdered by parliamentarians, finished off by the British. He added his stab to the wounds inflicted on our martyred land by the R.A.F. bombers, he attempted to sow dissension among Frenchmen desirous of working to make once more a decent France freed from Jewish lack of principle.'

It seemed that this general had made an appeal over the London radio. But very few had as yet heard of him. But as far as I was concerned it was from this *Au Pilori* that I first got to know about this man who was to make history.

On the morning of 1st July I was sitting at my desk in the director-general's office on the first floor of the Palais Garnier.

Suddenly repeated and hurried knocks on the door: before I had time to answer it opened and there was the *concierge*.

'Monsieur Lifar, Monsieur Lifar, a group of officers has arrived. They have asked for you. They are on their way up. I think they are important people,' he said breathlessly.

Officers. In those days it was hardly necessary to mention their nationality. In those first days of the Occupation the Germans were like men who have just bought a property. They were amused with and proud of their purchase, impatient to visit it and to show it while the old owners were still on the premises.

But I scarcely had time to think. I prepared myself to play the part I had thought out a short time before. My intuition —influenced no doubt by what I had seen during the Russian Revolution where *unkempt* was synonymous with *powerful*—

told me that this role was the most suited for concealing my real self and thus protecting me. So I leaned back in my arm-chair, put my crossed legs on the desk and busied myself with the first papers that came to hand.

Knocks on the door. It opened. A rustling of leather and boots, a clicking of heels—the ever-present sound in those years—invaded the room. One of the visitors stepped forward, pulled himself together and shouted:

'Monsieur Lifar, *Reichsminister* Dr Goebbels.'

I forced myself not to blink at the name which hit me like a point-blank shot. So they said I had done the honours of the Opera for Hitler whom I had not even seen, and that was enough for the B.B.C. to sentence me to death. Now the Propaganda Minister of the victorious Reich was in my office. Although I pretended to be occupied and did not look straight at him, out of the corner of my eye I could recognise a narrow figure draped in a long, leather great-coat . . . his livid, sharp-featured and nervous face under a crop of coal-black hair.

I remained in the position as they found me. What self-confidence the unmerited condemnation pronounced by the enemies of the 'Greater Germany' gave me! What I was paying most attention to was playing effectively my part as an artistic Bohemian, ill-mannered when anything else but his art is mentioned . . . it is only subject in the world which can arouse his wits, but for the rest a laughter-loving good fellow. This was the role to hide me, protect me from my timidity and allow me to evade embarrassing replies and extricate myself with a pirouette. This behaviour has often been useful to me so as to unseat an interlocutor, to make him swerve his line of attack. I got up slowly:

'But I don't know him,' I let drop, smiling and careless of all etiquette. 'I have never met him. What does he want? What can I do for him? Is he going to come to Paris?'

Then, glancing over the six persons who were there, I recognised Radermacher and then I noticed the minister's face change. It became inscrutable and extremely hard, his expression sharper still, under a large, intelligent forehead . . . the appearance of a sorcerer with a hooked hand.

'The *Reichsminister* is here before you, Monsieur Lifar,' said the same individual who had spoken before, while the minister took a step forward with his limping gait. I felt it was time to change my tone if not my register. I got up hurriedly and walked round my huge desk.

'What, is it you, Mr Minister? But it's not possible, I did not recognise you. We are all so preoccupied and hustled by things starting up here again . . . please sit down, Mr Minister.'

For a short time his face still remained hard and inscrutable. Then I noticed the moment when he decided to be cheerful and attractive.

'Monsieur Lifar' (the interpreter translated) 'do you know that I was one of Diaghilev's first great admirers? I was present in 1929 at the first performance of *Fils Prodigue* and *Apollon* in Berlin. I was in the *poulailler*'—'the gods' but he said the word in French—'and I applauded you.' I confirmed what he said. He seemed delighted, carried away by his memories of another age, another world.

'That is how I knew you, Monsieur Lifar, and I was able to appreciate your art as a dancer for which I have the greatest admiration.'

I bowed but said nothing.

He went on chatting in this way until abruptly he shot at me:

'Why did you stay in Paris when everyone else made off?'

'But to defend Paris against you, Mr Minister,' I replied with a smile. 'Moreover, I was mobilised at my job.'

'Mobilised? But you are a Russian.'

'All the White Russians were mobilised, Mr Minister, they did their duty, as was fitting, to the country which had welcomed them.'

Now he, in his turn, bowed without saying anything. Taking courage and relying, at the same time, on my 'personage', I went on:

'Let us say rather that I trembled when you Germans entered Paris.'

'But why?'

'Because you are the allies of the Soviet Russians and as a White Russian refugee I did not know what I should have to put up with.'

'Absolutely nothing.' Goebbels all at once became animated. 'The Russians work in *their country* and the Germans work *in theirs*.' He said *chez eux* in French and with his two hands made an energetic gesture conveying the idea of very distinct and separated compartments. From that moment I began to have some inkling of how fragile was the alliance whose announcement had stupefied the world . . . the alliance that allowed the rapid conclusion of the conflict's first phase and led the Germans to Paris and *Reichsminister* Dr Goebbels on an elegiac pilgrimage to the National Academy of Music and Dance.

We chatted for a good half hour in my office and then the minister expressed a wish to visit our illustrious house. Out of courtesy—and because he spoke German—I wanted to introduce to him Laly the secretary-general, so I sent for him that he might be with us during our visit. Then another of my collaborators turned up, one Dupont. A desiccated, austere-looking man, wearing black gloves, carrying an Eden hat in his hand and an umbrella over his arm. He greeted the minister with a resounding *Heil Hitler* which seemed to embarrass everyone. Goebbels gave him a brief reply while scrutinising him as an entomologist would an insect. During the visit Dupont was to keep on trying to get into conversation with Goebbels and to attract his attention. But the minister kept aloof from this individual he did not know and whom it seemed he thought of as quite insignificant. It was not my fault if Goebbels wanted to talk only to me.

We went into the Foyer de la Danse. I pointed out the portraits adorning the walls. Before that of Fanny Essler I stopped:

'A German, Mr Minister.'

Goebbels turned round and stood before me with his forefinger raised. He said very slowly in French:

'An Austrian, Monsieur Lifar.'

I still blush when I think of the lesson he taught me.

'And don't you figure among them yet?' he went on, guessing my embarrassment.

'Yes, here.' I had stopped in front of a large mirror and as a joke struck a pose like that of a dancer's portrait.

Later during the visit he asked me:

'Do you like the German ballets?'

'No, not at all,' I answered frankly, 'I detest German Expressionism. As far as I am concerned it may be good theatre but it is not good dancing for the Dance must be free of all elements but itself.'

'I know your ideas on the subject,' he said with a sly smile. 'I have read your book on the *Dance* written for the second International Congress of Aesthetics in 1938, Monsieur Lifar. By the way, that reminds me I'd like to see the library.'

We walked across the stage. As I had wished, stage-hands were at work putting up scenery and artists were beginning to rehearse the ballet *Giselle* with Dinalix.

'We want at all costs to get the Opera going again, Mr Minister.' He stopped and looked at me.

'Monsieur Lifar, I've told you we appreciate very highly indeed what you are doing and we are very glad you are here. We want to help you in every way we can. The best thing we could do would be to appoint a German manager who would be in a better position to keep in touch with our departments.'

'Mr Minister, if you put in a German here, I will at once resign.'

'But you are a Russian.'

'Forgive me but I am a French official.'

'Ah, but then why resign?' he said, obviously annoyed.

'First of all because it is the Führer's wish that the French theatre and French art should remain in French hands. Therefore it is a choice between you or me.'

'How do you know this view of the Führer?'

The idea came to me all at once. I had not seen him . . . but I retorted:

'But he himself was here last week.'

Clearly Goebbels knew nothing of Hitler's visit to the Opera and was piqued at not knowing. His face clouded over for a few instants—then he dropped the subject.

We entered the library rotunda. Dr Goebbels took an obvious pleasure in glancing at the rows of precious volumes. With a self-satisfied look on his face he walked about in the huge room. Then, as he passed by a window, he began to shout orders in German to the members of his suite. I was alarmed and wondered what on earth could have happened and on whose head would fall the punishment for some obvious misdeed. What had happened, however, was that he had noticed in the rue Auber the name-plate of the Calmann-Lévy publishing house—which is still there. Goebbels wanted the sign-board taken down at once. By the time he stopped in front of Renoir's portrait of Wagner, he had calmed down.

'The Führer is such an admirer of Wagner, you should present this canvas to him, he would be delighted.'

'Mr Minister, you can take anything, you can requisition, you can do what you like, but I can give away nothing of the French patrimony that does not belong to me.'

Goebbels walked on and said no more about the matter. The portrait has remained in its place to this day.

Then, abruptly, he got bored and gave the signal for departure. We were bewildered by the brilliant sunshine when we got to the entrance steps. For an instant the Opera seemed to me to be very far away. We walked down the steps with the minister. He stopped to admire the group of Carpeaux's statues. Goebbels seemed pleased but preoccupied with other things. He thanked me, congratulated me and said *au revoir*, adding that he would come back for the opening performance—which luckily he did not. Dupont appeared once more still with his hat and in the bright sunlight more than ever like a funeral mute. He went up to Goebbels and gave the Hitler salute. When Goebbels saw him, he turned to me and with a motion of his head drew me apart:

'Just who is this man?'

I said I had already introduced him.

'Whoever he is he is a *con*,' replied Goebbels in French. He then disappeared into his car that roared off through the deserted streets of Parisian indifference.

I felt more exhausted than after the longest ballet in my career.

3

LAVAL IN PARIS

So my credit with the German authorities was strengthened but in the midst of fortune's ups and downs and at the cost of this risk to myself. I had allowed myself to pass as a German 'agent' while I knew that I was doing what I wished, that is to say, working for France. But my official position was still precarious and, as I had guessed from the beginning, I would be in a better position to carry out my mission if I was backed up by a French director. To secure the appointment of one became not only essential for the accomplishment of my mission but also the most sure means of avoiding German requisition.

It just happened that Vichy asked me for a report on the most suitable candidate we proposed. Louis Laloy, the temporary director, made a report—as I was to find out later on—against Rouché's appointment to the post and also against Gaubert's, while I strongly recommended their appointment.

A few days after Dr Goebbels's visit I was summoned—without being told why or before whom—to the Villa Said, in the 16th arrondissement. When I got there I was ushered into the presence of Pierre Laval—who as usual wore a white tie—on a private visit and incognito in Paris. He embraced me in a familiar way and spoke to me in his usual simple and direct manner. He confirmed that the Marshal's orders were for the Paris theatres to be opened at all cost. And he added briskly, 'The Marshal hopes to meet you in Vichy as soon as possible. So get started. We will meet again there. But tomorrow I will receive you officially in the rue de Grenelle. Léon Noël will be there.'

The latter was the French government's ambassador in occupied France.

The next day, sure enough, I was received at 127 rue de Grenelle by Pierre Laval in the presence of Léon Noël. The Prime Minister gave me these instructions: 'Find a director, anyone you like will do, but above all not Rouché. He's a cunning old fellow who has managed to keep his head above water amid all the disorders and confusions. For the national lyric theatres I will accord you a subvention of twenty-five million francs.'

I took good note of the advice though remembering that my report had already gone off. Then Laval added, 'Keep in touch with me through M. Léon Noël.' But although the Prime Minister had seemed frank and open Noël appeared to me to remain inscrutable, unforthcoming. His only contribution to the conversation was evident ill-will. In a word, he inspired me with no confidence. Then, as I took leave, the Prime Minister said with humour which may have been only modesty, 'Above all, in so far as your influence reaches protect the Auvergnats, Chanel and all the others. Watch over them.'

I must say here that Coco Chanel's famous dress-making firm was the only one of the first-class *couturiers* not to open its doors during the whole of the Occupation.

On leaving the Prime Minister's residence I found in the hall two German officers who proposed to accompany me to the German embassy in the rue de Lille. In the grounds I soon noticed a man in shirt-sleeves and wearing braces. He would have seemed more suited to a country house than an embassy. He came towards me and smilingly held out his hand. Then he introduced himself, 'Otto Abetz, ambassador of the German Reich.' He added, later on, as he was showing me round the garden, 'You know I've always done what I could to encourage Franco-German amity and harmonious relations. I am very pleased to know you, that is to say meet you at last. Before the war I used to be taken here for a spy. But I was only a "collaborator" before the term had been invented.'

He expressed himself in perfect French. Later on he said, 'Now, I'm the chief. We are going to be able to do some good work. The Opera must be opened very soon—and by the French people.' Then giving me a quick, searching glance . . . 'But don't go to Vichy . . . it's for your own good that I forbid you to go . . .'

He interrupted the conversation to lead me into a drawing-room. But I shuddered. It had seemed to me he was answering my conversation with Pierre Laval. How could he have been informed so precisely and so quickly? There had been only one witness present at the interview.

Abetz introduced me to Grabowski, who was the senior counsellor and the power behind the throne at the embassy— as I found out afterwards. Then the ambassador's wife came in, Suzanne Abetz, who had been French before her marriage.

She explained to me how happy she was to be back in Paris although it made her sad also to return in such circumstances. But she hoped to make herself useful. She told how she had burst into tears at Compiègne after the fall of Paris and that it was the Führer who himself had comforted her, with much delicacy and courtesy.

At the end of August Rouché arrived to take over the management of the Opera. His title was director of the National Lyric Theatres. I told him how glad I was to see him in the position and to 'give up my post to him'—an expression that was, I noticed, hardly to his taste. The first measures followed at once. Rouché dismissed Szyfer (who had brought him up from Vichy in his Citroën) because he was Jewish. Laloy was also turned out because of the report he had made against Rouché and which the latter had got to know about. But the German authorities, for some reason unknown to me, would not confirm Rouché's nomination and it was only after my pleading with Abetz and his wife that they finally consented. In spite of that, or rather doubtless because of that—so paradoxical were those years—I remained in Rouché's eyes a power behind the German throne and that was why he was always a little suspicious of me. And this was in fact to turn to my advantage. Moreover, I had sworn not to save myself but the French patrimony. Etienne de Beaumont, released from the army, made his reappearance. He went off to Vichy to get himself made director of the Opera, of which he proposed to make himself the Maecenas. He failed in his attempt. Other efforts were made with the same object in view by Roger Capgras—helped by Henri Jeanson—this time with the German authorities. Capgras had finally to be satisfied with the Ambassadeurs Theatre, where, helped by the Germans, he got together a ballet troupe. He, and Kniaseff at the Marigny Theatre, started bidding against each other in order

194   LIFE WAS LIKE THAT

to attract to their theatres artists from my Opera Company. Darsonval and Chauviré at first yielded to temptation and I had to win them back.

But already as between these enterprises and the Opera there could be noticed signs of artistic politics, just as there were between 'Paris' and 'Vichy'.

The first aim of my mission had been achieved. French authority had been established. Rouché was director of the United National Lyric Theatres, Gaubert was director of the Opera and Henri Busser that of the Opéra-Comique.

Such a situation was going to allow us to set to work despite the tempest of war—a first step, maybe the most important one.

4

DANCING ON THE VOLCANO

During the first period of the Occupation the two most important men to hold authority in France were von Grote at the head of the *Gross-Paris Kommandantur* and Abetz the ambassador. In order to carry out my mission I had often to see both of them. But each one of them for different reasons did all he could to help me. I have mentioned the goodwill of von Grote—of Baltic origin—who showed kindness to the members of the White Russian colony who had left their country after the Russian Revolution. As for Abetz—who was aided by his wife Suzanne (who before the war was the secretary of Jean Luchaire and an active worker in the cause of Franco-German reconciliation) and his children Bernard and Sonia, they made the rue de Lille embassy a meeting-place for more French people than I can name. . . .

These were, then, the two 'heads' of the Occupation in the capital. But I was soon to get into touch with two much more powerful individuals who were to help me in accomplishing my task of defending the Opera and also in giving my life during those years a quite exceptional flavour of high adventure. I was, in those days, very often at the house of a Dr Zalewski, a gynaecologist and physician to the Russian colony in Paris. He had been a pupil at my college in Kiev and perhaps for this reason honoured me with his friendship. He was a very subtle man, very cultivated, in fact a survivor of that race of what used to be called *honnêtes hommes* ('gentlemen') and are now becoming so rare. In earlier days he had attended members of the imperial family, as well as Chaliapin and Benois. He had lived long in Germany, he knew a great number of people throughout Europe and he entertained a good deal at his Parisian apartment in the avenue Wilson. His great discretion emphasised rather than hid, for anyone who was intuitive, the role of intermediary which he must on many occasions play. It was at Zalewski's house that I met Professor Heim, who had been introduced there by Mme Bernhardt, a Russian refugee of Berlin and a patient of the doctor. Heim, at once, expressed the wish to meet me privately. He was a grey little person and quite simple, a real 'man in the street'—one of those who in the story-books appear suddenly at your side at a crucial moment and then disappear and get lost in the anonymous crowd in the streets . . . I can today recall only with the greatest difficulty what his features looked like. As a matter of fact also I was soon to discover that he was one of Martin Bormann's closest associates.

During some long conversations alone with him he was to reveal some of the Third Reich's hidden mysteries. I had the impression of lifting the corner of a veil and of entering the wings of a huge, black theatre. He expounded to me the political ideology of the New Europe as seen by the thousand-year Reich and its power behind the throne, Martin Bormann. He warned me of the rivalries that existed between the great ones of the regime, of the struggles for influence around the Führer—all under the cover of a State that was in appearance all of a piece. As from then he gave me to understand that, at Hitler's side, the man who really held the reins of power was Martin Bormann, although he was not the one most talked about. Little by little he told me more and more. He explained to me the complexities of the German political administration. Thus I learned soon enough that there were at least two Gestapos and that they must not be mistaken the one for the other. There was the Gestapo of the avenue Foch, the most talked about. This was the police for the repression of anti-German activities. It was under the orders of Oberg and Knechen, stylish individuals whom I was often to meet in society although I had never any direct contact with them. The other Gestapo was much more important, its agents wore civilian clothes and it held the real, secret political power which maintained the undisputed ascendancy of the Party. This was the Gestapo that could have a general arrested immediately without further ado even if he were the governor of the city or the ambassador himself. This Gestapo—the *Sicherheitsdienst*: S.D.—had its headquarters at the Hôtel d'Orsay with a branch at the Hôtel Lutétia. Heim, who was constantly on the move throughout occupied Europe, also had his Paris office at the Hôtel d'Orsay and he revealed to me that he had in his possession—with only a dozen other people in Europe—what was called 'the Führer's procuration'—that is to say, permission to sign even in the most serious cases.

However, he introduced himself first of all as a delegate for artistic matters. He took an interest in my work, he said, which he was well acquainted with, and for that reason had made friends with me. It was through Heim that I learned about the idea Hitler had of making Munich the great cultural centre of the post-war Europe—after the victory. In this matter, once again, he was inspired by Bormann with Goebbels and Goering dissenting. And in this connection it is droll to know that Picasso's works, officially condemned as aesthetically decadent, were being surreptitiously bought at very high prices from the secret funds and destined for this post-war cultural and artistic headquarters.

Heim introduced me to Zeitschel, his adviser on musical matters. When Heim was away, it was Zeitschel who took his place. Zeitschel was a great admirer of Herbert von Karajan, who owed, moreover, to this powerful protection the important position he enjoyed in the Third Reich. Karajan had a private plane at his disposal and lived a life worthy of one of the high dignitaries of the old princely courts. In this connection, moreover, it is fitting to note that during the Nazi era artists formed a sort of privileged caste. At least certain of them who were members of the Party or who had shown goodwill towards it enjoyed very great prestige, which the State encouraged so as to increase its own glory. Such persons, it must be admitted, were accorded advantages unknown in the liberal democracies. The artist was, it can be said, a member of one of the high castes of society in the Hitlerian epoch, and privileged as he still is in the Soviet Union. It was indeed to this condition of things in Germany that I owed both my influence with the Occupation authorities and also the rather exorbitant powers which were soon—without my having sought them—to fall to me and to load me with responsibility.

I had then gained the confidence of Heim and Zeitschel. Our long conversations strengthened this confidence. I realised easily enough that Heim had decided to attach me firmly to him, and this not so much by orders which he did not give, but, on the contrary, by the help he had decided to give me for my artistic creation which was the screen behind which I was trying to hide the national mission with which I had been entrusted. One day while we were talking freely and intimately Heim mentioned once again the complexity of the German State political machinery as well as that of the Nazi Party. He also drew my attention to the traps which could sometimes, in this connection, lie in wait for the unwary or those who just did not have control over the machinery. 'In case of necessity never hesitate to call on me. I want to assist you and always will help you in any circumstances. You must succeed.'

'Very well,' I answered, realising all at once the great support this would mean for me. 'There would be no difficulty while you are here in Paris, but you are always travelling about, you are summoned to all parts of Europe. If something happens while you are not here and while Herr Zeitschel is also away, and the matter is urgent, what should I do then?'

He seemed not to have thought of this possibility. He was silent, reflected for a considerable time, looked at me again and again. Then at last he said, speaking slowly:

'You are right. One must think of everything. I want to help you. So, here we are. If you urgently need to contact me while I am away travelling, you must get on the line at the German embassy and ask for the Reich Chancellery in Berlin and you will at once give the name "Mademoiselle Françoise". Remember that, then you will get a cleared line to the Chancellery and from there you will be put immediately in contact with me wherever I happen to be in Europe, you will not even have to say my name or your own. Orders will be given.'

I was dumbfounded. I felt I was living in a fairy-tale world of my early childhood days, with a wizard who appeared to give the magic formula that would help one to overcome the designs of the evil spirits. But, as I had already had experience of Heim's great influence, I did not doubt that what he now said would be quite possible. I carefully memorised this new-style 'Open Sesame'. I thanked him and was quite decided to try out the magic words at the first opportunity. On many occasions I had recourse to 'Mademoiselle Françoise' and always got Heim or Zeitschel on the line within a few seconds. And this astounded me more than once and sometimes afforded me a self-assurance that saved me. Right up to 1943, to the turning-point of the war, I felt this strange protection hovering over me. When I think back to those days it seems to me that not one of the least of the paradoxes of the time was that so much power should have been vested in an artist, a dancer, amid a deluge of steel and fire!

However, the epoch had not as yet assumed all its tragic grandeur. The war, after having submerged France, seemed to mark time before it flamed up again more furiously than ever. I had, however, to take steps at once. The first results of my mission were no sooner achieved than they were imperilled. I have said that at the same time that Rouché was appointed director of the National Lyric Theatres, Gaubert was nominated director of the Opera and Busser of the Opéra-Comique. I thought I would be able to take a breather since I was covered by the French authorities. However, attacks and intrigues put the whole set-up in danger. I learned that the appointments of Gaubert and Busser were not approved of by the Germans. They had been informed—by friends who wished him well!—that Gaubert had, in his fury at the defeat, lacerated on the frontage of the Opera the playbill announcing a performance of Mozart's *Zauberflöte*. Therefore Gaubert was an enemy of the Germans and must be dismissed from his important post. I called on both von Grote and Abetz—I had not at that time yet met Heim—and explained to them that the denunciation was not only odious but silly, since on the day of the incident Gaubert and I had been together and it was not he but I who had torn the playbill in an unconscious nervous movement, as though to shake the dust of the Opera from our feet, our Opera from which the disaster was evicting us—and also to show that the Opera was to be shut thenceforth. They believed me and as they did not want to blame me, Gaubert was confirmed in his post as director of the Opera. Busser's case was rather different, for during the war he had written an article in which he demanded that German works should not be played. I was not in such close touch with the Opéra-Comique and I had no time to do anything, so the job was given to Max d'Ollone, president with Florent Schmitt of the musical section of the 'Collaboration

Group'! But in spite of these changes the lyric theatres remained in French hands.

The influence I had with the Germans allowed me to come to the aid of a great number of artists. I was especially careful to see that nothing unpleasant happened to my friend Pablo Picasso—we may remember his fresco on Guernica—whose very advanced opinions might have made the Germans suspicious of him. I had spoken about him to Heim and had been assured that Picasso would remain perfectly free and unharmed throughout the whole war—despite the fact that he was anti-Franco, pro-Communist and partly Jewish.

As a matter of fact he lived quietly during the entire war at Paris, where he owned and occupied in turns two storeys at 23 rue de la Boëtie, and a whole 18th century building, rue des Grands-Augustins, just before you get to the quays along which he would walk with his Afghan hound. In this building—a palace crammed with unframed paintings—his taste for acting led him to play the part of a persecuted pauper.

Just one anecdote. To protect and preserve them, Picasso had insured and then deposited in a bank an inestimable treasure in pictures. The Germans were curious about Picasso's painting and also about the fabulous sum for which some of the pictures had been insured, so they ordered the strong-room to be opened and had the paintings displayed to them in the presence of Heim whose curiosity had also been aroused. He described to me, in humorous fashion, the Germans' disappointment when shown the pictures which they turned about in every direction without appearing to discover the slightest beauty in them. Everything was left as it was and the Germans withdrew without doing anything more in the matter.

When I learned that the splendid Turgeniev library, of some hundred thousand volumes, had been requisitioned I took action at once. But this time it was too late. The books had already been sent off to Germany. I had not got the news soon enough the keeper of the library, Odinletz, had been ejected some time before since he was a freemason. All I could find out was that the collection had been ear-marked for an *Ost-Europa* university Hitler wanted to create. He was already showing his interest in the Slav regions of eastern Europe. Grote himself seemed to be very sorry he had been able to do nothing. But never even after the war was any trace ever found of this precious library which probably perished under Allied bombing. However, it was not wholly destroyed, since in February 1965 Ilya Ehrenburg, the famous Soviet author, told me he had been able to buy from Soviet soldiers—who had been with the occupation troops in Germany, several volumes bearing the library's stamp. He added he thought the other books had gone up in smoke with the tobacco they had 'clothed'.

Since we are on the subject of Slav studies I may mention that Heim urged me firmly and, as he hoped, convincingly to sell Hitler my Russian library and also my collection of Pushkin manuscripts. I could not risk displeasing Heim so I consented, but revealed at the same time that the sale could not be completed until after the war, since my library was deposited, and so blocked, in the United States. I showed as proof of my statement the receipt from the exhibition where I had shown some pictures in 1939 in America. He was convinced.

Then one day I got a message that the house at Chambourcy of the great painter Derain had been requisitioned by the general commanding the region and, as a consequence, the artist had been expelled. It was added that works of inestimable value, which had been in the house, had been treated abominably and either thrown away or handed out to the neighbouring peasantry, who had not the least idea of the precious nature of what they had been given. This time, in my indignation, I appealed directly to Heim—who happened to be in Paris. Moreover, this was the first occasion on which I was able to note and measure the extent of his influence. I depicted for him the dramatic situation in which were Derain and his works. Heim got very angry and ordered his car so as to go and see at once the general in question. In my presence he spoke to him in Hitler's name and with no circumspection, but rudely, imperiously, as one might talk to an inferior who had been guilty of some outrageous blunder. Then he turned to me and said the requisition would be countermanded immediately. But as far as the pictures were concerned, the general denied having had them treated as I had been told, but he ordered an immediate and searching inquiry. Heim added he would have some of his own people follow the matter up. I was able to note that a huge picture from the studio of Jerome Bosch was in the house and had been untouched by the Germans who nonetheless parked their motor-cycles in the drawing-room.

A few days later Heim was able to tell me the result of the

inquiry. It was this—and he had checked it himself: it was not the Occupation authorities, but undoubtedly Derain himself, who in view of the German advance had distributed his paintings to his peasant neighbours so that they might preserve them. But these good people took no interest in the paintings that they did not understand and had in many cases left them exposed to wind and weather. Heim added that at the time he was speaking Derain was already in possession of his house once more. Also troops under the orders of the general commanding the region were engaged in collecting the scattered paintings, which, in so far as they could be saved, would be once more collected in the artist's house. Derain was delighted and soon afterwards went off to Germany on an official tour of artists.

On another occasion the International Dance Archives were threatened. I had spent much time in eagerly helping to build up this collection. They belonged to the Swedish art-patron Rolf de Maré. Tugal the keeper, who was a Jew, had left and the archives were abandoned behind open doors.

I appealed to Nordling, the Swedish consul-general with whom I was in contact, and put the archives under his protection. He was on good terms with the Occupation authorities and as he represented a neutral country he was able to save these precious documents. He appointed me keeper of the collection.

I remained then in close contact with Nordling and was from time to time a guest at his house during a period of four years. It must be admitted that this house was in storm and later on, during the food-shortage, was a haven of peace and abundance. His country's neutrality secured for him almost every sort of privilege as well as considerable prestige. Between ourselves we called his dwelling 'the caviar house'. Was it because of this abundance that so many people—French and Germans— eagerly accepted his invitations? I would not care to say. Maybe also his guests wanted to make contacts, much sought after in those days, or perhaps it was just curiosity that attracted them. At any rate, it is certain that for four years Nordling's good, even excellent, relations with the German authorities made him, in many cases, a precious intermediary. My only surprise was to see him, at the end of those four years, forget everything and to refuse to remember what I myself had, on occasion, been able to obtain for him.

I had also to go to the aid of Coco Chanel who had helped an English friend of hers, a Mrs Beet-Lombardi, to escape to Spain. She had been grateful enough to relate her escape on the Allied radio, but she had mentioned the name of Chanel. Coco was not disturbed. I can remember also how, together with Sacha Guitry, I stepped in to save Willy, Maurice Goudeket, Colette's Jewish husband.

Society people—the *monde*—gradually made their way back to Paris and resumed old habits. Paris was quiet. No vehicles, people learned again how to walk—and to take the Métro. I still keep the memory of that strange world whose *sound* was even so different and where it seemed that an old play was slowly struggling to recapture its rhythm. The countersign was to liven everything up, to revive everything as far as possible, so gradually people began to resume their old routines.

Society life, strange as it may seem, flourished again, perhaps since so many other pleasures had faded away. Society was more lively, more exciting, than ever. The two high-spots were Maxim's and the Racing. It was there that 'one' went in afternoons and evenings. There everyone who was 'anyone' in Paris went to see and be seen. The young counsellors of embassy, the young German officers—then in the heyday of their glory and displaying their version of distinction—crowded together. Green uniforms of the infantry, tank corps black uniforms, grey uniforms of the airmen. It was there also that the girls and women of Society, or of artistic Paris, came to enjoy one of the rare diversions left in a city that was empty and burning hot.[1] Fashions had not yet had time to change. Shoes however—for everyone walked—did begin to alter silhouettes and these new outlines lasted as long as the war.

I would spend long evenings in conversation with Chanel, who, because she had closed down her business, had returned to her first loves—music and song. Accompanying herself on the piano she would interpret the longest scores of the *bel canto*. I was much struck by her musical sense. She would also read

[1] But in conformity with Marshal Pétain's wishes there were, in everyone's mind, thoughts of the prisoners. The existence of the camps for which no end could be foreseen seemed an extremely harsh measure. Many Society women, even if they did compromise themselves with the Germans, so behaved only in the hope of getting husbands, sons or other relations liberated. Out of respect I will say no more.

aloud French classics to me. She was the first to extol and make known (as did also Braque and Picasso) to a wider public the poetry of Pierre Reverdy. She quarrelled moreover with Cocteau whom she accused of being jealous of Reverdy's poems.

At Maxim's in the evening, Germans and French still rubbed shoulders, but now, perhaps, with a little more constraint. Most often there were French tables and then German tables. More than once I noticed Goering dining there during his stays in Paris. At one of his first appearances he turned up at the Opera. His *Reichsmarschall's* white coat . . . his chest covered with decorations . . . I showed him over the building and then accompanied him as far as the entrance steps while he went on chattering away in French. He strolled off alone without showing much interest in what he saw—just as he had been inside the Opera. I followed him with my eyes. No one turned round or seemed to notice him as he was passing along. This odd vision remains engraved in my memory. I was to see him again at places of business—Lanvin, Lelong, Boucheron, Rochas, Pomba, Dior, Trémollet, Cartier, Hermès when he was with his wife Edda.

On 13th July was the first rehearsal of the first performance we planned to put on—*Prométhée*, *Giselle*, and the *Spectre de la Rose*. M. Darras of the Hôtel de Ville was present at this first display of the Opera in working order again. Thirty-nine artists and eight pupils were on the stage. On 26th July Radermacher came to watch the rehearsal. He was accompanied by journalists from *Paris-Soir* and the *Matin*, who were thus able to write their first articles on the Opera.

It was later on that I made the acquaintance of Arno Breker. He presented a good example of the high position some artists could reach under the Third Reich. Breker, whom Hitler wanted to make the 'sculptor of his regime', was most influential. He had at his disposal every imaginable opportunity for carrying on his work. He had the use of huge studios at Vriesen near Berlin and from them his monumental creations issued. Anyone he might choose to employ in his studios was at once free from any other sort of national obligation. He thus saved, I must admit, many Frenchmen by appointing them to his workshops even if they had never heard talk about sculpture before. His wife, Memina, who was a Greek by origin, had been at one time a model for Maillol (of whom Breker himself had been

a pupil) and then for Picasso. She was a close friend of the
Führer. So the wishes of Arno and Memina were real orders in
the Third Reich and because of this they were a Providence
for the French artistic world. In their rooms at the Ritz Hotel
the *Tout-Paris* used to flock in crowds. But I often saw him
alone. From the Hôtel de Castille in the rue Cambon where I
was then living it was only a stone's throw to the Ritz and I used
to cross the street and chat with them both—especially about
art, about his art concerning which he had a grandiose, an
heroic, conception, but who nevertheless—contrary to what
some people might have said who were unacquainted with his
work or knew little of it—remained a sensitive man. He at once
saw in me a possible subject, an ideal Daphnis he hoped to use
in a large sculptural composition.

It was he who, together with Heim and Zeitschel, gave me
the most help in accomplishing my mission and in saving French
lives. Thus one evening I got a telephone message that the name
of Henri Matisse's son figured in a list of hostages, that the man
might be shot at any minute and that something must be done
at once to save him. At so late an hour I did not know what to
do. Then I had an idea. I could brave the curfew, run across to
the other side of the rue Cambon and see Breker who happened
to be in Paris at the time. I peered about carefully to see there
were no patrols in sight and then dashed across the street.
When I got to the Brekers' apartment (which I knew well, for
Barbara Hutton had often occupied it before the war) by a
great piece of good luck General von Stülpnagel, commanding
Gross-Paris, was there with them. I explained the situation.
Arno and Memina told the general who Matisse was and pressed
him to do something. Stülpnagel at once telephoned some
orders. The next day Matisse was saved . . . by chance . . .
since the affair was, if I may so express it, a fake. My informer
had been misled and the man was not the son of the famous
painter.

'Be careful what you ask for,' warned Arno Breker, it is true
amiably enough. 'As you saw, I made a very strong appeal to
General von Stülpnagel, who afterwards did not fail to point
out to me that it was based on a misunderstanding.'

However, things were all right as they were—it was always
another human life saved. I should also mention that Breker
never refused to intervene when I asked him. But as far as I

myself was concerned, during four years I refused all privileged treatment whatsoever. In spite of German offers I had no house, no car, no heating nor any *Ausweis* (pass). And all the time the Germans wanted to push me into the place of Rouché whom they had accepted only unwillingly in the first instance. I had to resist this attempt to raise me to the heights and I never ceased to defend Rouché against the Germans.

Germaine Lubin and I did all we could to secure the countermanding of the order forbidding Frenchmen to play German music. We considered this prohibition to be a humiliating discrimination because it was injurious to art. Finally we were successful. Germaine Lubin had great influence with the Occupation authorities and with Hitler himself. She had before the war sung Wagner in German at Bayreuth in the presence of Hitler and had received his congratulations—much to the pride of the French.

On 28th August we gave our first Dance performance. There were, it is true, plenty of Germans in the audience, including Abetz and Stülpnagel, since during the whole Occupation one third of the seats were bought by the Germans, but we refused all the same to make this re-opening an official occasion, almost a festival. It was just that life was going on in a natural way.

However, on 3rd September, the anniversary of the outbreak of war, we received an official order to give, at the German embassy, a performance in honour of General von Brauchitsch, supreme chief of the German General Staff, who was passing through Paris. It was impossible for us to refuse. I considered this obligation as one of my tasks, one of the roles I had to play as an actor in life. On the appointed evening, then, we danced. Marshal Goering, who had announced he would be present, did not turn up. After the performance the artists of the troupe, the musicians of the Opera and myself were invited to stay and have supper. I had to accept because of my role, which now was more than that of a simple artist. And then, in German eyes I was not a Frenchman. But I must admit that I was inwardly displeased that no artist of the troupe excused himself on the grounds of quite comprehensible fatigue after the effort of dancing. All stayed and rushed to the sumptuous buffet. I remained on one side and looked on the scene. It seemed like a dream to me. A year before it was war, the end of a world . . . and no one appeared to think about it. They were all making merry. It seemed to me I was witnessing a banquet while the plague was raging.

It was, however, true that social life had started up again. At the receptions in the German Institute given by Dr Karl Epting and his wife (she was of Swiss origin) there crowded a mass of 'intellectuals' and artists among whom were Metternich, the German responsible for all the art treasures in occupied France— Giradoux and Etienne de Beaumont. The latter's mansion in the rue Duroc was wide open for Franco-German intellectual contacts which were much encouraged by Marie-Laure de Noailles, Marie-Louise Bousquet, Antoinette, Duchesse d'Harcourt at the head of the writers and by Georges Auric as the leading musician. Their especial darlings were Friedrich Sieburg and Herbert von Karajan.

Elsewhere, and especially in conversation, people were 'pro-' or 'anti-' (that is *phile* or *phobe*-) for these pre/suffixes had by now made their appearance. After Dunkirk and Mers-el-Kebir everyone was anti-British (*Anglophobe*) but gradually people became forgetful, so it was that some were quickly dubbed 'pro-German' because they tried to maintain some French social life while those who condemned them thought they were being very superior when they declared themselves 'anti-German'. It is true that others spoke only with great contempt of the 'pro-British'. All this was handy enough. It applied to sentiments attributed to others and not to one's own activities, which one avoided taking into account.

In the night of the 13th December, a hundred years to the day after the return of the 'Eagle' (i.e. Napoleon), I witnessed the return of the remains of the 'Eaglet' (i.e. the *Aiglon*, Napoleon's son). In the icy chill of night the bronze coffin moved along escorted by six pieces of ordnance and motor-cyclists of the *Wehrmacht*. Paris was deserted but there were a few policemen who saluted. A handful of passers-by hardly stopped to look. Behind the coffin where Hitler and Pétain were to have been (the latter decided at the last moment not to be present) walked Admiral Darlan between Abetz and General von Stülpnagel. Then came a small group of official personages. In the courtyard of the Invalides were drawn up Republican Guards in full uniform. I noticed Maurice Rostand shivering in the cold.

The night seemed still emptier and more sombre around the torches carried by the guards, while clouds of incense swirled up from a huge vessel and mingled with the snow-flakes that now began to fall. The cold became almost palpable. This was no festival nor was it a funeral. It seemed like something seen in a dream. That night you could realise that war had its grim, gloomy, 'Wagnerian' beauty.

❦ 5 ❦

WITH MARSHAL PÉTAIN

It was cold everywhere in that winter of 1941. Real war conditions were beginning to prevail. But we were only serving an apprenticeship to their hardships, to penury and to what were then called 'restrictions'. Consumer goods and foodstuffs became scarce. The towns were cut off from the countryside. The demarcation line between the two 'zones' formed a redoubtable barrier. Cards and tickets made their appearance. But the 1400 calories daily to which they entitled each person did not suffice even for adults. And not every citizen received the parcels which began to be an institution. Coal, fats, oil and soap were in very short supply. Prices rose much more quickly than salaries. The life we led was made up of strange contrasts as between dullness and privations on the one hand and on the other an unbridled curiosity, a taste for the motiveless, for adventures of the mind. Just as Paris was empty, dismal, and forced all of us to walk, so also it had never been so beautiful, freed from vehicles, stripped, grandiose. Paris lived by Berlin-European time. The twilights and dawns were jostled. No more old habits, everything had to be discovered anew.

New fashions suited to the circumstances had had to be adopted. The women wore thick wooden soles whose tap-tap on the Paris streets lingers in my memory. Hair was dressed up into very tall coiffures and topped with huge hats. Skirts were short and jackets long. The 'zazous' tried to impose their style, long hair, long coats, tight, short trousers. People turned all the more to trifles since they lacked the real necessities of life. The black market had soon appeared. The Métro had perforce become fashionable and the most important people could meet each other there. The only ones who could escape the Métro were those who had a gasogene car (petrol was reserved for war needs), or who had the means to take a *vélo-taxi*, the modern version of a rickshaw, the Western version. These were later on suppressed by arbitrary act of the Occupation forces. The filching of jobs was in full swing. Some people elbowed their way pretty ruthlessly in order to get a position in the public eye or a situation at Vichy or Paris. Some went so far as to denounce those who had collaborated with . . . the Third Republic! There was fear that even within the new regime some measure of instability might creep in.

Thus at the end of 1940 Pierre Laval had been replaced by Pierre-Etienne Flandin as heir apparent of the old marshal and as Prime Minister. In February 1941 Flandin, in his turn, was succeeded in these positions by Admiral of the Fleet Darlan, who seemed to usher in a new era.

Some havens, however, subsisted where there seemed to be preserved something of the atmosphere of those happy days before the war. I have mentioned Maxim's. To this must be added the Montmartre restaurant that Vaudable had just opened in the rue de Clichy. This place became a veritable Franco-German club. The life I led, the 'role' I played in Parisian artistic circles (and which obliged me to help out-of-work artists to earn some fees), forced me to frequent these places. And I must admit that in this way I was a privileged person during a time that was so harsh for most people. At the Racing, in this period, I often used to meet a small group of people who forgathered there. I was on very friendly terms with Corinne Luchaire, the daughter of Lucien Luchaire who 'discovered' the cinema and was to show later on great courage in the face of disaster . . . and also Geneviève Vaudoyer, the daughter of the manager of the Théâtre Français. Around these and a few others there gravitated a whole collection of handsome young officers from the smartest units, the Panzers, the *Luftwaffe* or the *Kriegsmarine*. Americans were still to be found in Paris. They were very objective observers and made continual trips between Paris and Vichy. Bullitt himself had very soon been dismissed—and in cavalier fashion—because of his anti-German remarks. The new German time made night come very early. But in the evenings it was in a gay atmosphere that small groups of people often, after dinner at Maxim's, met at the Lido, the Schéhérazade or at Monseigneur. They were the most flourishing night-clubs where the Germans went to find women, listen to Tzigane music and drink champagne. Sometimes when the fun was over a few would go up to Montmartre and, in the cold and rarefied air, gaze at the too early 'Berlin dawn' rise over Paris.

So it was that by close but surreptitious attention to the profound changes taking place, I was one of the first, as early as the beginning of 1941, to think I could discern a great movement occurring in the foundations of the German organisation. Little by little, unit by unit, the youngest elements of the German Army, the crack troops, were recalled toward Germany and the eastern frontiers. Everywhere in Europe there was noticeable a general movement towards the east, a movement on a much greater scale than would have been justified by the campaigns in Yugoslavia and Greece. German troops were unceasingly crossing Europe. I remember having said as a joke, in those days, that the Greater Reich had, through its conquests, become a new Cook's travel agency. Even the officers to whom I mentioned these things, very discreetly, appeared much astonished. Either they did not realise or they did not understand what was going on. But soon—and thanks to my informants in Heim's circle—I fancied I could see plainly enough what was going on and why. Things were to become still more serious.

In May I was invited by Abetz to go to Frankfurt. The pretext for the journey was an 'artistic' one which I did not very well understand. After having called on Herr Kwiring, the consul-general, and having obtained my travel documents, I took the train. At the frontier I was literally carried off by some people quite unknown to me. They asked me to get into a car. We drove away at a great speed to some place I did not recognise. Here we met a collection of people. Half of them were soldiers and the other half civilians who spoke to me, with great seriousness, as a 'friend of Hitler'—as they expressed it. I could not make out what it was all about and began to be vaguely anxious, so weird did everything appear—and so far removed from the 'artistic object' mentioned by Abetz. At last one of the men came straight to the point and proposed that I should become the *Gauleiter* responsible for the Russians in France and, it was added, my prestige would aid much in securing that my task would be successfully accomplished.

I was totally flabbergasted, but then I recalled my intuitions of the last few months and my fears which were being fully confirmed. After pretending to reflect for a few instants I naturally refused the offer though quite seriously and with due deference. 'I would be quite incapable . . . it would be a delicate task demanding experience—I am just a dancer and no politician and moreover I am quite unable to become one.'

They accepted my excuses.

On the morning of 22nd June I was in my room at the Hôtel de Castille. About ten o'clock I went out to go, as I did almost every Sunday, to the Racing. Hardly had I taken a few steps than I ran up against a man I knew. He said abruptly, 'Do you know that at dawn the German troops invaded Russia?' As I have indicated I had been expecting this news for a long time. But what a long way it was from the idea to the brutal fact. I felt completely broken. So my country was once more at war. What would happen to it—and to me? For what I was trying to do for my adoptive country might also be threatened. The rue Cambon had become unrecognisable. The sun had been extinguished at high noon. I walked on like a robot, so giddy that I no longer felt the weight of my body.

That evening I met Heim who took me to the German embassy: 'Come with me,' he said, 'there at least you will get the news. Anything is better than solitude and uncertainty.' I followed him, for I was indeed greedy for news. Otto Abetz and his wife greeted me with the greatest kindness. 'We quite understand how you feel,' they said when they noticed my dismay, 'but cheer up, it means the end of Bolshevism.' Indeed there was a strangely festive atmosphere in these rooms where only a few weeks before I had met Bogomolov, the Russian ambassador to Vichy.

Later on, when I got back to my hotel, and the excitement caused by the meeting had worn off, there I was face to face with myself, distressed, without resistance.

The next day I learned that during this same night some hundreds of Russians had been arrested of whom the Germans doubtless thought they had reasons to be suspicious. Among them were Korvé and Prince Vladimir, the son of the Grand-Duke Andrew, who had been taken prisoner in the absence of the governor of Paris. I escaped probably because I was considered to be a Frenchman. As soon as the governor, Radermacher,

got back, I contacted him and all were immediately released—
with excuses. Later on they all had important jobs in German
departments dealing with Russian affairs or were put at the head
of purchasing units set up by the Germans. But all of these
people—still later on—discovered they had been keen resistants
and hastened to remember that one night's imprisonment—
due to a mistake!

During the very next days there came into operation the
'war' regulation respecting Russian citizens. Madrach took up
his appointment and installed his offices in the rue Galliéra. A
census of all Russian nationals was at once ordered and their
banking accounts were blocked. I myself was without resources.
Rouché told me: 'This time, Lifar, you are done for. You must
stand up for yourself.'

In the 'free' zone still harsher measures were adopted. All
Russians, indiscriminately, were arrested and were all treated
in the same pitiless fashion—no distinction was made even
respecting those who had fought in 1939–40. All were suspected, out of hand, of being Russian patriots.

For my part, I very soon got into contact with some Russian
friends. We were later to be called 'The Six': Baron von Pahlen,
Baron Wolf, Baron Lamsdorf, Dr Zalewski (who had become a
patriot), my brother and myself. We met to consider means for
combating the actions of the Russian Führer and to prevent
him from acquiring too much influence among the Russian
colony in France . . . we also did what we could in Paris to aid
our fellow-countrymen in the other zone. In these efforts we
were helped by Heim and Fernand de Brinon who had succeeded Léon Noël as French ambassador in the occupied terri-
tories.

20th September. Kiev my city is in the hands of the Germans!
This was for me a day of mourning.

All around me, however, was joy. My group that I had got
together for the purpose of defending Russians—I will not say
for resistance, that word has been too much bandied about—
were enthusiastic. I was a little stupefied (I have already said
that I was not politically minded) when I heard them all explain
to me that this time victory was in sight, that Bolshevism was
finished, that dear old Holy Russia would rise again and that
we must be present on the day of the great victory. One after
another they all left me except one of the Lamsdorf brothers. I

did not share their enthusiasm, I do not know why, perhaps from having seen too much, perhaps because my temperament does not allow me to go into such raptures. So I became suspect in their eyes . . . as I was in the eyes of certain French people though for quite other reasons.

I want now to forestall events somewhat. The war in the East was in those days presented as an ideological crusade against Bolshevism. Hence the enthusiasm in certain Russian circles where the war was regarded as a struggle for the liberation of their country. Many of these Russians volunteered for service in the German Army—so that the sole honour of such liberation should not be left to others. But very soon when they got out to Russia they discovered how things really were. Gradually, though not so very slowly, they came to understand that the campaign was not being waged against the Bolsheviks but against the Russian people regarded as inferiors, as a lower type of Man, the *Untermensch* in the sense that *Mein Kampf* and the Nazi doctrines had given that word. The struggle carried on in the name of the 'white man' had degenerated into a war against certain sorts of Whites who did not present an ethnic type arbitrarily defined by the Nazi cliques. And, sick at heart, I had to witness a double death, if I may so express it, both the tragic deception experienced by my Russian fellow-country-men (many of them among the best) and also the disappearance of what might have justified the German campaign. But it was not easy for my compatriots, who had been carried away by their first enthusiasms, to reverse engines when the light dawned upon their minds and souls. More than one of them paid with his life for such obstinacy and that when his sacrifice had lost most of its meaning.

Thus, one day I learned that Pahlen, who had set out so full of ardour, had been condemned to death in Russia. He had, in a fit of anger and lucidity, thrown a portrait of Hitler on the fire. He was to be shot. At once and as vigorously as possible, I applied to Heim. By stressing Pahlen's nervousness, his fatigue and indeed almost his irresponsibility, I managed to save yet another human life. But this incident made me still more distressed by the tragedy of those tortured Russians who could no longer have any hope of the Bolsheviks' downfall, of the dis-appearance of the men who had seized their country. How ever the war might end, in one way or another these Russians

Giselle (1932) (Photo Condé-Nast)

'I adored loving in *Giselle*, and in that love I consumed my strength' (Photo Teddy Piaz)

The prodigious leap of the
Czardas (1934) (Photo
André Steiner)

1935 With Toumanova
(National Photo)

Icare Orchestrated by Honegger (Photo Lipnitzki)

Above left   With Coco Chanel (Photo Schall)
Above right   With Jean Cocteau (Photo Marcovitch)
Below   During the Occupation (Coll. Lifar)
Opposite above   With Picasso (Photo Marcovitch)
Opposite below   1942 At Vriesen with Arno Brecker, a pupil of
Maillol (Photo Rohrbach)

1942 At the Opéra in *Joan de Zarizza* by Werner Egc (Photo
Teddy Piaz)

Rehearsal at the Opéra
(Photo Serge Lido)

At the Liberation (Coll.
Lifar)

1955 at Eden Roc
(Photo Serge Lido)

1963 with General de
Gaulle (Photo Pic)

were in any case deprived of their country itself or of their own loyalty.

One day I heard on the radio Stalin's speech in which he announced the revival of such values as Russian patriotism, religion and the usefulness of those for a patriotic war. I heard all at once such national heroes as Peter the Great and Suvorov extolled in Russian speech once more. I then guessed vaguely that we were at a turning-point of the war, of an epoch whose developments it was not possible to foresee. Moreover, in the following months I was able to note the progressive and ever-increasing importance assumed, until the end of the war, by a national Russian resistance movement; it was the first in date on French soil, where as yet the only resistance was that of the Jews who were personally threatened and where there was to be a Communist resistance supporting the Soviet cause. De Gaulle, indeed, was as yet totally unknown to the mass of the population.

All this, however, did not take place without clashes in which I was involved nor without twinges of conscience, as I have already mentioned. When the fall of Kiev became known, Fernand Divoire, the poet and a friend of Cocteau, asked me for *Paris-Midi*, of which he was the editor, to write an article on that city, my own city. I could not refuse and was indeed proud to speak of Kiev, especially as my worst fears had not come true. We heard that Kiev had not suffered much during the operations. So I wrote a eulogy which I intended to be somewhat equivocal. The theme was 'I am proud that my city of Kiev has not been destroyed.' Thus I celebrated a Russian town, the town I passionately loved, while at the same time I hinted that it might one day be allowed to continue to live a free life. On 21st September the article, under the title 'Kiev, my native City', appeared on the front page of *Paris-Midi*:

'Kiev, my native city . . . there I lived a happy and joyful childhood, then an anxious adolescence tormented by war and revolution and finally an early manhood full of adventures. I left Kiev in 1922 for a new world, the world of the Dance. I carried with me a love for my native city. I love it still and always will love it with all my heart and soul. Until my dying day I will be an ardent "patriot" of Kiev.

'There were in Russia three sorts of "patriotic" citizenry—that of St Petersburg, that of Moscow and that of Kiev.

Between St Petersburg and Moscow there reigned a ceaseless rivalry, a spirit of jealous competition I would even say. The inhabitants of these two capitals tried to dazzle each other. They boasted of the beauties of the city where they were born and the citizens of each place professed a sort of haughty contempt for those of the other.

'The people of St Petersburg were proud of their river Neva the beautiful, of its quays so broad and splendid, of the Summer Garden, of their *corps de ballet*, the finest in the world, of their refinement, their culture, their intellectuality.

'The Muscovites retorted by extolling the Kremlin, the St Basil cathedral, the "forty times forty" churches (the number indeed had greatly diminished since the city had been burned in Napoleon's time), the *avant-garde* spirit that reigned in Moscow, their own good nature, their lavish hospitality in the old Russian tradition—it is true that this hospitality had become less profuse with the passing of time.

'Kiev, situated far from these two capitals, entered into no sort of competition with them. Though the men of Kiev despised the "Northerners" just a little, the Kievans, instead of spending their time vaunting the merits of their city, were satisfied enough just to love it with all their hearts, souls and bodies. They were hardly concerned at all to dazzle the people of St Petersburg and Moscow, although they could well have done so. They could say with legitimate pride that their city, set on lovely hills from which the eye could rove over vast landscapes, was the mother of all Russian cities, the cradle of our civilisation, the nucleus of the Russian State and its Christian culture.

'The inhabitants of Kiev—the Russian Rome—could boast of their Dessiatiny church built in the 10th century, of the St Sophia cathedral, of their monasteries, of the Lavra that was the sanctuary of Holy Russia, of the immense catacombs where lay the bones of forty times forty saints.

'The Kievans could be proud of their St Vladimir cathedral —radiant in the sunlight, its walls covered with paintings by Vasnetzov, Nestenov and Vroubel—and of their St Cyril church, much more sombre but adorned with the finest frescoes of that Russian genius Vroubel.

'The Kievans could boast of their University Centre, their eighteen theatres for under a million inhabitants, of their superb monuments recalling both Byzantium and Renaissance Italy, of the magnificent gardens—those of the Tsars, of the merchants as well as the Botanic Gardens and the *Château des Fleurs*.

'And then they could glory in the majestic Dnieper, the superb Borysthenes that linked the Vikings with Constantinople and compared with which the Neva in its granite cuirass is but a small stream.

'However, I repeat, the inhabitants of Kiev sought in no way to astonish the men of St Petersburg and Moscow—they were content just to love their city as the most beautiful in the world.

'In the last twenty years during my travels, I have seen nowhere else a city so fine, one which combines in so felicitous a way, both the past and the present, the works of Man and those of nature, where one could breathe so easily, where the eye could discover vast horizons and where everything was not only sun-lit but warmed by sun-light. Is it not for that we all love our cities? Is it not that warmth which gives their beauty to our women and which gives us our love of music and dancing? The famous Nijinsky also was born in Kiev.

'Before the Germans troops occupied Kiev I was full of foreboding. I feared that the Soviet troops, as they retreated, might destroy the city's beauty, our pride. . . . May Kiev flourish for ever in its age-old loveliness. . . .'[1]

As can be seen, I did not want to do more than to express the feelings of a 'patriotic citizen' wounded in his heart and soul. Unfortunately this was not understood—or people did not want to understand it. It was declared that I had celebrated the German capture of my city and that I had congratulated them for having saved it. It was perhaps this article that was, later on, to cost me very dear. I was accused of having treated lightly the harsh realities of war and the fate of my fellow-countrymen under fire . . . this was the exact contrary of what I had wanted to express. Such was the horror of the times . . . I was once again condemned to death by the London radio—Gaullist this time—together with the Comte de Castellane—the brother of Boni—the Marquis de Polignac and Sacha Guitry. However, this new resistance movement, as I have said, did not get moving at a moment's notice. I was myself present at more than one demonstration that shocked me in my turn. Thus it

[1] As a matter of fact the Soviets did mine the most important buildings, so that when the Germans had got the central electric station working, everything blew up.

was that I saw with my own eyes the Metropolitan Evlogii of the Russian church in the rue Daru at Paris bless the Russian soldiers who, in German uniforms, were preparing to leave for the eastern front. This time it was my turn to feel some embarrassment at this spectacle. It was a feeling I had already experienced when I saw Frenchmen in foreign uniforms— German in France, supported by Pétain and Laval—and British across the Channel who had answered de Gaulle's appeal.

To be fair I must add that from 1942 onwards the attitude of the metropolitan changed entirely. He came out in support of the 'national war' and hailed the renaissance of religion in Russia. After the war's end he enjoyed the reputation of having been an oustanding resistant and in Stalin's good graces.

So confused were men's minds at that time, that everyone was at the mercy of some blunder arousing misunderstanding. Thus, in my own case, the 'crime' I had committed by my article on Kiev was confirmed and rendered even more heinous by a telegram of congratulation I had sent to Abetz on the occasion of my city's 'liberation'. Evidently this was a serious matter. But what dumbfounded me amid all the rumpus that rumbled around me was that I had sent no telegram to Abetz at all! After the Liberation I made enquiries into the origin of this affair and I soon discovered the explanation for something which might have had horrible consequences. The whole business was due to a dreadful blunder made by my brother Léonide who (without consulting me in any way) was so carried away by his own recollections and his anti-Bolshevik sentiments that he did indeed send a telegram to the German ambassador and signed it 'Léonide Serge Lifar'. That was enough, double Christian name or not. What attracted attention was the 'Serge Lifar'. Needless to say, I remonstrated with my brother in a manner that befitted the circumstances. However, the time that had elapsed helped me to forgive him. But he had risked nothing at all whereas I had been exposed to risking everything —such were the hazards of being a prominent individual in troubled times!

He was not, moreover, the only one to have these ideas, and thus involve me in difficulties. One day when we were all— artists and stagehands—rehearsing on the Opera stage I was told a German officer wanted to see me. This made me feel rather disquieted. I was just going to leave the stage and meet this visitor when I saw a German army captain in brand-new uniform come on to the stage itself, rush up and greet me warmly as an old friend. When I had recovered from my surprise I recognised Neumann, my old Russian caretaker for whom I had got a job with the Rol de Maré Archives. He was about to leave for the eastern front. 'It's my duty,' he said simply. 'I must take part in the liberation of my country.' I could not help showing him how moved I was also. Then he left. We started up rehearsing again. But for some time the atmosphere was chilly. The rupture of the Germano-Russian Pact and then the war between the two great totalitarian regimes had changed the psychological and ideological data of my mission. The Opera staff, for instance, who up to then had been all on my side because I was a Russian and because they were Communist-collaborators, became more and more inclined to see in me a collaborator henceforth to be damned. But in other circles, on the other hand, there was to be noted a new and reinforced approval of the German struggle to free Europe from the Communist scourge. The Legion of French Volunteers (the L.V.F.) was created and despite what was afterwards alleged, it did not by any means consist only of outcasts and ex-convicts. Among those who joined the L.V.F. were the son of a future Marshal of France, the grandson of a celebrated general and the son of a manager of a large business concern . . . there was, indeed, throughout Europe, a short period of collective enthusiasm which led to the raising of 'legions' in various countries—Spain, Belgium, etc. For some people a new Crusade had begun with the 'Barbarossa Operation'.

As for myself who was not at all so won over as people were ready enough to say, I lived in continual fear of hearing that the Japanese had come into the war against Russia and at the side of their German allies.

General Schmitke, chief of the *Propagandastaffel*, whose offices were at the Hôtel Majestic, was very annoyed with me, no doubt because he was not very sure about the sincerity of my attitude. Under Schmitke's orders were Colonels Baumann and Lucht, and under them again were Pierzig and Heinrich Strobel, the writer, a passionate devotee of Debussy's music and a Jew who, however, was 'protected' all through the war. Schmitke had had the idea of forbidding all Russian works in France. I was at once informed of this scheme by a woman friend who during these years gave me some efficacious protection. She was the wife of a famous French theatrical producer and the mistress of the general. She tipped me off soon enough for me to be able to take steps and prevent the scheme being carried out. Authorisation was given again to put on Russian performances and to play Russian music. Through the Germans in Berlin I had won a victory over the Germans in Paris.

A short time after this incident I was summoned to the offices of the *Propagandastaffel*'s 'Musique-Théâtre' section at 52 Champs-Elysées. Captain Lucht was then running this office instead of Baumann. Lucht was a Prussian and by no means pro-French. He received me in the presence of an individual to whom at first I paid no attention. 'Monsieur Lifar,' said Lucht, 'henceforth it will be one of your compatriots who will be entrusted by us with all artistic matters which may concern Russians. He will be able to help you in your work whenever you have needs to have recourse to our services. Here he is in fact.'

And whom did I see? One Konstantinoff, a composer and an old acquaintance. I bowed to him but did not say a word. This was the only time I met him. I did not have occasion to see him again. I never dealt with his department. In fact, I openly refused to do so. I got into touch directly with the highest authorities. I could never understand how Konstantinoff got his job, especially since I knew he was Jewish and his real name Schreiber. Obviously he did not have to produce so many proofs as I did. Since the Germano-Russian war had begun, I was once more, in the eyes of the administration, a Russian—a fact which before one had been only too willing to forget—and sometimes Jewish.

One day Rouché called me into his office and said, with obvious embarrassment:

'Lifar, they say you are Jewish. I must have some proof to the contrary. You are in a very awkward position indeed.' He added he knew quite well I was not Jewish and that never before had he taken any interest in such questions. But, once again, I saved the situation and managed to come out on top thanks to the help of Heim and Zeitschel.

On 24th August I reached Vichy. I had been summoned to an audience with Marshal Pétain. I was rather affected when I got to the town that through tragic circumstances had been promoted to be the seat of the French government. Vichy was already invested with a kind of legend. Vichy was a world apart. It was a 'state of mind'. It embodied what had been called the 'National Revolution' with the new motto 'Work, Family, Country'. Some people were already opposing *Vichy* to *Paris*, although as far as collaboration went *Paris* only wanted what *Vichy* declared officially that it hoped for.

But Vichy was all the same a little more *France*. Once the demarcation line was crossed there were no more German uniforms to be seen. It was with some emotion that one noticed French uniforms again. They seemed like relics surviving from a world that had been thrown back into a far-distant past.

I was to meet Gaston Bergery in Vichy. He was getting ready to leave for Ankara where he was to be French ambassador after having occupied a similar post in Moscow until the German troops entered Russia. We talked for a long while about the way the war was going as one might get an idea of it beyond the French frontiers and in a country that was not yet belligerent. But the whole world was at this time under the influence of the German victories. The German Army was thrusting forwards all the time and driving before it or capturing hordes of Soviet Russians completely routed.

That same day at Vichy there was to be a great sports parade. I was present with Bergery. Everyone who was anyone at Vichy was there grouped around Marshal Pétain. I got Bergery to put names to the faces I did not know, names which then were in the news and filled the Press. It was a festive occasion intended to honour young people and to stress their outstanding part in a new France which according to the doctrines of the 'National Revolution' had ceased to be a republic to become the French State. It was perhaps all a little ingenuous but I was sincerely happy to find a France which, as I was not slow in realising, was far removed from Paris, despite the efforts we made to keep Paris French. Here was a France, maybe a little provincial and screened from the great clashes and the harsh realities of the time, but still a youthful—and apparently care-free—France.

The next day but one, the 26th August, I was accompanied by Dumoulin de la Barthète, Pétain's principal private secretary, and by Dr Ménétrel to the Hôtel du Parc, the marshal's residence. I have no need to say how moved I was on entering this building, which in Paris was regarded as legendary—the Hotel du Parc, a sort of *Côté de Guermantes*, a mythical place where one could not imagine that one day one might land up there in real life.

I waited in the marshal's anteroom. I saw Admiral Darlan pass through. He had come to work with Pétain. Then General Huntziger was announced. Everything took place simply, with hardly any ceremony, as in a family circle. During an interval between the audiences I heard Pétain's voice raised. He had been presented with a request that decorations should be given to Mrs Corrigan and Mrs Hoity Wiborg, two of the numerous American women who were then making themselves busy at Vichy. The requests had been brought by Mme Nicole, the wife of the general and a member of the French Red Cross. The marshal grumbled in a loud voice, 'They make me sweat, all these amazons with their Legions of Honour and their War Crosses. Let them see the *maréchale*. I've got no time. Let them all have decorations anyway.'

At last I was ushered into the marshal's room by Dumoulin de la Barthète without more ado. The Chief of State, in uniform, entered by a little door cut into the panelling opposite to me. He looked at me for an instant and then held out his hand.

'So here is the man condemned to death,' he said, 'but I too have been condemned to death by my old friend General de Gaulle.'

I looked at the noble visage under silky white hair and the blue eyes I shall never forget, so bright and clear were they. He seemed suddenly to be astonishingly young. I did not know what to say. His hand that kept hold of mine trembled a little. He went on:

'Lifar, I am glad to shake your hand, I congratulate you and I thank you. I know what you are doing in Paris and I know that it is you, a man of foreign origin, who holds the French flag when it floats from the Opera over occupied Paris.'

And he added in a lower tone of voice:

'We are performing the same task, Lifar.'

Then he embraced me . . . his eyes were wet. A certain kind of look in the eyes—whatever may be their colour—always reminds me of Diaghilev and memories of him revived within me.

The marshal went on:

'France will show herself grateful to you, Lifar, you will be decorated.'

Then I heard myself say suddenly:

'No, sir, not now. It would be better to wait. It would hamper my work in Paris.'

I cannot say just why I refused the distinction. Maybe because deep down within me was the realisation of my essential solitude.

'Sit down,' he said, 'and tell me about life in Paris.'

So I remained three-quarters of an hour in conversation. At one moment Admiral Platon put his head round the door to see if I was still there.

'Lifar, how bored I am here!' Pétain said suddenly, perhaps gripped by memories of Paris, 'and my diplomatic corps is also bored. I am saddled with them and I do not know what to give them to do. I have only one real friend and that is Lequerica.'

I realised how often he must be tired and sick of everything. He went on:

'Do not leave. Tomorrow there is to be a gala here and I want you to dance, Lifar. I will be delighted to see you—and they during that time will not be intriguing.'

I was touched and promised that the next day I would dance for him *L'Après-Midi d'un Faune* which decidedly was a great help to me in such circumstances. I was preparing to withdraw and was rather embarrassed at having stayed so long chatting, but when the marshal got up he said:

'Wait for me, we will go down together.'

He called for his stick and képi. Then we walked down to his car while white-gloved guards presented arms and very smart motor-cyclists got ready to escort him. They were among the first, and appeared just as their successors do today.

The next day, the 27th, I did dance at the Casino in this gala performance to which crowded 'all Vichy', attracted by the prospect of seeing an artist from Paris dance with the local *corps de ballet* which included then Audran and the star Mlle Cassini. I threw my whole heart into the dancing in honour of the marshal surrounded by his government and all the diplomatic corps.

Ever since the preceding day I had been astonished at not having seen once among all the various personages the figure of Laval that I knew so well. He was not present at the gala either. This puzzled me. I asked the reason for his absence and was told that he was in Paris. During the interval I saw everyone's face bore a look of consternation. Again I asked the reason for this and was told that during a review at Versailles of the first units formed of the L.V.R. a young man had fired at Laval who was undergoing an operation the result of which was not yet known.

The gala slipped from everyone's mind. However, it was decided that it was not worth while spoiling the marshal's evening since he was taking such obvious pleasure in the performance. During the interval when Pétain came behind the scenes to congratulate the dancers, Admiral Darlan, accompanied by Chauvet, the manager of the theatre, whispered to me, 'Above all, not a word of this to the marshal.' So I danced before an unsuspecting Pétain while I knew of the serious incident he would learn about soon enough and which might have such grave consequences.

The next morning I called at the Hôtel Sévigné where I was to take leave of the marshal. He congratulated me again on the performance and said how much pleasure it had given him. He made me promise to come back again soon to Vichy 'with your *danseuses* of the *corps de ballet*. Are they pretty? I'd like to know them.' But the news, by now released, of the attempt on Laval's life preoccupied everyone's mind and upset all the work routine. I saw pass by Jaujard, Carcopino, Hautecœur, and Georges Hilaire. Pétain asked me what I was going to do next and I answered that I planned to take advantage of a few days' freedom to go—since Venice was inaccessible—and visit the South of France that I had not seen for two years.

'But in that case take a car,' he said paternally while making a sign to someone of his suite.

Then he gave me one of his photographs, signed it, and had a *francisque* pinned on me. So it was that I had a car and a chauffeur at my disposal. They came from the Chief of State's own car-park and I left Vichy in this almost official vehicle at the end of the morning.

On my way south I thought I would pay a visit to my friend Lily Pastré who was then at her country property at Mondredon. When I got to her house I was given to understand that she had friends with her, friends she had taken in and had been keeping for a year in her château. So I decided to surprise her. Without allowing time to be announced I pushed open the dining-room door and stood still under the lintel. Thirty faces turned towards me and froze into amazement. I recognised Bérard, Boris Kochno, Lady Abdy and her son, the pianist Youra Gouler, Ira Belanine, Stravinsky's niece and Edith Piaf. They all seemed terror-struck as though the devil himself had made an unannounced appearance in that room.

'Serge . . . you!' the mistress of the house mumbled as though choked by the effrontery of a man calling on her, a man whose conduct had been so scandalous in Paris. I realised the barrier that existed henceforth between Paris and what was called the 'free zone'. No one dared to speak to me or to say good day.

'How do you come to be here?' Lily Pastré managed to articulate all the same.

I was delighted to keep them guessing so I just said with a perfectly relaxed air:

'But I've come from Vichy and in one of the marshal's cars, in fact I saw him only this morning.'

I had pronounced the words of exorcism. They were all relieved at being no longer confronted with Hitler's friend who had been condemned to death by the Allies. They got up, ran towards me, embraced me and asked, as with one voice, 'What nonsense! You've seen the marshal? Tell us all about it!'

So I spent a short but happy time at Lily's house and then went on towards the Riviera. I revisited Nice, Cap d'Ail, Cannes, Eden Roc and Monte Carlo. I began to think I had not seen the Mediterranean for centuries. There was quite a new spirit abroad. Life in the free zone was marked by a certain dignified austerity but the Riviera was a different world. To begin with there was not the same population as before the war. There were plenty of people who did not belong to the region but who had not come necessarily to seek the sunshine; they were refugees from the occupied zone who had taken up their quarters here or who were waiting for a suitable opportunity to move on farther afield, to cross the sea. I was touched on seeing Monte Carlo again, the place where I had passed my first years near to France. I met quite a number of friends, among others the Adjemoffs. They were all astounded to see me there. Paris seemed to them so far away behind an impassable wall. I caught sight of Philippe Erlanger. I ran after him while he fled as though terrorised by my reputation. That evening we dined together. I saw Philippe de Rothschild and explained to him the meaning of what I was doing in Paris. I met also Baba Lucinge,[1] who had, in company with some Italians, taken refuge on the coast. As she seemed to reproach me with my presence in Paris and my activities at the Opera, I replied, 'What about you? You are ready enough to meet Italians. They have occupied the Riviera. And your husband? He's running a requisitioned hotel in Paris!'

A little later on we were to meet again at Maxim's.

Then I went back to Paris for the season that was opening.

After the departure of Louis Jouvet the German control over travel became more strict. He had, indeed, obtained for himself and his company an exceptional *Ausweis*—and even a special train packed with scenery and costumes—in order to undertake a tour in Switzerland for the glory and prestige of French culture. But once he was there he went off with his company by plane for South America, where he remained until the end of the war. So all permissions for foreign tours and performances abroad were suppressed.

Another small incident made some stir in the theatrical world. On 12th September there was held at the Ambassadeurs a Maurice Chevalier gala. The *chansonnier* and mimic enjoyed a real triumph. I could not help thinking that on this occasion Chevalier had, in his own fashion, made a more solid bridge between the two zones than any of those the diplomatists had been able to construct.

But Charles Trenet had the greatest success in Paris. Chevalier realised this and confided to me in the presence of Mistinguett: 'There you are, my time is over.'

Mistinguett, Piaf and François Perier enlivened the Parisian stage, while on 18th September the *Fledermaus* by Johann Strauss was put on sumptuously at the Opera. On this occasion a reception was held in the rotunda. General von Stülpnagel, the governor of *Gross-Paris*, and Otto Abetz, the Reich ambassador, were present.

Such were the festivities in Paris. They were also German festivities since all the national theatres had to accept once a year a German company giving German performances. Thus Heinrich George came with the troupe of the Berliner Theater to play at the Comédie-Française, Karajan conducted at the Palais de Chaillot, and Germaine Lubin sang in German *Tristan und*

[1] The late Princesse Jean-Louis de Faucigny-Lucinge née Erlanger.

Isolde at the Opera. When the next year I asked the famous Wilhelm Furtwängler in Switzerland why he did not come and conduct in Paris, he told me, 'I do not wish that bayonets should seem to impose what I have obtained and want only to obtain by art alone.' He never appeared in Paris during the war years.

On 27th September I went down once more to Vichy in order to accept the invitation Marshal Pétain had extended to me. This time I was accompanied by the Opera *corps de ballet*— as he had kindly requested. In the presence of Pétain I danced with Solange Schwarz, Yvette Chauviré and Efimoff while the orchestra was conducted by Roger Desormières. Now we in our turn, though in a different style, enjoyed a real triumph that warmed our hearts. After the performance the marshal came to congratulate us. We gathered rather timidly around him while he said how happy he was to see us there and thanked us for the work we were all doing in Paris to maintain the French 'presence'. The youngest *danseuse* of the company presented, with a curtsey, a bouquet of red, white and blue colours. She was to become celebrated. It was Colette Marchand.

I was during this journey the object of an 'attack' by the Resistance. I learned about it later on, after the Liberation, and from the mouth of the man who had organised the business. Guillot de Rode. He, at the head of a group which had founded at Lyons the review *Confluences*, had planned to kidnap me, nothing more or less than that. The idea was to divert, at Saint-Germain-des-Fossés, the *wagon-lit* carriage in which I was with the Opera troupe. I was then to have been put on board a hydroplane—which was to be waiting on the surface of Lake Paladru in the Isère—and after that handed over as 'artistic asset' to the Free French Forces in London. At the last minute the operation had to be called off because of a hitch in the arrangements. Guillot de Rode told me how the plan had been concocted with a certain M. van der Welde—whom he knew only under the name of 'Vignon' and was unaware that he was one of the most important individuals in a Franco-Belgian network that was among the first to get into action.

During this year 1941 the Dance maintained its rightful position. It was moreover in my eyes quite inseparable from my mission and from that form of Resistance it demanded in order to protect the French patrimony and its artistic traditions.

In 1941 also, despite all sorts of difficulties, there was created at the Opera *Sylvia* by Léo Delibes with Dignimont's décors and danced by Lorcia, Darsonval and Schwarz.[1]

But what marked the year especially was the creation of *Le Chevalier et la Demoiselle* by Philippe Gaubert. It had been planned two years before. In the presence of Jaujard, Coco Chanel had introduced me to Cassandre from whom I commissioned the décors, while the costumes were executed from documents provided by Prince de Faucigny-Lucinge. The orchestra was conducted by Louis Fourestier. With me danced Schwarz, Chauviré, Peretti and Goubé. The performance was under the patronage of Marshal Pétain, Admiral Darlan and the ambassadors Brinon and Scapini.

But this ballet is always associated in my mind with tragedy. In fact, by its very success it brought to its author Philippe Gaubert both happiness and death. He (who, as I have mentioned, was on my recommendation appointed manager of the Paris Opera) loathed the Occupation authorities and pretended to have been put in this position against his will. But, in reality, though he said this, he was extremely flattered to be applauded by the men in green whom he declared he despised and at whom he thought it smart to gibe.

He was, however, very nervous when his ballet was created— and it was a triumphant success. On the day after the first performance we all dined at Laurent in the Champs-Elysées, a restaurant then very fashionable. We were the guests of Gaubert's friend, Allisalde, a Spanish musician.

In his joy at his success and no doubt to calm his nerves that had been for so long frayed, Gaubert drank more than was reasonable. Outside the restaurant while we were moving away, he broke out into almost incoherent remarks, aggressive as are so often those of a drunken man, and dangerously anti-Boche. It was late at night and a German patrol was drawing near . . . thereupon he shouted still louder, saying, 'I don't give a damn . . . I'm French, a Frenchman of Cahors, of Verdun' . . . we did not wait to hear any more for the patrol was by now quite near us. We hustled him along to his home. The next morning, while he was telephoning to me to say something I will never know, he fell down dead from an attack.

[1] Later on I gave the role to Yvette Chauviré when I appointed her as a star (*étoile*).

He had to be replaced as manager of the Opera. By my influence with the Germans I got Samuel-Rousseau appointed and he kept his position until the end of the war. It was a post he had long coveted. He was no doubt a second-rater but had the advantage in my eyes of being French. Henri Rabaud, the director of the Conservatoire, having reached retiring age (he was pitilessly deprived of his apartment), Claude Delvincourt, who up to then had been head of the Versailles Conservatoire, took his place. Delvincourt still held the job at the end of the war when he was made much of for 'having saved his pupils by accepting the position'. For once, anyway, the merits of collaboration were recognised by the Resistance. Max Aldebert was in charge of the Palais de Chaillot. Emmanuel Bondeville was artistic director of the national radio at Vichy. Finally René Nicoly's *Jeunesses musicales de France* made its appearance thanks to the support (which I obtained for it) of the Secretariat of State for Youth, and of Emile Vuillermoz, the eminent musicographer.

It was at this time that one of my Jewish friends had been denounced by his own son: he admitted to me, 'Serge, it is appalling, it's like a Greek tragedy, but I love my son and I forgive him.' He was to die in a concentration camp. He was René Blum, the brother of Léon.

On 31st December there was yet another festival—but a solemn one this time—a great gala in aid of the *Secours national* (National Relief). For the first time the programmes were adorned with a French flag draped around Carpeaux's statue of *La Danse*. It was a gala in the presence of Marshal Pétain's wife. The programme included the creation of Ravel's *Boléro*, with Lorcia, and Vincent d'Indy's *Istar*, with Chauviré. It was this last ballet that earned her the title of *danseuse-étoile* (star dancer)—the fourth of my stars at the Opera. We also revived *Oriane et le Prince d'Amour* by Florent Schmitt (with Darsonval). I was both choreographer and dancer in all the ballets of that evening. My enthusiasm and my youth lent me wings both in real life and on the stage—two worlds merged into one.

After the performance we watched the Old Year out, that strange year 1941, black and red, night and blood, but also with the German colours, for it was the year that marked the culminating point of German glory. We had supper at Maxim's together with Madame Pétain, Georges Bonnet and Flix de Lequerica, the Spanish ambassador, who often came up to Paris from Vichy.

Later, for the night seemed as though it would never end, I was with some friends at the Schéhérazade. We were laughing, a little nervously. Suddenly a German general, who was there with other soldiers, got up and walked towards me:

'Monsieur Lifar?' he said in a half-questioning way. As I bowed he went on, 'I watched you dancing, Monsieur Lifar, and I admired you. My second son has just fallen on the Russian front. I wanted simply to tell you that he has died for those essentials of civilisation which we share, which are ours.' He hesitated a moment. 'Even if the means seem different,' he added, checking his tears. He bowed and disappeared in the semi-darkness. I was never to forget that moment.

6

BEFORE THE DESCENT INTO HADES

The year 1942 was that of the German's zenith of power. The conflict had by now spread over its greatest extent of territory. The year of these triumphs was for me the year of descent into Hades.

The military triumphs of Germany I have mentioned. But there were artistic triumphs also. There was the Arno Breker exhibition at the Orangerie.

But, no doubt, the most brilliant success was that of Werner Egk's ballet *Joan de Zarizza* created on 10th July. The décors were by Yves Brayer and Louis Fourestier conducted. The work was ample, lyrical and powerful. The success was so overwhelming that even those who had held aloof had to admit it. Critics and public were unanimous. The French—and I do not mean the musicians whose talents were well displayed on every occasion—wanted to emulate and play their part worthily. *Les Animaux modèles*, a most charming ballet by Poulenc— with décors by Brianchon—was created on 8th August, thus shortly after *Joan de Zarizza*. Poulenc's ballet, though highly appreciated, was somewhat thrown in the shade by the enduring success of the dazzling German work, just as Egk's ballet had relegated to a second place my ballet by Gaubert *Le Chevalier et la Demoiselle* which, however, up to then had been considered as a masterpiece.

I would also mention that this was the year of my film *Symphonie en blanc* made in collaboration with Henri Saugert and Roger Desormières. It was also the year of an exhibition I organised at the Musée des Arts Décoratifs and was opened in the presence of Paul Valéry, Brinon the ambassador and Professor Gregor of the Vienna National Library. The subject was the inexhaustible one—the 'Romantic Ballet'—always so evocatory of reveries. After a visit he paid to the exhibition on 14th April, the minister Carcopino, who had come up from Vichy, wrote . . . 'To Serge Lifar who organised this remarkable exhibition devoted to that great art which he is renovating before our eyes—a mark of esteem from a grateful visitor.'

In the spring came the performance of Tchaikovsky's *Roméo et Juliette*. Not often had an audience at the Salle Pleyel applauded an artist as enthusiastically as they did Ludmilla Tcherina, then hardly fifteen years old. This wonderful and highly gifted child-artist had achieved her first triumph.

Thus, even outside the Opera, I kept in touch with young artists such as Ludmilla herself, Janine Charrat, Roland Petit, Renée (later Zizi) Jeanmaire and Alex Kalioujny. I helped them to find their real paths since I was, as always, convinced that the influence of the National Academy should be exercised outside its walls, often to attract to it the best artists, or, again, to guide others.

However, although all seemed smiling enough, relations with the forces of Occupation became, almost imperceptibly, more strained. Certain events were to reveal suddenly this state of things in a more noticeable way.

After the first performance of *Joan de Zarizza* a big reception was given at the Ritz. There were present the composer, Werner Egk, the performers, the musicians and representatives, in full uniform, of the Occupation forces. The party was brilliant. The champagne flowed copiously. But still a certain, and novel, nervousness could be felt. Otto Abetz, already in disgrace, was present. And I think that this nervousness could be explained thus. Despite the victories won in the east, the German Army was meeting an ever increasing resistance. The Germans were getting farther and farther from their bases. The conflict had assumed the tragic extension of war on a planetary scale. And everyone, from then onwards, realised how dangerous things had become and how great were now the risks involved. So amid the delights of Parisian life hidden apprehension betrayed itself by a muted nervousness.

The party went on. Plenty of toasts were drunk. I was to some degree, and with the author, the hero of the evening, since

I was his artistic interpreter. After a great number of toasts had been drunk, to me, Herr Knote, the German consul-general, who, as friends had told me, was Hitler's choice as the Otto Abetz of occupied Britain, made us fill our glasses once more and got up in front of me, I followed suit. We held out our glasses. Then he said he was drinking to the health of the great artist, the great dancer, etc., but added with a sardonic look and lowering his voice, 'Still, you are a Bolshevik.' What was the matter with him? What did he mean to say? Ought I to have taken all this as a joke? All the same—no doubt the prevailing nervousness played its part—I scented a danger that must be warded off at once or I was a ruined man. I reflected only for a second and then without taking a sip I threw my glass on the ground. What a hullabaloo! People rushed up from all over the room, they fluttered about trying to efface the memory of my act, the consul-general and I were the centre of a crowd. Talk was about the heat in the room, about an artist's nervous fatigue. In a word, other glasses were put in our hands and it was proclaimed that all must be forgotten. Once again Herr Knote was in front of me, we raised our glasses, once again he spoke of the great artist, the great dancer, and then a lower voice and with his eye more steely than ever, he added, while giving me an evil look . . . 'But you are a Bolshevik!' Once again my glass splintered at his feet and amid general confusion and a great uproar I rushed into another drawing-room. I was perplexed and a little afraid. What did all this mean? Was the man just tipsy and in a bad temper? If he was not, I was lost. So I made up my mind to go away at once. To take French leave. Then whom did I see on the staircase but the German consul-general, Herr Knote. He also was leaving.

Inspiration—or a fit of madness—seized me. I rushed up to him and gave him a punch with my fist.

Now my escape route was cut. The consul (luckily in civilian clothes) had seen me. Either I would be imprisoned—or perhaps shot—or I had at once to take the offensive and make full use of the proofs I possessed. Now or never was the time to rely on my protectors Heim and Zeitschel. I went to see them and explained the unspeakable provocation to which I had been subjected. I added that Knote had sought in this way to get rid of an embarrassing witness who knew Knote had a mistress in Paris who was a half-caste with 'yellow blood' in her veins—

and it was true. Very soon afterwards Knote was dismissed from his post and sent back to Germany. Once again I had just managed to escape the worst of dangers.

But, as a matter of fact, the incident helped to increase my influence still further. The consul-general had lost out to me. On one occasion when joking with an officer I patted his epaulettes and asked him whether another pip would not suit him. Some time afterwards I called to congratulate him on his promotion.[1] I owed this favour to Heim, but afterwards the officer could refuse me nothing and others soon got wind of what had happened.

Again, I obtained permissions for marriages with foreign women which were normally forbidden to German officers. In these ways I accumulated prestige that was all the greater for no one being able to define exactly—or even imagine—the part I played inside the huge war-machine. No one could have ventured to guess the truth. I played no part at all. It was simply the protection of some chiefs enamoured of the arts that made me taboo. I played the game.

Another incident, less serious in its possible consequences, illustrates clearly enough the times we lived in. In the month of March I had a visit from Schmidloss, the manager of the Zurich Opera, who asked me to take part in the international Music and Dance Festival which was to be held at his theatre in June. I accepted with great pleasure, for I had already danced several times in Switzerland and had been able to see for myself what a splendid welcome is there accorded to artists. Furthermore I was particularly happy to dance in a country which had been spared the horrors of war and under the direction of that admirable conductor Ernest Ansermet whom I knew well. I was also looking forward to taking part in a festival where would appear my great friend Arthur Honegger. The German, French and Swiss authorities granted me quickly the necessary visas and I obtained a special authorisation from Rouché and from the secretary-general of the Fine Arts Department. All this after Jouvet's adventure, which I have mentioned, seemed to me a victory that confirmed my influence. I left on 4th June and, finding that life was splendid, decided to exhibit in Switzerland my art at its best. On 6th and 7th June I danced with marked

[1] Thus I made the acquaintance of Lieutenant Lucht, director of the *Propagandastaffel*, 52 Champs-Elysées.

success at Zurich. Many official marks of satisfaction were received by me as were also wreaths with the national and cantonal colours.

It was on the return journey that the incident occurred. Ludmilla Tcherina, my partner, had finally worn out her shoes in Switzerland so, taking advantage of the abundance prevailing in that country, she had bought herself another pair which she had been wearing for some days when together with her mother and myself she set off on her way back to France. But at Geneva a Swiss customs man noticed the shoes and roughly pulled them off her feet. Then she was obliged, barefoot and in the rain, to cross the station platforms in order to give an account of herself. All this much to the amusement of a crowd of passengers.

I was furious and began to insult the customs men. Carried away by my anger, I addressed the crowd and asked if the Swiss were so frightened of shortages that they did not like to see one pair of shoes leave their country. Someone called out, 'It's war-time.' 'What war-time? It's not for you, anyway.' I added just for the pleasure of striking an additional blow that I hoped they would soon lose their avarice. And, declaring I would not like to deprive them of anything, I threw out of my compartment's windows all the wreaths I had received. They crushed down on the soaked platforms. Admiral Bar, the Vichy ambassador in Switzerland, Arthur Honegger, and the Swiss ambassador in a foreign country had come to wish us goodbye. The ambassador, whom I did not know, tried to butt in, but in my rage I crowned him with the last remaining wreath. The ambassador stood there without moving, a Hawaiian of another world, with a laurel wreath around his neck!

But I had gone too far. There was a diplomatic incident. The Swiss Press took the affair up and showered abuse on me. The *Weltwoche* published a sizzling article in which it transpired that the Swiss had acted like champions and heroes and I like a cad. I should be banned from Switzerland for ever.

Almost immediately on my return I made a detailed report to Laval, and also one both to Rouché and to Mlle Augassis, secretary at the Swiss legation in Paris, who had taken part in the organisation of the trip. The matter was even referred to Vichy, an ambassador had been insulted. But the damage done, the export of a pair of shoes from Switzerland was too slight to move hard hearts in wartime. I think that, under the usual diplomatic civilities, the incident just caused shrugged shoulders at Vichy. Both Pétain and Laval had laughed about it. The Swiss had forgotten it by the next year when with the Paris Opera I again visited their country.

But from these journeys I brought back something else, a more vivid vision of the contrasts between war and peace. I found once more lights and words that did not cause fear. I saw once more towns illuminated, shop-windows full, stores well stocked. Before the evening dance performances a reception had been given by a certain M. Egley where in a fine display were all the things which for us had become 'pre-war'. We seemed to have travelled back in time. I saw the Aga Khan at this party and I never afterwards forgot how, later that evening when eating strawberries, he said to me in a calm voice: 'Lifar, all the same, it is Russia that will win.'

After my return to Paris the *Action artistique* of the Vichy government delegated to the Opera M. Favre-Lebret, who became secretary-general and the power behind the throne of the National Ballet and he has since remained such. Jean Mouraille was appointed principal private secretary to Abel Bonnard, the Minister of National Education, and he protected the national Ballet of the Opera in every way he could.

The Paris atmosphere had changed, my little escapade abroad made me very sensitive to the difference. On all fronts the German Army was still victorious. The Germans were in sight of Leningrad, in sight of Moscow, the Caucasian oil-wells were within the range of German guns, and the Germans were at the gates of Alexandria. There was just one great effort to be made and victory would be in the hands of the *Wehrmacht*. But it was just in this last effort, when it tensed all its muscles, that the Third Reich grew stiff. Gone were the young heroes with winged feet of earlier years. Now it was hard-bitten warriors who could not both smile and conquer. The German war-machine was becoming weighed down. The ambassador Abetz was in disgrace. Joachim von Ribbentrop's people in Berlin accused him of having shown himself too weak with regard to the French and with having failed in all his political manœuvres. Several times I had to pass sleepless nights in the police-station at the Grand

Palais since I had not been able to obtain an *Ausweis* especially when I was in company of Bérard after the party at Christian Dior's.

At the *Gross-Paris* command, von Stülpnagel, the uncle, had been superseded by the nephew. The name was the same and the Parisians did not seem to notice the change except that the vice of repression was gradually screwed tighter. Stülpnagel's signature appeared at the foot of the first hostage-lists which now made their appearance on the walls of the capital. In Berlin the elder Stülpnagel was also accused of letting himself sink in the delights of Paris, the modern Capua. The alarm was given when British planes came very low sweeping up the Seine valley, too low to be hit by German *flak*, and machine-gunned the 'Palais Rose', the residence of the governor. This was too much and the governor must be reminded what war was really like in 1942. Furthermore we were already exposed to more and more alerts and to the curfew.

Karl Epting, who was admirably acquainted both with the language and the literature of France, was called to Berlin for consultations and to report on what he had accomplished in France—he had managed in a very liberal spirit the German Institute that was housed in the former Polish embassy, rue Saint-Dominique.

It may have been due to the tact that Epting showed in his job but certainly he was a success in Paris. The German Institute became a popular meeting-place and the visitors-book contained a fine long list of names belonging to the most outstanding personalities in Parisian artistic, literary, scientific and Society circles. Epting, by the way, took this book with him at the end of the Occupation and kept it in his possession and thus, it was said, saved himself from all sorts of trouble. Jean Giraudoux who earlier on had been often at the Institute now showed up less often, but he always asked me to go and to report to him what was happening there. So regularly when I left the Institute I went to his room (next to mine), at the Hôtel de Castille and told him and his friend and secretary André Beucler what I had seen and heard.

It is worth noting that during the years when the war became more and more harsh, cultural relations between French and Germans instead of slackening were as close as ever. Everyone who was anyone in Paris flocked to the concerts at the German

Institute. These were also the years when François Mauriac warmly dedicated his book *La Pharisienne* to Lieutenant Gerhart Heller of the *Propagandastaffel* who had obtained for the publisher Grasset enough paper for a spectacular send-off on the market. These were the years when I saw Jean Giraudoux and a group of German officers signing the contract which provided for the publication of his works in Germany. At this epoch also Marie-Laure de Noailles published her second book— but in the unoccupied zone at Clermont-Ferrand—and Paul Claudel, diplomatist and great poet, who had addressed one ode to Pétain and was later to address one to de Gaulle, got into contact with the authorities of the Théâtre Français to arrange for a performance, later, of his magnificent *Soulier de Satin* which was to be put on by Jean-Louis Barrault, with music by Honegger and on the stage Marie Bell, Jean Yonnel, Jean Chevrier, Marie Marquet and all the great artists of those days. It was the time when I worked enthusiastically with Raimu, Pierre Fresnay, Gérard Philippe, Maurice Escande, Bérard, Darcante and François Périer.

Paul Valéry handed me the theme of a ballet he wanted to see created under my direction but I turned a deaf ear to the suggestion since it meant a return to *Giselle* and the purely classical which had struck and marked so many sensitive imaginations. So many artists had dreamt of returning to, no doubt surpassing, this dream. But I knew that way had reached its ending, and I was looking in other directions.

Max d'Ollone was president and Florent Schmitt the vice-president of a musical group at the German Institute. I refused to join.

Dr Goebbels's *Propagandaministerium* had arranged two large-scale trips to Germany, similar to those of 1941. One was for writers and the other for painters and sculptors. I do not know why these trips have remained so celebrated and are so often referred to or why they made such an impression on people. Most probably it was because of the standing of those taking part —or maybe because the journeys had an idealistic character and were entirely devoted to Art amid the clash and clamour of war. I took no part in these excursions but for the sole reason that I disliked group-travel, moreover I was preparing to go soon on a journey alone.

At that time Georges Auric also wanted to work with me. He

sent me the subject-matter of a ballet thought up by Céline. Auric wanted to write the music for it while I was to be responsible for the choreography. Once more I refused, since once more, it was only a question of the *Giselle* aesthetic. For the rest, Céline, whom this project had no doubt pleased, was to conceive, because of my refusal, a bitter hatred against me. Indeed he did not hesitate to intrigue against me and to support those who, with the aid of the Germans, were trying to lure away some of the best artists from the Opera. They did not succeed for I managed to put up an effective resistance to German requisitions at the very moment I had to affront these same Germans in another field.

My plans pointed to a quite other direction. I was then preparing to put on a ballet by a musician who had been killed in the war. It was *Le Jour* by Joubert who had fallen in 1940. I succeeded in getting the authorisation for this and also permission to mention on the playbills 'died for France' after the composer's name. This was a reward from the Germans in whose eyes I had the great merit of putting on *Joan de Zarizza* and assuring its triumph. Jacques Rouché, however, out of prudence, had the words suppressed. The musician's widow——who was later active in the Resistance—never forgave the director of the Opera—such were artistic politics in those days!

7

FACE TO FACE WITH ADOLF HITLER

In that year 1942 I was to undergo my descent into Hades. I
was once more in Germany, a country I had not visited since
1929. Now was the great adventure of my life. But though in
the course of 1942 I was three times in Germany, I will for
the sake of convenience group the three visits together in a
single account. The goings and comings are of less consequence
than what I saw and heard in that country—in the heart of the
great adventure, in the heart of the drama.

One fine day I received, sent on to me by my friends Heim and
Zeitschel, an invitation from Dr Erich von Prittwitz, the general
manager of the Preusissiches Staatstheater, to visit Germany and
to consult with him in Berlin about certain artistic problems.
Having in mind my adventure in 1941, I hesitated a little, but
there could be really no question of refusing or evading the
invitation which had been made in somewhat ceremonious
fashion. I was to be the guest of the Deutsche Akademie. And
to this invitation from *Propagandastaffel* were attached letters
from Baldur von Schirach (the supreme commander of the
Hitlerjugend) whom I had met in Paris, and from Arno Breker.
Furthermore, I must confess that curiosity urged me so strongly
that it was not altogether disagreeable to give way.

On 12th August and for the last performance at the Opera
before the holidays we played *Istar, Les Animaux modèles* and
Le Chevalier et la demoiselle. Then I left Paris in company with
Zeitschel who had offered to go with me to the end of the world
—Berlin, where we arrived on the 15th of the month.

No sooner had I set foot in the great city than my eyes and

mind were assailed by what might be called the living image of militarism. Everyone was in uniform—flags, music, the stamping of boots, the war flags. One huge clockwork was pitilessly grinding down all reality. In that year of apogee of German might I could actually see with my own eyes the 'war machine' in action.

I was put up at the Hôtel Adlon, that great Berlin hostelry, traditionally reserved for diplomatists and distinguished guests. Indeed, in the hotel, except for a few foreigners passing through Berlin, was only a swarm of generals, of high dignitaries of the Party and of very pretty women.

Soon I was discussing the artistic problems which had ostensibly justified my journey. I met the two great general managers on whom depended the Arts of the Third Reich, Tietjan and Prittwitz. They were, moreover, in a state of constant rivalry, for if the former 'belonged' (as was said in the time of the Cardinal's and the King's musketeers) to Goering, the latter 'belonged' to Goebbels. And there was a race between them as to which of them should outdo the other in ostentation and prestige. It was not always easy for a foreigner to find his way about among mysteries full of traps for the unwary. In any case, I was offered the direction of the Dance in Germany and with a large allocation. I asked for time to think things over, actually to find a valid pretext for refusing the offer.

A big luncheon was given in my honour at the Academy. I was glad to discover there an old familiar acquaintance, Karl Epting.

Before we sat down I had had some conversation with a group of prominent German architects. They spoke freely about the orders they had all received from their government to prepare sketches for monuments to the dead of the glorious *Wehrmacht* which were to be set up soon in all the towns of colonised Russia. This reminded me of the scenes at the railway stations. I had seen a convoy of cattle-trucks full of starving, miserable human beings wearing yellow arm-bands. I had walked towards them. Efforts were made to stop me but I pushed through the barrier and got near enough to talk to them. They were Ukrainians being deported to somewhere far from their fields and homes. On their yellow arm-bands was the word *Untermensch*—'Subhumans'. The Germans did not seem to be particularly embarrassed. They spoke to me freely about their plans against the Russians . . . and I said to myself, 'They think I'm French,

they don't know I am a Russian too!' . . . all this besmirched
my heart and mind.

Then followed a lot of long speeches about Art and the future
Europe, about civilisation and culture. I guessed that all these
aged academicians were jittery with joy and greed at the prospect
of the great victory that was almost within their grasp. There
were forty persons present besides the chairman and myself. On
my right had been placed a ravishing young woman who was to
be my hostess during the trip. This Baroness Knorine, a Balt by
origin, and speaking excellent Russian, plied me with fulsome
compliments.

We drank a lot, especially myself—no doubt so as to forget
the slight uneasiness I felt. Little by little my mind became
somewhat fuddled and I was so frightened of saying something
stupid, imprudent and dangerous that I clenched my jaws. Then,
suddenly, I realised there was no way for me to escape making a
speech in reply to the president's words of welcome. I was
filled with anguish when I rose to my feet and began to string
together a lot of hollow and inoffensive remarks while I slipped
like a dancer in between words and pirouetted among insignificant ideas. When I thought I had talked enough, I dug about
for some spectacular sally to end up with . . . then I heard
myself announce in a persuasive voice, 'What has to be done is
to destroy the spirit of Bayreuth!' If I had shaken the pillars of
the Temple the effect could not have been more astounding.
Each one stared at his neighbour with consternation.[1]

I realised what I had done. I had blasphemed the Wagnerian
god of the Third Reich! Luckily my very insult brought me
back to my senses. I started off again to explain that it was the
dusty, old methods of presentation at Bayreuth that must be
reformed and made more lively, more aggressive, more this, that
and the other! I finished up under a thunder of applause from
the relieved audience when I declared in rousing tones that
Wagner was a god equal to Bach and Mozart.

That evening, with several other persons, I was invited by
Baroness Knorine to a party she gave at the Russian cabaret-
restaurant The Bear which I visited again with some emotion
since it was there that I had met the Russian poet Maikowski

[1] I repeated these remarks of mine about Bayreuth to Wieland Wagner
when, at about this time, he came to Paris to be present at a performance
of *Tristan und Isolde*.

who shortly afterwards committed suicide in Russia. The party
was brilliant. Dr Brandt, Hitler's personal physician, was present.
We drank little kegs of vodka. We began to be rather tipsy
and it seemed to me that Baroness Knorine kept on filling my
glass very rapidly and diligently. I still had in my mind the
memory of my blunder at the luncheon and although I was
nearly overcome there still remained within me some shred
of sense . . . 'Don't say anything stupid . . . don't be led into
expressing your real feelings . . .' Later on a few of us moved to
the Baroness's house. When the last guests had gone I remained
alone with her. Her intention now became more and more
obvious.

It was eleven o'clock when I woke up in my room at the Hôtel
Adlon on 16th August. How I had got there I was quite unable
to remember. There floated only in my mind a vague memory
of my outrageous but reassuring declarations and their loving
conclusion.

I was to learn later that Baroness Knorine worked for the State
Intelligence and that she had been placed next to me only in
order to test me. I still dream of the report she was certainly
able to make about my real sentiments as revealed in intoxication and intimacy.

At eleven o'clock someone came knocking on my door. It was
Zeitschel who pitilessly interrupted my musings on my astonishing adventures of the day before. 'Hurry up,' he shouted at me,
'hurry up, you've got to be at the Chancellery in less than an
hour.'

There was no time to be astonished, I had to make haste as
fast as I could. I heard Zeitschel walking about impatiently in
the adjoining room and explaining to me, though I did not understand very well what he was saying, that the Führer had expressed a wish to see me and that Zeitschel was to go with me
on this visit. As soon as I was ready he led me off downstairs.
In front of the hotel was waiting one of Dr Goebbels's cars. It
was a powerful open automobile with two pennons on the wings.
On the one side were displayed the colours and emblems of the
Third Reich—eagle and swastika on a black and white ground.
On the other side a yellow flag with Goebbels's personal badge.
Zeitschel hurried me into the car. He was in a splendid full-
dress uniform (adorned with four SS insignia) which I had never
seen him wear in Paris.

We drove through Berlin. I do not know why but I could not help thinking of a slow procession, a sort of ceremony that had to be performed before arriving at the Holy of Holies.

Finally we got in sight of the massive Reich Chancellery. We drove along the main frontage with a monumental door opened only on very great occasions. Lining the frontage were soldiers with their legs apart and rigid in the German position of standing at ease. They were the guards. We turned left into a narrower street, the Wilhelmstrasse. In this thoroughfare there was, as Zeitschel explained to me, on the right the Propaganda ministry, Goebbels's domain. Facing it and at the side of the huge Chancellery I noticed a small, low house, looking more 'human' though imposing all the same. Opposite us the bronze door of the Chancellery opened. Our car drove into a small courtyard. I got out still accompanied by Zeitschel. Guttural words of command ripped through the air. As we passed two soldiers of the *Leibstandart Adolf Hitler*, in smart black uniforms, came to attention, clicked their heels and presented arms. I just had time to notice that behind us the Michelangeloesque twin bronze doors closed shut. In this courtyard were several gigantic statues by Arno Breker, typifying, it seemed to me, the warrior, the fighter, the man who combats because life is not neutral, the racial type also that must triumph, in a word the human hero whose definite predominance must be assured by Nazi victory. On the far side of the courtyard was a noble flight of steps. This time Hell was upstairs!

A German officer stepped up to us. His name was Bormann (the brother of Martin, the power behind the throne of Hitler and the Reich) and he was one of Hitler's secretaries. He seemed to be no fool and spoke perfect French. Zeitschel told me later that one of this Bormann's daughters was a dancer—under an assumed name—and was a pupil of Tania Gzovsky. He led us to the foot of the steps and after having exchanged a few words with us asked us to go up. He remained below. An orderly officer, Zeitschel and I then began to walk slowly up, step by step. I felt perhaps more moved, more disquieted, than I have ever been in my life. It seemed to me, in fact, that it was not a descent but an ascent into Hades that I was undergoing. I reflected on the history of the last few years. I remembered the day when Gustave Roussy had asked me to save that national heritage the

Opera and its treasures, and had said to me, 'You've got *carte blanche* to do anything you think ought to be done.'

I had not guessed then that this mission would lead me right into the whirlwind of war, would get me condemned to death, taken for a traitor by some of my adopted fellow-countrymen and would lead me on this day into the heart of Europe at war, into the Reich Chancellery, into that utmost cavern where, according to some, was to be found the absolute Good, and according to others the absolute Evil.

We entered an immense gallery, a sort of modern edition of the Galérie des Glaces at Versailles. This corridor had tall, light-curtained windows and was furnished and decorated tastefully in tones of beige. Zeitschel and I walked on. The orderly officer asked us to wait a short time. At its farther end the vast gallery led into a large room. The general effect made by the yellow marble was certainly very imposing and I knew Hitler had been his own architect.

The orderly officer pointed out one of the two doors in the long wall facing the windows. He explained that it gave on to a staircase the Führer had designed specially to link the Chancellery with the little house I had noticed on arriving. This was none other than Hindenburg's former residence where the Führer had chosen to live. It was from that direction he would arrive.

Then the officer opened for us the other of the two doors. It was just before the corner formed by the gallery and the room that led out of it. He said, 'The Council of Ministers Chamber.' I could not resist a temptation to go in. The others followed. A wide, almost square table occupied the centre of the room. Around the table were red-leather armchairs and on it only ink-stands and blotters. I walked round it and read the names in gold letters that marked each place—Goebbels, Goering, Ribbentrop, Speer, etc. Once again I was filled with a holy terror.

Except for this table the only other object in the room was a gigantic globe, more than six feet tall, which on a mobile stand occupied the right-hand corner facing the door by which we had come in. I went up to it and then saw that a great number of small swastikas flags was dotted over it. The state of the world was inscribed there. I began to twist the globe round, not so much to find out more as because of a kind of unconscious revolt that filled me. I aroused a muffled clamour from my companions. 'Stop. Are you crazy? If it is noticed that anyone has touched that . . . !' They both appeared to be terrorised. I withdrew my hand quickly and contented myself with staring at this globe, a strange and beautiful symbol that glowed softly in the indirect lighting falling from ceiling-lamps hidden at the top of the wood panelling and irradiating all this secret and secluded chamber.

I was still dreaming when my companions brought me down to earth.

Suddenly I felt tension around me and I turned. The door that the officer had said gave on to the stairs had opened and there was the Führer in front of me.

My two companions snapped to attention like robots, thrust their arms out and I heard only one *Heil Hitler!* I remained motionless watching the figure I knew so well from having seen it reproduced in the newspapers, but which, all the same, seemed to have come from another planet. He walked up to us. He appeared quite calm. He wore black trousers and a light brown coat on which only the Iron Cross stood out. His hands were behind his back. When he got quite close to us he gave my two companions a casual salute, the sort of salute he used in private—the palm of the hand rather listlessly raised to the level of his eyes, his arm kept bent. Then, while the orderly officer presented me, he gave me a handshake that struck me by its flabbiness. I think I can still feel it today. I bowed and said nothing. When I straightened up his gaze was striking, it was a look—how can I describe it?—both unseeing and piercing. It was a look that held you but at the same time appeared to be directed far beyond you and incapable of adjustment. The eyes were glaucous, of a light, watery green. They reminded me somewhat of those of a Siamese cat, or perhaps still more of what I had always been told were those of Rasputin. Hitler seemed to me as . . . yes, as sorrowful, maybe sorrowful from solitude. Even today if I think about him that is the impression most fixed in my memory—a strange, magic power and the solitude caused by it, a power for good or evil according to circumstances.

Under his black lock his face was pallid and more puffy than I had expected. Only his eyes struck me—and his nose. But if the eyes attracted me, the nose, rather long and pointed, displeased me at once—and violently. It looked to me geo-

metrical, made of some different stuff from the rest of the face
to which it was attached without really belonging to it. I do
not know why it fascinated me. I know it was stupid but I
could not take my eyes off it. Some vision came to me, perhaps
from my childhood . . . a wolf, that was it, a wolf . . . and the
Charlie Chaplin moustache . . . the middling stature. I do not
know how long I thus observed him. My recollection must be
that of a momentary surprise—that lasted however all the time
of the interview. He spoke in a low voice and in German. I
was brought back to earth when the orderly officer began
translating Hitler's remarks. The Führer spoke quietly, calmly,
said how sorry he was not to have met me when he visited the
Paris Opera. He remembered each incident of that morning.
I understood he had been informed of who poor Glouglou was
and had also been told of his unawareness and of his later fears.
Hitler told me he had been amused by Glouglou and added:
'But you yourself were not there although you had been
informed of my visit. Were you also afraid of me?'

He spoke in a familiar, almost paternal, manner, with a
slight smile and in the least official way possible. I had not
time to reply before he went on to tell me how highly he appreciated the work I was doing at the Paris Opera which he considered
was of a nature greatly to aid in furthering Franco-German
understanding.

'I have learned,' he went on, 'of the great success Herbert
von Karajan, Arno Breker and Werner Egk have had in France
. . . the privileges of Art,' he murmured in a musing tone.

The four of us walked through the vast gallery. Exceptionally
for me I was quite silent. In spite of my close attention I did
not even manage to take in everything. Then, abruptly, he
said, 'How greatly I admired your Opera! I am an architect
myself.' Then he pointed out to me some details of the Chancellery building which, as I had been told, he had himself designed.

Then his whole personality seemed to change. He appeared to
be dreaming, as though he were alone, and he said, as if to
himself, 'We will give magnificent festivities here in order to
celebrate the peace. You will help us. You have a feeling for
vast settings. I will entrust the task to you. You will be able to
celebrate the victory in a fitting way . . . peace, victory, the
New Europe, the new era that will be ushered in.'

He was another man. As he spoke of the future, and of his

M.V.—R

vision of victory, of an all-powerful Germany, he stiffened up, his voice became rough and hard, his face assumed a brutal expression, his footsteps beat the floor with an energetic, military rhythm. One personality had given way to another. A brutal vision of things, that demanded and permitted all things, had transformed a mediumistic nature that was more apathetic when in repose. Then he calmed down, put his hand on my right shoulder. I had to restrain myself not to give a start. He looked me in the eyes:

'On 20th August you will come with me to Moscow. That day the city will fall. Stalin has already left his capital. I invite you to witness my triumphant entry into Moscow. You will be my guide.' I looked into his eyes. I wanted to speak but could not. At Hitler's contact, I too had been transformed. I gazed at him and became another man. All I had heard and seen since I had been in Berlin came into my mind and I said to myself: 'No, this man shall not tread the soil of Moscow, of my country. If I am by his side, very well then, I will kill him before he sets foot in Moscow.'

My mind was made up. In the space of a second *I had become an assassin.* Visions of destiny surged in my mind . . . Glinka's 'A Life for the Tsar', Pilsudski's dragoons before Kiev, Yusupov liberating his country from the Spirit of Evil. All my destiny was swaying . . . as though I had always been prepared . . . as though it had at last assumed its real meaning.

Then, abruptly, he snapped:

'You can go to Vriesen, to Breker's . . .'

After that he saluted; energetically this time, but he did not shake my hand . . . he disappeared through the same door by which he had come . . . a vanishing phantom.

He withdrew without saying a word . . . and then, there I was at Zeitschel's side in the sunny streets of Berlin. . . .

8

I AM NOT AN 'ASSASSIN'

The car let me out at the Hôtel Adlon which struck me as though I had left it months and years before. I went into the hall and looked at all the people there as though I had been a blind man who had just recovered his sight.

'Serge! Serge!'

Suddenly I heard someone call my name. I turned round and there was Memina Breker, Arno's wife, who was coming towards me. I was glad to see her again, especially as, to my great astonishment, I had heard nothing from her or her husband since my arrival in Berlin. We sat down. And she spoke to me as though we had parted scarcely two days before. She seemed to be aware of my slightest deeds and acts. She spoke to me of the Chancellery before I had mentioned it at all. She questioned me about my opinion on the architecture of the place, about the impression made on me by those buildings designed for pomp and ostentation. While she chatted away I noticed she did not let drop one word about the Führer who had, after all, been the cause of my visit. I did not say anything about him either.

'Your suit-case is in the car and I have come to take you to Vriesen where Arno is waiting for you.'

Then all at once I remembered Hitler's words, 'You can go to Vriesen, to Breker's', which had struck me as being without rhyme or reason since such a visit had been suggested, but I had soon forgotten what he had said about this, the rest of his remarks had driven this one from my mind. So, then, my stay in Germany had been much more minutely organised than I had suspected.

Memina and I left in a car for Vriesen. It was about 38 miles from Berlin and at Vriesen were the house and the work-shops of Arno Breker, the official sculptor of the regime and a great personage in the Third Reich. We were spinning along a main highway when, at some twenty miles from Berlin, we passed a huge dwelling in an immense park strongly guarded. Memina mentioned that it was Hermann Goering's residence. In three-quarters of an hour we got to Vriesen and drew up before a splendid country house, of classical proportions and in the taste of the finest French 18th century châteaux.

Arno Breker came to meet us. He was simple and friendly in his sculptor's working clothes, and he also greeted me as though he had left me only the day before. I was curious to get a good look at the place. He at once took me off for a stroll around the property. With great unconcern he showed me everything. The house, which had a very 'lived in' look, was, he said, 'a present from the Führer'.

Not far from the house were Breker's own studios and farther away, about a thousand yards or so off, were other work-shops that it would not be unfair to call 'the Breker factory'. For it was indeed in this real State 'factory' that the models Arno created were reproduced on a gigantic scale so as to be ready to adorn the palaces and official emplacements of the Third Reich. He himself conceived 'monumentally' but then his creations passed into the 'factory', where they were enlarged so as to give the public an image of the National-Socialist Man on a heroic and gigantic scale. There was a station just completed which was the terminus of the private branch-line serving this artistic factory. Arno Breker noticed my astonishment at the noble splendour of his dwelling. As he was explaining to me how his studios worked, he added, in a lower voice as he bent over towards me: 'This is the ransom. They've stolen the soul of my works from me...' and that was the only remark about himself that I was to hear him mention during those years.

The work-shops over which he ruled as an absolute monarch were an asylum for Frenchmen, many of whom, as I have said, had not the slightest notion about sculpture, but who had been welcomed at the time of the 'relief' and the S.T.C.

Among themselves this favoured spot, almost at the gates of Berlin, was known as the 'Little Switzerland' and there I met, on this visit, war-prisoners transformed into workmen without

their knowing the first thing about any of the techniques
employed. Arno Breker arranged for me to contact these people
who, since I had come from Paris, welcomed me most warmly.
I could have thought I had suddenly become the good God's messenger to suffering souls in Purgatory. Officers who were excused
from work but who were the guests of the master of the house
gathered around me and were only too happy to see an envoy
from another world. They said they knew all about what the
marshal was doing, how he was protecting France and how
much they were in his thoughts. They asked for my autograph
and so as to make the souvenir more expensive—or just because
they had no other paper—they made me sign on the special
notes that served as money among the prisoners. I remained
talking to them for a long time and since I had told them
about my meetings with the Chief of State, some of them said as
I was going away, 'Tell the marshal that we are confident,
thank him on our behalf!'

I was very moved to find in this way France so near to
Berlin, at the other end of the continent. I felt I must say to
them, when I took leave, 'Have confidence, courage!'

A number of Arno's relations from the north of the Ruhr
had taken refuge with him. They did not say much but it was
easy to guess that life had become intolerable under the Allied
bombardments which had by now started up. And I began to
realise just what this meant. Despite what Goering, the grand
master of the *Luftwaffe*, had promised, the air-space of the Third
Reich was not inviolable. The first of the Allied planes had
already pierced it to drop their bombs. And this was only a
beginning. A warning whose gravity was clear to me when I
thought of it. And in this connection I may mention that I
witnessed, as it were beyond the war, the first bombardment
of Berlin. We had gone out to look on and I must admit that
the spectacle was one of tragic beauty. In the black night we
could see the projectors, the outlines of the planes, the light
clouds from the German *flak* fire, we could hear the crashing of
the first bombs. It was a ballet of light and death against the
background of the night's dark screen. We were all out of doors
gazing silently at the spectacle.

In those days when I was no doubt the only one of our small
circle to realise the gravity, the tragic gravity, of what was
happening. Arno Breker did my bust. While I posed I had plenty

of time to reflect. He kept on saying to me all the time, 'Serge, why are you so melancholy?' Then when I had finished sitting to him, I met all sorts of important persons in the Reich who had come to greet the great artist.

One day it was the great chief of the Reich armaments and industrial production, Speer, who had taken Todt's place. He had just come back from a tour of inspection at Kiev and in all the region of the Dnieper's loops. I was keen to question him. I was filled with emotion at the thought of meeting someone— even if he was a German—who had just seen my city much in my thoughts in those days. The minister willingly spoke about his trip. He was proud to have so quickly repaired the Dnieprostroi barrage and all the industrial and power installations of an area which had evidently been hard hit by the fighting. He was full of enthusiasm and kept repeating cheerfully, 'Victory is in our hands.' I thought once more of my visit to the Führer and said to myself, 'The 20th August is near, within my reach also.' A secret fixation had formed within me. How could I get hold of a gun? And I looked at my hands that seemed unfamiliar, and repeated to myself, 'I am an assassin.' And to achieve my aim, I must smile, seem happy and fool people. And I asked myself, 'Why me, why should this task fall to me?' Such greatness was not what I desired. My decision was however irrevocable. I then thought of asking Speer to search out my father and have him brought to me, if he were still alive. Speer promised.

In the evening of the 18th August I was again in Berlin. With much fear and trembling I prepared myself for the 'event'. Then it was that a great rumour spread abroad and I guessed that something quite extraordinary was about to happen. I ran off to Zeitschel. He said a special communiqué had just arrived from the Führer's G.H.Q. All radiophonic communications had been cut to allow of the communiqué being read. It was a song of triumph. The swastika flag was flying on the summit of the Caucasus. The Germans were in sight of Baku— the heart of the Russian oil production—the fall of Baku and that of Moscow would seal the definite victory. Baku was within range of the *Wehrmacht*'s guns.

Zeitschel, perhaps to make me share his joy or maybe to convince me, if there were any need, of German might, led me to a place that was supposed to be reserved for the military. There, on a wall, projected directly by a system of 'belino'—a sort of forerunner of television—he explained, hung a huge map kept up to date according to the communiqués and showing the German flags advancing little by little over the territory of Russia. At the announcement of the new thrust forwards enthusiasm knew no bounds. And I, the only civilian among all the soldiers, witnessed an extraordinary scene. There were no more ranks, no more precedence, it was an orgy of joy. French champagne flowed like water. Three times in three centuries my country, Russia, had been in danger of death—from Charles XII, then from Napoleon and now from Hitler.

The dawn of the 19th August had hardly broken on this day of enthusiasm which had not left me a moment of sleep. I was nervously awaiting my departure for Moscow. Then a great hullabaloo again shook the hotel. In this world of high personalities of the regime and of officers and officials in touch with them, every event found a resounding echo. This time once again I suspected at once some quite exceptional upset. Something in the nature of the rumour that filled the hotel warned me of this. I rushed down. My nerves were on edge through waiting.

The first scraps of information I got left me sceptical. Then they were confirmed. An Allied landing had taken place on the French coasts! So the other end of Europe was on fire. Then further news arrived. The Führer had given orders to hold up the attack on Moscow and to keep troops ready to be switched over westwards. I would not go to Moscow and the city would not fall by 20th August. Everything had to be reconsidered, anything again became possible, nothing was irreparable.

I fell asleep feeling that, in spite of everything, I had done my duty.

It was becoming broad daylight when I awoke. The first thing I remembered, strangely enough, was that it was the anniversary of Diaghilev's death. Gradually reality formed itself again around me. This was a day certainly decisive for me. And what was the night's news for Europe? The Allies—Canadian commandos—had indeed attempted a landing near Dieppe. They had been repulsed. It was admittedly only a raid, a probing of the German defences, but a probing which all the same suggested other attempts would be made. Henceforth a permanent menace hung over western Europe. The German troops could not any more engage themselves thoroughly on any one

front. Fate hovered in the balance. After this slight but sympto-
matic military action and after the death of some hundreds
of Canadians Hitler began to lose the war.

During the days which followed there was intense political
activity. On the morrow of the Dieppe operation, German
propaganda had defined its position with regard to France.
Since the local population had remained calm and had taken
no part in the few engagements which had occurred to throw
back the Canadians towards the sea, the *Wehrmacht* High Command decided to proclaim that the population had been most
loyal to the German troops which were defending Europe.
The French inhabitants were thus showered with loudly
proclaimed compliments.

This was the official attitude. But secretly there were being
prepared quite different measures induced by the anxiety felt
at the prospect of further attempts at landing. Thus I heard that
a decree of the Führer was ready to be issued. All private
wireless sets were to be requisitioned in France. As soon as I
learned of this I hurried off to Zeitschel and pointed out to
him how dreadfully maladroit such a measure would be. What
greater proof of weakness could be given, at the very time when
so many compliments were being addressed to the population!
The decree was never published.

Before I had left Paris, Otto Abetz, as I have mentioned,
confided in me how anxious he was. I learned in Berlin that
von Papen, back from his post as ambassador at Ankara, was
about to be nominated to Paris, in place of Otto Abetz. Papen
was indeed to have been, rather than an ambassador, a kind of
Gauleiter for France. He was to have full powers for taking
any measures to maintain order in the case of further attempts
at landings. Berlin desired that a strong, tough man should
succeed Otto Abetz who was accused of weakness and of being
too lenient with the French. Papen would have been the tough
man—but he forgot that and denied it at the Nuremberg
trials.

But Papen lost out. Abetz came back to Paris.

I also frequented Russian circles. Some of my compatriots
were then trying to imagine what the future of their country
would be after the war and they were sincerely persuaded it

was their patriotic duty to believe in a German victory, which, in fact, at that time looked probable. General Krasnov was the leading figure among those who thought thus. I was present at an evening meeting of these people. A Russian emperor was proclaimed, one who after the end of the war was to occupy the throne of Peter the Great. The candidate was a certain Prince Bagration, the descendant of a Georgian royal house and whose sister had made a second marriage with the Grand-Duke Vladimir. In this way it was sought to establish a continuity with the ancient dynasty of the Romanovs. The Russians present at this meeting called Bagration 'Your Majesty' and attempted a farcical revival of the former Court etiquette. I was not much impressed by these efforts made to revive a dead past. I must admit indeed that I was very sceptical, for in my heart of hearts I did not think that the future was likely to be influenced by the dreams of a few men isolated amid the turmoil of a terrible war. General Krasnov protested energetically because Hitler refused to use Vlassov's troops against the Communists and they were employed only in the auxiliary services.

At the request of Dr Goebbels I had to witness a showing in the Propaganda ministry of a film I had made shortly before in Paris. In this I traced the history of the Dance and the Ballet from their origins to the present day. It was called *Symphonie en blanc*. It had been ordered and financed by Jaques Thibaut and had just been shot by Ardoin and Chanasse in the Pathé studios at Paris.

The film was a great success. Goebbels made no secret about his enthusiasm and, on the spot, gave me permission to show the film in France where there was a German censorship, but he by-passed it. I learned afterwards that, although he did not ask my consent as the author, he ordered dozens of copies to be made and shown in schools throughout the Reich. But, anyway, his was a decision which was to establish the great influence of French ballet on the Dance in Germany.

This time the Minister of Propaganda spoke to me in French, slowly and a little jerkily, but correctly enough. He said:

'I am in agreement with *Reichsmarschall* Goering that after the war you should become director of the Dance.'

I should explain that Goebbels had under his control the Kroll Oper at Charlottenburg while Goering was responsible for the Deutsche Oper, Unter den Linden. After the end of the conflict the two *corps de ballet* were to be known as the 'New Europe Ballets' and to be placed under a single director.

Then, abruptly, he asked me what my immediate plans were. I replied I was getting ready to leave for Venice. 'I'll meet you in Salzburg,' he said, and then without waiting to see how I took this remark, he bid me goodbye.

But before leaving Berlin, I went back to Vriesen where Breker finished off my bust. Dino Alfieri, the Italian ambassador at Berlin, and Della Porta, his first secretary, gave me the necessary visas so that I could visit Italy before returning to France. A German came with me. He was to keep an eye on me and also to act as a guide. As a matter of fact he was quite useful since he dealt with all the day to day difficulties incidental to travel in those times.

What had struck me in Berlin was a military, mechanised aspect of war while at Salzburg it was a pathetic and painful appearance, that of the day after the battle. The visage of a sick Reich. The town was one huge military hospital. The whole population hobbled on crutches.

Baldur von Schirach had organised a reception at the Town Hall, where he received the guests. I had some conversation with him and with Goebbels at the supper that was provided. Goebbels began almost at once making ill-natured remarks about France and pointed allusions to the cowardice of those people who were not taking the side of the New Europe in the conflict that threatened it and where others were shedding their blood in torrents. Baldur von Schirach changed the conversation by congratulating me on the work I was doing at the Paris Opera. He wanted to organise for the following year, at the same date, a magnificent festival at the Berlin Opera to mark the tenth anniversary of the formation of the *Hitlerjugend*. He suggested that I should take part with the Opera *corps de ballet*. As I saw in this proposal only the opportunity for a large-scale artistic achievement, and as, moreover, I found no reasons for objecting to it, at least there and then, I went on to talk about the spectacle that might be arranged to the glory of European youth, youth linked with beauty. I waxed quite enthusiastic and addressed myself to Goebbels. I mentioned that for such a performance I would need all my dancers and then reminded him of a promise he had given me in Paris some time before, that he would liberate two of the Paris Opera dancers, Legrand and

Romand, who had been held prisoner in Germany for the last two years. At these words he burst out into a fit of anger. I tried to remind him that it was a matter of a definite promise made a considerable time before. But he was no longer listening. He was back on his old subject—the cowardice of those who were not fighting. Those dancers were where they were because they had not fought honourably. They were better off where they were than the Germans soldiers on the eastern front who did not ask to come to Paris or Berlin but were satisfied with defending those towns. 'Our people can die, but yours want to dance!'

My impression was that he was raging like a wounded beast. Had he been victorious he would not have adopted such a tone in which bitterness was plain enough. It was clear to me that he, at the very summit of the Nazi hierarchy, was beginning to feel anxiety and anguish.

The next day at six o'clock in the afternoon there was given for wounded officers a performance of the *Magic Flute* at the Festival Palace. As we went on foot to the building we passed a great number of these wounded who were either making their own way or were being driven to the show. I felt very ill at ease. All these maimed men, who were going to watch a festival, stabbed me to the heart, especially as I caught some of their looks. These crippled officers stared fixedly at Goebbels. I read in their eyes aloofness, often hostility, sometimes real hatred. I do not want to generalise, but I myself could not help hearing, 'He is always talking to us about heroism being necessary for the survival of a nation. But he is crippled because of an accident whereas it is fighting that has made us what we are. He has nothing to tell us whereas we would have a lot to explain to him, to tell him about "things he knows nothing of".' These expressions of hatred I found very hard to support. I was next to Goebbels. A few days before I had taken the decision I have spoken about. Fate alone had held my hand. And today I, who had been lured here only by the desire to help my adoptive country, felt myself to be, quite unjustly, the object of a hatred which concerned me not at all . . . 'Get away! Get away!' that was the idea that racked me. I felt a little reassured when, on arriving at the Festival Palace, I met the celebrated conductor Ernest Ansermet with his new wife. He was conducting some of the season's concerts at the Mozarteum. So he, although a Swiss, was also there. So I was not the only one. This thought comforted me.

I stayed in the same hotel as Dr Goebbels. That evening, while I was dining with him and members of his staff, the sirens went off. After a moment of amazement, the minister started up like a madman, almost pulled the cloth off the table in his blind haste and, crazy with panic, his face drawn and haggard, he dashed down to the cellars like a wounded rat. For some moments we sat there, in silence, stupefied. Then these Germans and I came to a tacit agreement. We would not go down into the shelters. We would remain where we were, since we experienced, maybe, some aesthetic pleasure in finishing our supper with death as a possible companion. We talked about quite other things than the war while in the far-off distance we could make out the sound of bombs. We learned later that Munich, in its turn, had had that evening its first serious bombardment.

An hour and a half later Goebbels reappeared. He was pale as death, white as a corpse. Conversation did not get going again. He quickly bade us good night. As he was leaving he said to me, 'I'll take you tomorrow in my plane to Venice' . . . I thanked him but asked to be excused as I did not much like flying and would rather take the train.

As I was going to stop in Vienna, one thought filled my mind. I do not know whether it was due to the nearness of the great Russian plains, but in any case the desire to save my father from the dangers that threatened became very strong. I foresaw, confusedly, that the world was moving towards afflictions still more tragic than those it had hitherto known. It seemed to me that near me my father would be in greater security . . . and since the opportunity presented itself, I remembered that the minister Speer had told me that he was returning to the Dnieper loop region, that is to say Kiev and its neighbourhood. Through my guide-guardian-secretary I planned to send Speer a letter for my father. My guide agreed to accept it and I gave him a long missive. I knew well enough the German authorities would read it and that if I wanted it to have the least chance of reaching its destination I must be very careful. So I declared my 'European' sentiments most heartily and asked my father to come and join me in Paris. The letter went off. But I heard nothing more and thought it had gone astray until one day I did get news. The letter had arrived all right; it had gone from my

'secretary' to Speer's staff and from them to Kiev right to my
father. But he replied he was too old to leave his native land
and the grave of his wife, my mother. He sent me his blessing.

This answer left me in a state of mind that was both deferential and dreamy. I understood more clearly the way people's
opinions were moving in Russia.

I crossed over into Italy and experienced, when I got to
Venice, the same emotions as always. The city was lovely in
the sweetness of a summer's end. But Goebbels was already
there—I met him at the Lido. With him were Conte Volpi,
Toscanini's daughter and a crowd of Italian aristocrats. I
also found José Maria Sert and Frau von Stohrer, the wife of the
German ambassador at Madrid. Sert felt himself obliged to
take me on one side and whisper in my ear, 'Serge, promise you
never saw me here.' . . . I could hardly refuse to do him that
good turn.

At a party given by the Contessa Castelbarco, one of Toscanini's daughters, at the Lido, I met once more all my old friends
—the Morosinis, the Vendramins, the Viscontis, the Robilants,
the Brandolinis, and, of course, the Volpis. But how well
guarded Goebbels's cabin was! It was from this same cabin
that, after the war, I saw Winston Churchill bathing for the
last time. He was with Lady 'Clemmie'. I saw him also at
Torcello—a legendary figure with cigar and parasol at his easel.

In the Piazza San Marco I heard Goebbels speak before the
large crowd that had gathered but did not applaud though the
whirring of the microphone did give an imitation of enthusiastic
clamour. Farther off, in the port, were the outlines of the laid-up
liners. Along the horizon they were like empty tombs awaiting
their fate.

I went to Diaghilev's grave there to commune with myself and
to meditate.

Then I set off for Paris. I had in my pocket all the necessary
papers. They were quite in order and had been got for me by
Dino Alfieri and my Italian friends. However, at the frontier
occurred an incredible drama. Not only was I prevented from
crossing the border but I was arrested and sent to San Remo
prison. And there, as though to end on a Stendhalian note a
succession of days passed between festivities and hell, I was
put on a diet of bread and water. I could make out beyond the
bars of my cage a patch of blue sky and the throbbing, frothing

sea. I did not know what to think, so just resigned myself to fate. However, in two days' time I was released with the excuses of a very embarrassed young prefect. I was free, he said, but I had not yet permission to cross the frontier. I then began to lose my head. I telegraphed to Berlin, to Rome, to friends in Paris. No answer. Even my friend Grabowski, whom I had known well when he was on Abetz's staff in the German embassy and who was now consul at San Remo, admitted he could do nothing for me. At last, one morning when an isolation for reasons of sickness, a sort of quarantine, threatened Grabowski's house I managed to escape and got the authorisation to enter France that I had so much desired.

To this day I have never been able to find out the reasons for this fantastic episode. Was it just administrative muddle within the formidable machine of Europe at war? But I rather believe that it was a secret revenge taken by Ciano who remembered my remarks made to him in 1939. Proof of an odd self-conceit— and very Stendhalian at that—surviving in the midst of such dramatic events!

Hardly had I got to Lyons than I met Dumoulin de la Bar- thète who was waiting for me. He accompanied me to Moulins on the demarcation line between the two zones. I told him about my journey but gathered he was already fully informed about my adventure in Italy. I had once more the strange impression I had so often felt that everything was tabbed and known by a few people amid an apocalyptic chaos.

9

LOVE STRONGER THAN DEATH

The year 1943 was the turning-point of fate. During the last days of the dying year, the myth of German invincibility had faded, and other myths too. The difference of position as between Vichy and Paris was now only ideological. Under the blows of Zhukov's counter-attacks the *Wehrmacht* had lost all hope of capturing Moscow. The battle for Stalingrad had ended in disaster for the Germans.

The great retreat began. By about the middle of the year we could see Allied victory begin to dawn on the horizon. The gigantic battles in July, the vigorous thrusts made by the re-suscitated Russian Army at Kursk, Orel and Kharkov, sounded the first peals of the German Army's death-knell. Soon the Allies landed in Italy. 'It's only the third front, the second will come later,' announced Churchill. From now onwards the Germans would be everywhere fighting on the defensive. Once more the eastern front was on the Dnieper, my river. There was soon to be struggle on the *Ostwall*, the 'Eastern Wall' as the Germans called their defence line. Kiev, my town, was again under fire.

It was during this month of March that I met 'Sonia'.

At a gala film showing in the place Clichy I had noticed a young and very beautiful woman who had several times tried to get near me and be introduced. I had at once spotted her game and for some reason I could not define, it made me suspicious. I was determined to adhere to the rule I had adopted—remain alone with the minimum of personal contacts. It was this condition of work and freedom that kept me from many worries and much loss of time. More than ever I felt I must stick to my rules and that this person had quite other aims. For this reason also I enquired from friends present (who were in close touch with the organisers of the evening) who this very striking young woman was. I heard she was not very well known but that she was called 'Sonia' Olpinska and that just for something to do she was playing a small part in a film being shot with Madeleine Sologne in the leading role.

I saw her again at the Opera. Each time I appeared there she was in the front row. Then she tried to get into my dressing-room. Her presence became part of my daily life. I knew I should find her always in the same place. She would be alone and pay close attention to the performance. She was like a milestone of destiny. She was running after me. That was certain. And I was giving her the slip, fleeing from her, but it was as in those dreams where the pursued is little by little paralysed and the pursuer gains on him inexorably. My intuition told me that I should undoubtedly fall, and soon, but she left me in ignorance as to whether she was engaged in a chase after love or after death. From that time I would see no one, so my door stayed shut even for my dear friend Florence Gould who could only get to see me with great difficulty.

As soon as the footlights were extinguished and the stage-hands had taken possession of the stage so as to remove the scenery after a performance at the Opera, I would dance for them, despite my extreme exhaustion—for it often happened that I danced in three ballets during one evening. Then it was that in joy and exaltation I would give the best of myself. I was freed from all constraint and of all responsibilities towards this public. Then it was that I reached the peak of my technical and physical possibilities. Their approval, their applause, touched my heart, for I knew that I was dancing before the most merciless of critics.

A month went by in this way. Then one day I was in my room at the Hôtel de Castille. I had the flu. I was in bed thinking of nothing, letting my mind just wander. Suddenly the telephone rang. The man at the reception desk told me that Boulos wanted to see me.

'Ask him to come up.'

A few minutes later, a floor-waiter opened the door—and in walked 'Sonia'.

I must say she was very beautiful, very intelligent and charming. You could try to avoid her but once you had met her . . . I got to know her sumptuous apartment in the avenue Malakoff just opposite the Palais Rose where the governor of Paris, General von Stülpnagel, lived. And I must admit that in her house I spent some very delightful moments. a little removed from real life, when she did not know what to invent next so as to make time pass in the most enjoyable manner possible.

One fine day 'Sonia' disappeared. A short time before she had said she must go away but she did not mention where or why. Then she was not there any more. I waited and sometimes said to myself I would never see her again—but without quite believing it.

A month later she rang me up and asked me to call at her apartment. I rushed off. I was filled with a sense of foreboding. She seemed another woman, completely upset. I pretended not to notice anything, but hardly had I said a few words than she burst out sobbing. She told me everything including the reason for her absence. She had come back from Berlin where she had been to report on her activities for the Gestapo. She worked for the highest rank of the organisation—that of the Chancellery. And on this visit she had learned definitely that orders had been given to 'suppress Lifar' whose name figured on the black list of the Berlin Gestapo files. She added that she had been caught in her own snare. She cried, 'Serge, I love you, escape while there is yet time, flee! . . .'

I was torn between blank astonishment and a feeling that my intuition had been justified. I mastered my emotion so as to get her to tell me why I had become a suspected person. I thought attack was the best form of defence. She must surely know, at the level where she worked, the names of the Gestapo informers. I overcame, therefore, my repugnance, pretended to be affectionate and asked for further details.

Then it was I learned that, on the pretext of cultural exchanges and humanitarian sentiments, one of my own acquaintances was taking part in a very big affair of selling arms to the Germans . . . and it was he who had denounced me to the Gestapo. I was the 'collaborator' sold out to the Gestapo in the Chancellery of the Reich at Berlin—and I was learning all this from the mouth of one of their principal agents!

However, as it was, 'Sonia', who had wanted to destroy me,

saved me. Thanks to her I was able to take the necessary measures. At once I tipped off 'Mademoiselle Françoise', that faceless and soulless goddess who dominated my destiny during those years. Just a call in the night to some secret power which protected me from afar. It was just at this time also that Gustave Roussy was arrested by the Germans. It was at this period again that, by a strange chance, I met in the corridors of the Métro my comrade Bourischkine who, as I knew full well, belonged to the American secret service. Each of us, as though sensing a common danger threatening us, was silent. Only our eyes were eloquent. After the war I met him again. By then he was a real hero and martyr, three times parachuted into France, arrested, tortured and condemned to death. But he had always managed to escape.

By this time I was no longer seeing either Heim or Zeitschel in Paris. I had lost contact with them. Were they still watching me from afar? But their places—as far as I was concerned—were taken by Herren Wenger and Schumann who belonged to the Gestapo organisation on the Quai d'Orsay. At this time they were all-powerful. I also had recourse to my friend Korvé, a kind-hearted man and a great scrounger. He was, during all this period, a real Providence for his Russian fellow-countrymen whom he never failed to aid and to protect. Korvé had great influence on Wenger whom he often met at the lavish parties put on by a business man in his house with a dance studio.

This individual owned what in those times was known as a purchasing business with two branches. Such organisations bought in the occupied countries (and ostensibly for civilian needs) goods destined for the Germans. In this way huge fortunes were amassed by the operators. With the complicity of Korvé and the secret help of Wenger, this Monsieur, a Lithuanian by origin, piled up treasures only a tiny part of which he expended on his parties which, however, were sumptuous enough. Such proceedings constituted one of the strangest and most immoral features of the war years.

As I felt myself in rather a strong position owing to common interests gained during the festivities, in August I asked for a visa to go to Germany, so that I could, following Otto Abetz's advice, accept an invitation sent to me by Arno Breker. I would moreover, have been able to exonerate myself better in that country. However, I was refused a visa. Himmler's office had

turned down my request despite support from both Abetz
and Breker. I realised that the situation was even more serious
than I had thought.

But I did not for long have to puzzle my head as to what to do.
Abetz sent for me to the embassy. I rushed off. Abetz did not
give me time to regain my breath.

'Lifar, what on earth have you been doing?'

His terror-struck appearance would have, at any other time,
made me smile. But this was not a time for smiling. He went on:

'They are coming from Germany to judge your case . . .
Himmler's people . . . right here . . . but I can do nothing for
you . . . my department is kept completely out of it . . . even
if it itself is not already suspect . . . and this court of inquiry
delivers a judgment without appeal. What *have* you done, Lifar?'

I did not know what to reply. I had realised the gravity of the
situation and reserved my explanations for Wenger. He listened
to what I had to say and when I had finished just stated:
'Lifar, don't worry, we won't let you down. You'll be all right,'
and although I knew well enough the hazards of those troubled
times, I was nonetheless a little reassured.

The hearing took place at the embassy in the presence of
Heinrich Himmler, though I was not there.[1]

That evening I learned that the Berlin authorities had referred the matter to those in Paris and that a 'verdict' had been
pronounced which freed me from all suspicion. The Paris
Gestapo had saved me from that of Berlin.

I will speak in its right place of the tragic close to Gustave
Roussy's career. The fate of my 'Sonia' was hardly less tragic. I
found out that she was actually a Frenchwoman, had been the
mistress of a Polish officer in the Resistance. He had been shot
by the Germans for whom she had agreed to work in order to
save her own life. After the Liberation she committed suicide
in Morocco. The only act of love and life that maybe she had
ever accomplished in her existence was for me. She saved my
life and I can never forget that. The false Swiss passport she
gave me to help me to escape, if need be, is there to remind
me of what she did.

[1] Himmler was to spend the evening of the next day at the *Lido* where
my friend Skibine, the father of the dancer I had taken to Australia with
me and the Basil ballets, was the choreographic director. At the Liberation
the son, in American uniform, came to give evidence in favour of his father.

After the Liberation—and now I am anticipating a little—
when I had been treated as a criminal, I was one day summoned
to the rue des Saussaies where I had, in the past, met the French
and then the Germans who had spoken harshly to me. Now I
found the French much more pleasant. I could not think why
I was there, when, to my astonishment, a certain Captain
Delettrez congratulated me. My name had just been discovered
on the black list of the Berlin Gestapo. Suddenly my past—
disguised as though to be recognised by me alone and winking
—seemed to come back and make me a sign. The officer, in a
deferential manner, asked, 'And what did you do to merit
that, monsieur?' . . . 'Well, I just danced,' I replied.

Life became more and more harsh. The Obligatory Labour
Service was extended. Each day tragedy entered more and more
into our lives. Even the Opera troupe was threatened with
requisition for the benefit of the German troops. I did my best
to protect my dancers. Thus it was that I saved Serge Peretti,
Jean Babilée and many others. One only was lost—or rather,
lost himself. Gustin wanted to leave and I could not hold him
back. He was to die at Buchenwald. Efimoff, the leading dancer
(*premier danseur*) at the Opera and who had appeared with me at
Vichy, made some violently anti-German remarks . . . 'Boches
bitched . . . Russian win . . .' to someone he did not know but
had met in a bar. This individual egged on Efimoff by saying
that he himself . . . then sharply flipped up the lapel of his coat . . .
Polizei . . . follow me. Luckily before he was hauled off to the office
of Knochen and Oberg, Efimoff managed to inform me and
I pleaded for him with Wenger.[1] Efimoff was liberated after a
month's detention in the Cherche-Midi prison and after having
been condemned to death by a court-martial. I took him on
again at the Opera. He was a simple modest man and, after the
war, never received any official mark of gratitude.

Social problems sometimes made one forget political anxieties
—and then led back to them again. Thus at the time we were
dancing *Joan de Zarizza*, the social climate was tense. The stage-
hands had presented a list of grievances and thought the administration lagged in considering their problems. The men got

[1] I have never been able to understand up to now why Oberg and Knochen
were so readily released.

tired of waiting and so as to force a decision, they struck for half-an-hour while the orchestra played soft music.[1] The Germans imagined it was a political strike, got furious and talked of nothing less than of shutting the Opera and deporting all the staff together with the recalcitrant stage-hands. I had to rush off to the Germans and explain that it was all a terrible misunderstanding, that it would be most tactless to make claims against the French authorities on an evening when the performance was devoted to the work of a German author. I stressed that a tragic situation might develop. The Germans understood. But in their eyes it was too late. They would not back down for fear of being fooled. I had once more to intervene in very high quarters to get the truth about the matter accepted and all plans for repression called off. I took all the blame on myself and said the trouble was due to a technical mistake I had made. I had saved all the stage-hands and I owed this to Wenger.

At this time also I would receive little model coffins accompanied by a variety of threats—but this was a custom that season. One evening on the stage when I had unexpectedly changed my variations in this same ballet, a block of cast iron, serving as a counter-weight for the scenery, dropped down from the flies right on to the spot where I should have been. The audience stood up. They also had understood. I went on dancing. Lysette Darsonval, my partner, although alarmed at having also risked her life, accompanied me heroically. Outside the stage-entrance there was a crowd of ordinary folk. They were shouting they wanted to cheer me. I slipped out through a side door.

It was in this sort of atmosphere that I created *Suite en blanc*. On account of this ballet—the most sincere of all my works—I was, moreover, attacked in *Aujourdhui* by that eminent musician Louis Beydts.

The year 1943 was also for me a turning-point. For us Russian emigrants the war had all at once assumed a new face—was entirely changed. I have spoken about the hopes, and indeed the enthusiasm, excited among the Russian refugees by the entry of German troops into the Soviet Union. Now colours had changed sides as I saw in the case of the Georgians in Paris. The White

[1] It was what is called a *grève à l'italienne*—'a strike in the Italian mode'.

Georgians henceforth formed a solid block with the Germans' Georgian prisoners whatever might be their origin—and what I say about the Georgians held good for all the Russians though I was able to observe the Georgians closer at hand, since during this year I began to work on the longest ballet of all my career— *Chota Roustavelli*, based on 11th century Georgian folklore. For this work I had as collaborators Arthur Honegger, Tcherepnine, Goncharova and Djordana. The ballet was subventioned by Beridzé, an extremely wealthy Georgian business man. In this way I was able to get together a second company, on the fringe, so to speak, of the Paris Opera which carried on with its usual work. It was a troupe of young people into which I had introduced Georgian folklore elements. If this was to the advantage of art it was also to that of the struggle, for very quickly this company became the spiritual and physical kernel of the Georgian resistance to the campaign of propaganda carried on by Vlassof, the ally of the Germans. In my working studio, 36 rue de Ponthieu, I lodged, I hid, I supported a number of compatriots in difficulties. Little by little my 'mission' had changed. I had been doing all I could to protect the French artistic inheritance and I was to go on doing this, but henceforth I was supported by another 'family' that understood my sentiments and which, I hoped, would defend me with greater steadfastness and courage.

It was through this group that I discovered Antonio—this was the only name I knew him by—'the man with the red hand'— on whose head the Germans had put a price of a million marks. He was a Spaniard from the International Brigades. He had joined up with this group that was dominated by the personality of Gegetchkory, the former Georgian ambassador at Paris. The ideologist of the group was a certain Gégélia, known as 'Gustave' in the Resistance. He had already been a delegate of Stalin's in pre-war France.

I managed to get some arms for them. I possessed a 'permission to carry arms'—in blank. That is to say I had a permission, in those days a very rare thing, since I had to go home late at night and had received many threats, but the permission did not carry any mention of the number of the weapons. So, for a year, I literally pillaged the cloakrooms where the officers and gentlemen left their belongings while they were making merry at Maxim's, Schéhérazade, Monseigneur, Novy, the Café de Paris,

Dominique and other places. While the fun was at its height, I would filch a weapon and carry it away with me—covered as I was by my permit—and thus built up my friends' arsenal. But all that had to stop when in March 1944 during a reception at the German embassy Rouché said in my presence and in front of Abetz and Knochen, 'Oh, don't be fooled, Lifar is a very smart fellow, he is armed in ordinary life.' This was said in a tone of playful humour but what did it mean? I was caught, so I risked everything and with a swagger whipped out my gun which I presented before Abetz who smiled in a rather constrained way, he was as much embarrassed at the possible effects on his party as for anything else. After all, a weapon in war-time . . . but I had noted Knochen's baleful eye that nothing escaped. As soon as I could I made off, rushed home and typed on to my permit the number of my latest gun. I was in order now, but I had to tell my friends Antonio, Skobline and Gégélia that my carrying fire-arms was henceforth 'off'. I had not remembered that a few days before I had forgotten my briefcase in Rouché's office. He had handed it back to me with an expression in which fright and deference were mingled. No doubt he had been looking inside and had at the embassy party made that indirect allusion, that bloomer, as a sort of joke. At the Liberation I had to save Rouché from my Russo-Georgian group who wanted to execute him for having denounced a patriot to the enemy.

Number 100 rue Réaumur (today the offices of *France-Soir* and some other newspapers of the same group) was then the headquarters of the former chief of the Deuxième Bureau of Wrangel's army. He had gone over to the Germans and directed one of their secret services beamed on Russia. He had at his disposal very powerful receiving sets which intercepted all the code messages emitted by Stalin's general staff directed to the generals in command of the different sectors of the Russian front. In the rue Réaumur the information was regrouped and attempts were made to decode and complete it. One day I was summoned to these offices where I had to listen to a proposal to give me a visa and a mission. Under cover of my artistic activities I was to go to Spain and then to London where I was to get into touch with some Englishmen in connection with attempted negotiations for a separate peace between the Anglo-

Saxon allies and the Germans against Russia. Was this already a beginning of plans made to follow on after the attempt on Hitler's life that was being prepared? I never knew. In any case my decision was soon taken. I would do anything to sabotage this double treason against my country.

I left for Spain where I had not been since the early days of the war when Nazi Germany was young and brilliant and victorious, and when I had returned to France amid catastrophe and to witness the distracted flight of French armies and populations. This time everything was very different in Spain, 'the nest of spies'. I had met in the train Colonel Pascot, then High Commissioner for Youth and Sports and successor of Borotra. Some way after Bordeaux our train had blown up and I had to get to Hendaye by makeshift means. At Madrid I met Piétri the French ambassador and again saw my friend Franco Lecchio, the Italian ambassador. The latter informed me that he had taken sides against Mussolini who had just been arrested by Badoglio.

Lecchio had already got into touch with London. That explained to me the strange Madrid atmosphere. Just as in 1940 when we listened to the war communiqués of all the Powers, it was in Spain better than anywhere else one realised that the fortunes of war had indeed changed and that despite the enthusiasm, and loyalty, of some who were marching to disaster, blindfold and with songs on their lips.

At the Ritz I found Jacques Truelle, a very old friend whom I had known in London before the war when he was first secretary at the French embassy. He had gone over to de Gaulle. We chatted quite openly for a long time and swapped news and information; I realised that the stupendous American warmachine was at last moving forward on its irresistible course and that the result of the conflict was certain—sooner or later. At the end of our conversation he said, 'Go to London, why do you want to return to France?' Then I said the Opera troupe needed me—after perhaps a few seconds' hesitation . . . my presence in Paris protected my dancers and that I could not desert them just to save myself alone . . . that I would go on carrying out my mission which, it was true, had now outstripped the man who had originally entrusted me with it . . . and even if the man who had betrayed me was a scoundrel.

In Barcelona I broached the question of an official visit from the Paris Opera. I would have been very happy if it could have taken place. Everyone agreed to the plan—only Rouché was against it despite the facilities offered us by Felix de Lequirica, the Spanish ambassador at Vichy, by Pétain, by Abel Bonnard, now Minister of National Education, and by Jean Mouraille his principal secretary.

Rouché, as he admitted, feared desertions. However, acting within my powers, I signed a contract for the year 1944.

I was at Barcelona when I heard of Mussolini's liberation and of his being rescued from the Gran Sasso after a marvellous display of skilful flying by Skorzeny. On the Ramblas there was a scene of joyful frenzy. The exploit had style, brilliance, it was the act of one man alone but it was like a cavalcade. One might have imagined oneself back in the heroic times of long ago. I really think that on that day the Germans were, for the last time, admired by the whole world. A friend had hurried to a friend in distress. Some people began to hope once again.

It was on the Ramblas that I ran up against an old friend, Sayag, who had formerly been manager of the Ambassadeurs and artistic director of the Monte Carlo casino. At first his greeting was rather constrained: 'How is it possible that you, Serge, have come to think like a Nazi?' I explained to him how things really were, what my position was and what the situation was in France; for people outside France it was difficult to know just how complicated the situation was. At the end of our conversation he embraced me and exclaimed: 'Ah, that is just what I thought, Serge, I could not believe you had changed so much! Now again you are like a brother.' And I also met Trémoulet, formerly French minister in Australia whom I got to know on my trip with *L'Oiseau bleu*.

He told me he wanted to get to London and join up with de Gaulle. I suggested he get in touch with my friend Truelle.

In order to return to France I had to take a little German pursuit-plane with black swastikas painted on the wings.

Hardly had we crossed the Pyrenees than we were followed by British planes from Africa. For half-an-hour, in a crazy dance, my plane rolled, dived, pitched and tossed so as to escape from the attentions of the hostile pursuit plane. Once more I thought my last hour had come. But I escaped again though we had to make a crash-landing in a field near Lyons for the town itself was expecting an air-raid. I had come through with my life and there I was thumbing a lift from the side of the road. Finally I did get to Lyons and went to see Pierre Brisson. During a private conversation that lasted an hour I told him all I had seen and heard. Then I set off for Paris and crossed the demarcation line without an *Ausweis* while reflecting that I might finish up my astonishing escapade in another world, by landing in prison on a charge of vagrancy. However, I did get back to Paris which, it seemed to me, I had left years before. A few days later I could still dream while I started up my exercises again in the *foyer de la danse*. Once more I was at home facing my work, my soul, myself freed and serene. *My mission had been accomplished*—the sabotage of a task that was not mine![1]

Lucht of the *Propagandastaffel* (for whom I had obtained promotion and permission to marry a Belgian woman) summoned me. He was furious: 'I forbid you to leave Paris like that without my authorisation. You have been in Spain.' I smiled and answered very calmly: 'But, Colonel, who has told you I have been in Spain? Maybe I went to spend a few days in London.'

He seemed dumbfounded as he looked at me. He must have been thinking again about the exorbitant advantages I had been able to obtain for him from his superiors and from General Schmitke who was all-powerful at the Majestic. He decided to treat the matter as a joke and with an aloof smile let me go.

[1] In exchange for the permission (at last accorded) to take the *corps de ballet* to Spain during the following season, I had to accept the arrangements made by Vichy for an official performance at Berlin under the auspices of the *Kraft durch Freude* ('Strength through Joy') organisation which was to celebrate its tenth anniversary. But before the appointed date (November 1943) the first large-scale bombardment of the Reich capital took place. The performance was called off. The honour of the Opera was safe.

Some people might still be deceived. But one had only to be in
direct contact with the Occupation authorities to see quite
clearly that a spring had undoubtedly been broken. The immense
façade was still standing but behind it was nothing but tatters,
expedients and improvisations.

In February 1944, after I had danced with Darsonval at
Marseilles, Admiral von Spiegel invited me to dinner and told
me of the extraordinary odyssey of his submarine during the
First World War. It happened that the vessel exploded and all
the crew were reported missing, but when Spiegel got back to
Kiel after the war he was welcomed by all his crew down to
the last man! During this same dinner Rommel declared that
Germany was done for.

After that I ran along to Monte Carlo where I heard that orders
had been given to evacuate the population. That same evening,
in the Casino rooms, I came across the most extraordinary
collection of people it would be possible to imagine. There were
English regular visitors, Lady Champan, Prince Radziwill, a
Pole, Sandra, a Russian, and German officers cheek by jowl! So
I approached Admiral von Spiegel and asked him to annul the
evacuation order, which he did on the spot. The next day I was
able to announce over the radio, 'I am not an apostle, but the
dove of peace that tells you that you will not have to leave.'

When I got back to Paris I created *Guignol et Pandore* with
music by Jolivet and Dignimont's décors. I also prepared
Sauget's *Mirages* with *Cassandre*, while Louis Fourestier and
Roger Desormières rehearsed. Raymond Rouleau, his stage-

hands and electricians got the lighting in order in spite of alarms and stoppages.

Then on 6th June at dawn the Allies landed on the Normandy beaches. Curiously enough my recollection is of a great apparent calm that suddenly settled down on the city. The dice were rolling, destiny was moving forwards. Gestures had no longer any meaning. The only thing to be done was to hold one's breath before seeing a god's iron gauntlet come crushing down.

There was hardly any more electricity or gas. For the first time the Métro stopped running. Everyday life staggered on but the end was in sight. All the same some routines were still obstinately followed. The theatres, when they could, removed their roofs so as to play by daylight. For some people a world was about to be born which they awaited full of hope. For others a civilisation and all its values were about to collapse in bloody revolution.

The Allies were drawing near. On 28th July I lunched with some journalists in the rue Henner. Many of them were already preparing to leave. Robert Brasillach was there. It was the first time I had seen him. Several of those present talked about going off to follow the German troops in their possible retreat— or to seek refuge in a neutral country. Brasillach declared that he had committed no crime. His offence was that of holding certain opinions . . . he added, 'I am French and I shall remain in France.' He was to die for having been unwilling to quit his country.

After the general rehearsal of *Mirages* (the story of a man struggling with his conscience and then being dominated by it), when I danced for the last time for a very considerable period, the Paris Opera, on 23rd July, shut its doors after having given sixty-one ballet performances.

Four days later, at a dinner party, Lequerica begged me to accompany him to Bilbao. I refused but I was touched by his vigilant friendship since he foresaw revolution and all its excesses. However, I said that come what might, it was my duty to remain. Still, when I learned that Georges Hilaire, the Minister of Fine Arts under the Vichy government, was about to be arrested I went off to warn him at the ministry in the rue de Valois. At this time I also met Edouard Bourdet who was already thinking about the reopening of the theatres and we often talked about it together.

The executives of the Opera remained where they were. We
gave each other the impression we were waiting for some miracle
and were all ready to celebrate it on the stage. The artists used
to turn up and seemed to find some comfort in their 'home'.
I took advantage of the time at my disposal to work on com-
pleting *Chota Roustavelli* in my studio, 36 rue de Ponthieu. My
Georgians would be with me. Despite the interruption of normal
life, despite the dangers, the confusion, the alarms, the D.C.A.
firing, or maybe because of all that, these performances became
a pole of attraction as one of the last manifestations of living art
in a respited city. 'All Paris' turned up at my rehearsals in
the presence of Honneger, Charles Münch, Vuillermoz, Larionov,
Roland Petit, Tcherepnine, Gontcharova, Felix de Lequerica
(who had been appointed Spanish Minister of Foreign Affairs),
Nordling and the critics. So as to be able to get about in a city
with no means of transport, I decided to learn to ride a bicycle
for the first time in my life. The courageous Olga Adabache—
the leading *danseuse* in my Georgian ballet—lent me this machine
on which I performed successfully my first exploits. The streets
were deserted. More empty than ever. They were in fact as they
had been during the very first days of the Occupation.

One day in June when my rehearsal was nearly over I saw
come into the studio an individual who at once attracted my
attention. He was small, thick-set and I felt instinctively there
was something suspicious about him. This was not because of
his dirty shave or his burning eyes. However, in those unsettled
days when anything was possible, when blind hatred broke
loose, I at once guessed the man was full of passionate revolt,
making him doubtless a bird of ill-omen. He looked on at my
work from a corner of the room. All I could do was to go on.
Once again I realised that my possible safety lay in my art.
So I threw myself into it body and soul. I bounded about and
warmed up to the dancers and the musicians—Adabache,
Charrat, Skouratov, Algarov, Nicolas Stein[1] and Kabakize,
my Georgian assistant, they all followed me as though they
guessed something, they were galvanised by my dynamism and
danced in frenzied rhythm and with brilliant brio. All the time I
watched the man out of the corner of my eye. He followed our
movements as though enthralled. I felt he was caught and was

[1] Thanks to this work, Stein's wife and children were able to go and hide
at Tours. She was Jewish.

being carried away by the rhythms, the tambourines, the music. The more time went by the more I knew he was at my mercy. As long as I kept dancing I was safe. But my dancers were getting exhausted and I had to bring the rehearsal to an end. I was unarmed but I could not keep my artists there. Gradually they went away one after another. Night was coming on. The stranger still remained.

When we were quite alone he came towards me. His hands were in the pockets of his rain-coat. I no longer had any doubts and was waiting for the critical moment. Then he raised his voice. He spoke Russian with a Georgian accent.

'Congratulations. What you are doing is very fine. But tell me for whom are you making this ballet? For Hitler?'

Without a moment's hesitation I shot back at him:

'And why not for Stalin?'

I saw a face transformed, lightened up and he burst out:

'You are a brother. Kill me, I am guilty, I was in doubt . . . I came to kill you.'

He opened his rain-coat and showed me his weapon. He had been a prisoner in Rumania. He had escaped, gone back to Russia and then was parachuted into France where, on Stalin's orders, he was to kill me. Later on, I hid him, protected him and put him in touch with my group (Antonio and Gégélia) and other anti-Vlassof groups. He was Prince Nizéradzé. Much later I saw him again, during my last visit to Soviet Russia. It was at Tiflis where he is now director of the State radio. Gégélia, by the way, is a professor at Tiflis University.

Those were really violent days. A little while after this incident with the Georgian, I happened to leave my studio rather earlier than usual. The next morning my telephone awoke me at day-break and I got the news that my stage-manager, Nicolas Kremiof, whom I had known for a very long time and who had also been Diaghilev's stage-manager, had been attacked as he left my studio. His skull had been smashed in, and he had died in hospital. I was not only very sad, but also very puzzled. Kremiof had no enemies. Who could have wished him ill? I was turning over this problem in my head when, as I looked at his body, I suddenly realised that a resemblance had led the murderers astray. They had mistaken his figure for mine. At the time I usually left the studio, they had taken him for me. I was the one they were after and had thought they had struck down. Once again death had brushed by me and had spared me but at the price of Kremiof's life, the life of my old and incomparably loyal companion.

The Germans by now were beginning to draw out. What we had never thought we should see was taking place under our eyes. Those who had arrived as proud conquerors were going to retire extenuated and vanquished. They had lost everything. The last units fit to fight had been sent to the Normandy front. It was only the scattered fragments of an army that were pulling out. They piled up in old cars, dilapidated trucks, sometimes in carts, some men were even on bicycles. Everything that was going to move on the roads was camouflaged under branches of trees in an attempt to escape from the continual pounding from the Allied planes that commanded the air. The most varied rumours circulated about the position of the Allied armies. Gossip, or what was called the 'pavement-radio', reported the vanguards as nearer and nearer, nearer than they really were. One day I heard on the radio that was said to come from secret advanced units at Fontainebleau these words, among a flood of threats against the most varied collection of individuals who had remained in Paris at the moment of danger. The words were: 'Monsieur Lifar, prepare to hear your requiem Mass. You will not be shot on the place de l'Opéra but handed over to the Russian people, by whom you will be tried on the Red Square.'

On 11th August, 1944, Nordling came to see me at the rue de Ponthieu. He begged me to take him, without delay, to Otto Abetz. But the embassy was closely guarded—a speaker on the radio had been assassinated that very morning—and it was six o'clock in the afternoon before we were received. Nordling talked privately to Abetz in an effort to save the hostages and the last of those deported at Drancy and Compiègne. Abetz was very harsh while declaring that the Germans were effecting only a temporary withdrawal and were relying on their new weapons which were going to attack the Allied troops in the rear. Still, at the embassy, people were already beginning to leave.

On the morning of the next day Nordling came to fetch me at the Hôtel de Castille so that I might accompany him to the Hôtel Meurice. This I was able to do through Spiegel and

Choltnitz's aide-de camp. Then followed the famous conversation, so often reported, between Choltnitz and Nordling who 'saved Paris'. The same evening Otto Abetz and his wife left by car. Several years were to pass before Nordling had got his file nicely in order and was able to pose as a hero. Unfortunately the part I had played was blotted out and forgotten. It is true that I was then a 'living corpse'. When later on Nordling sent me an invitation I refused it.

Now came the last spasms of agony. All the violence that always accompanies great historic changes could now burst forth. On the one side as on the other the temptation to indulge in repression was strong. I did not go out much. I kept in touch only by telephone with Rouché and the scattered staff of the Opera. On one of the very last days, however, the 11th August, I went out to meet my Georgian group. On my way back to the Hôtel de Castille, unlighted in a city without lights, I noticed as I turned the corner of the street that a German army car was drawn up there. The engine was not running and in the car sat four mute and motionless officers who seemed to have been waiting for a long time. I took in this sight without thinking much about it. I had come alongside my hotel and had already turned to enter when I caught a glimpse of the manageress, Madame René Walpen who was in the shadows but at her reception desk. She made with her head an imperious movement indicating that I should clear off. In a flash I saw again the car I had just perceived a moment before—and I understood. I made as though I had only glanced into the hotel out of curiosity —and continued on my way. Then I began to run in the falling darkness of night. I slipped into No. 31 rue Cambon, the Chanel shop, and I was saved. Later Madame Poisson, the owner of the hotel, confirmed my suspicions. The Germans had come to invite me to accompany them—by force if need be—in their retreat. I never did find out what they already knew of my activities. Protection or punishment? Maybe there was also doubt in their minds. As I saw the old janitor shut Chanel's door, I murmured to myself, 'No, it's not death even this time!'

From Chanel's house where I was looked after by her, by Léon her butler and Germaine her lady's maid, I witnessed the end of the Occupation of Paris, the fighting of the F.F.I. and the arrival of the Allied troops. I saw the last German tanks leaving the Tuileries and another tank burnt out on the place de

l'Opéra. The firemen hoisted French flags on the building. I
heard the 'International', sung in Russian, rise from the Ministry
of Justice occupied by Soviet partisans.

Now appeared the armlets that served the Underground
fighters as uniforms. Finally on 25th August, after Leclerc's
armoured division, whose tanks were cheered by the population
but which went on to further combats, came de Gaulle's entrance
hailed by the pealing of all the bells in the capital. He was not
known. Many caught sight of him for the first time. But he
walked in triumph down the Champs-Elysées and crossed the
place de la Concorde. I could not help seeing in my mind's eye
that same people of Paris that four months before, on 26th
April, had extended just as enthusiastic a welcome to Marshal
Pétain. I remembered this procession as I had seen it from the
windows of the Opera rotunda. The marshal's car was mobbed
by an exultant if thoughtful crowd which saluted the French
flag. This time the lorries were also decked with flags—red
ones. The Communists felt they were in their own realm as
they never had done before. Shots could be heard, fired from
the roofs it was said, mysterious stray shots aimed at de Gaulle
and the crowd, it was also said. But there were no victims. But
all this enabled some people to intensify their pseudo-police
measures. So was ushered in the reign of Communists and Resistants ready to indulge in every sort of excess. The F.F.I.
controlled the streets and searched suspect buildings. But with
a people in a frenzy of excitement, the *Marseillaise* sung or
played served to cover every kind of injustice. Rouché telephoned me, once more: 'You are in danger. Don't move. I
will ring you again.' I had nothing to fear in Coco Chanel's
house where I was lodged and fed. It was the only house in
Paris that received me and maybe saved my life, for I was an
undesirable everywhere. A sort of living corpse.

I could not count much on those who had, nevertheless, always proclaimed their friendship and affection for me.

I had seen a great deal of Misia Sert. At her house, in the rue
de Constantine, she was not at home on fixed days and at
fixed times as social tradition demands, but all day and every
day. Diplomatists and artists met there in charming 'confusion'.
International personalities and bohemian aesthetes, members of
Society from South America, London and the United States,
gathered together in her drawing-rooms. She herself was indeed

M.V.—T

a celebrity who, in her time, had aroused the admiration of painters, musicians and authors. She was a friend of Ravel, of Diaghilev, of Proust and of Bonnard. Berthelot, also, was often at her house.

Her father, Godebski, was a Pole, her mother a Belgian and Misia had all the Slav charm. She was married three times. First of all to Nathanson, then to Edwards and finally to José Maria Sert, a Spanish painter—and a violent opponent of ₁Picasso—who owed in part to his wife his brilliant career and his international reputation. It was she who obtained for him such important commissions as those for the gigantic frescoes—painted in the manner of the Mexican artist Rivera— in the Waldorf-Astoria, the cathedral of Vich in Catalonia, the Rockefeller Center in New York, as well as the decoration in the drawing-rooms of Princesse Edmond de Polignac, avenue Henri-Martin, and in the mansion of the Wendels in what was formerly the avenue de Tokio. Sert's success for a time diverted all Paris but the compliments were mostly addressed to Misia.

But Fate dogged the footsteps of this happy couple. Sert was to divorce and marry 'Princess' Russy Mdivani whom Misia and he had adopted and who was to die soon afterwards. To occupy her mind and to help keep an aura around her I often visited Misia in company with my Russian friends, Meyerhold, Tairov, Ehrenburg, Rachmaninoff, Chaliapin, Prokofiev . . . from Diaghilev's time, Stravinsky had been one of her closest friends.

Misia, who would cast away one day what she had adored the day before, loved passionately only her husband, for, like a true Society woman, she was kind and pleasant only on the surface.

During the 1939–45 war Sert was appointed Spanish ambassador to the Holy See and there served often as a link between France and Spain. He died before Misia and after her death my friend Boulos, Misia's adopted son, inherited the property of both of them.

It was in Sert's house in June 1944 that I met Zeitschel for the last time. He declared that Germany was going to lose the war and he wanted to take me away with him in the private plane of the celebrated conductor Karajan who was present at the meeting.

On 14th July of the same year, at a last reception given by Marie-Laure de Noailles in her house where I was present with her friends among whom was André Dubois, she gave me a copy of her latest book *L'An quarante*. In it was a dedication 'To Serge with all my affection'. As she handed it to me she said, 'Well, Serge, how do you feel? Get ready to stand up for yourself.' On these words I left that house.

But I did not feel in the least guilty and was not at all inclined to remain cooped up during those feverish hours. I soon got an opportunity of going out.

Someone who, on my behalf, was keeping in touch with the hotel where I had stayed up to the time I fled before the Germans, reported to me one day that there had been a telephone call for me at the hotel and a message left that I was to go to an appointment in an F.F.I. office near the Austerlitz railway terminus. This made me very alarmed and I had no wish to fall into what looked uncommonly like a trap. I had heard plenty of the stories that were current as to what went on in F.F.I. premises.

The message was that instead of a meeting being fixed I was to ask for 'Mademoiselle Claude'. Finally my curiosity got the better of me and I made up my mind to call on Mademoiselle Claude. I felt I had nothing to be ashamed of and that, after all, my group would be there to defend me, and that also perhaps this was an opportunity of getting my personal position put straight. And, then, as I have just said, I was getting sick of being closely confined.

That 5th September I took my bicycle and rode through a marvellous Paris until I got to the address I had been given. It was a dirty and miserable-looking little place. That made me feel a little less confident, but all the same since I had come so far I went inside and asked one of the hang-dog-looking men who were moving about where I could find Mademoiselle Claude. He pointed to a staircase leading up to the first floor. While I was walking up I heard cries that made my blood freeze in my veins. Obviously someone was being tortured.

Those howls of pain and terror in that lugubrious and sordid spot, that hell at the end of the night—I had not heard worse during the Russian Revolution, in the days of my youth amid the horrors I had experienced and which now came suddenly surging up once more. I went into a room containing only a chair and a desk. While I was waiting and cursing myself for my folly in rushing helpless into the jaws of a wild beast, the door opened and in came walking towards me a very beautiful girl, young and fair. In that suburban gehenna a Walkyrie dressed in a skirt and pull-over. She wore an arm-band and had a large automatic tucked into her belt. I was more astonished than alarmed. In fact I felt once more how strong was the power of beauty to reassure me. By the time she spoke I no longer quite realised where I was.

'I know all there is against you. People are terribly incensed against you. You are accused of every sin and are regarded as a typical light-hearted collaborator who had an easy time with the Germans. It is your blood they want, but I am an admirer of yours. I know you are innocent and I want to save you. Here, take these papers. Keep out of the way but if you get into any sort of trouble show them at once and they will protect you— for you will be brought to me.'

She held out what I guessed was a pass established by the Resistance authorities. I took it without looking at it or answering. Then she pulled from the desk-drawer one of my photographs, she tendered it to me and asked me to sign it. I raised my eyes to the martial figure, the lovely, young, hard face—to the girl who had just saved me. I took the photograph, leaned over the desk and wrote, 'To Claude de France from Serge Lifar'. I then left without saying a single word. Sometimes I think of her. I never saw her again.

So Paris was liberated.

There was a new Press born of the Liberation. All the old papers (with the exception of the *Figaro*) which had appeared during the Occupation were suppressed. And these new publications invented the wildest stories about me. The columns headed 'Purges' were always long and announced arrests which were, alas, most often justified enough. But my fate was always in doubt or it was just reported, 'Lifar arrested', 'Lifar in South America', or 'Lifar, the multi-millionaire, in Monte Carlo'—after having wallowed in champagne during the whole war—or again, 'Lifar at the Vel' d'Hiver', or 'Lifar at Drancy'. These latter were places where prisoners were parked who had perhaps been denounced by some house porter's tittle-tattle. Rumours spread that I had been shot in the provinces or beaten to death at Drancy. Friends began to be very anxious about me. I was most touched to hear that, among others, Janine Charrat and her father (who commanded the Paris fire-brigade) had gone out to Drancy so as to get news of me and try to help me. One day when I ventured to take the Métro, all at once I noticed that the man by my side was reading *Franc-Tireur*. In it was a large portrait of me. It dated from before the war and showed me in the attitude of a 'Führer' and I guessed only too well that it was accompanied by vindictive comments. I pulled up my coat-collar and tried to get lost in the crowd before the reader of the paper raised his eyes to me. I was filled with anguish as I waited for the train's next stop. I did manage to escape that time but I vowed I would never be so foolhardy again. Once more I took to my bicycle.

Now that I had the pass from the Resistance I yielded to a temptation to visit the Opera. It was just at the time these stories were being concocted about me. People were looking for me at Drancy and there I was on my way to the Opera. The streets were bathed in sunlight. On the place de l'Opéra the remains of a burnt-out tank enhanced by contrast the beauty of a Paris that had been saved. Here at least the war was over. The capital was intact. Had God been in Paris all those years?

I found the Opera deserted, abandoned like a wrecked ship except for a few members of a mutinous crew. I skirted around a group of people on the ground floor and climbed up to the storeys above. It was with stupefaction and emotion that I gazed at the scenes I had left so short a time before but which now seemed to me to have been blasted by the wave of some evil spirit's wand.

I fancied I was returning to a ruined castle which in the days of its splendour had sheltered the glories of a childhood love. Then everything shone and glittered around the crowds that filled the place. I thought I could hear coming from the theatre the sound of a distant orchestra's music, waves of cheering. As I moved unconsciously towards the director's office, I could not repress a feeling of pride. I said to myself that it was, in great measure, owing to me that the Opera had managed to survive during the storms and keep its treasures unharmed. The silence was only temporary. Life would start up again tomorrow and I would be justified.

As I put my hand on the door-knob, I recalled that it was not so long before that when agreeing with Rouché or arguing with him we had on the poop-deck held the tiller of this ship amid tempests and fierce seas.

The door opened. I walked in. There before me were Rouché and Samuel-Rousseau. They looked round towards me. They were as amazed as I was. They stared at me. It was a situation like some others I had known in my lifetime, a situation in a way familiar to me. For them it was as though Lucifer had appeared. Nevertheless I walked in, closed the door behind me and advanced towards them.

'You here!' they murmured with one accord.

I decided I must play it cool—and cheerfully.

'And why not?'

'But . . . weren't you in the Intelligence Service?'

I knew Rouché was expressing a thought that had always lurked in his mind.

'If I had been,' I answered with a sardonic smile, 'it would certainly not be to you gentlemen that I would admit it.'

All the same, Rouché and Samuel-Rousseau calmed down. We chatted for a few minutes. They told me how anxious they were, but it was in such general terms that I could not make out whether the anxiety applied to me or to them. They seemed, at times, to forget that they also had kept their jobs right through the Occupation that had barely ended.

As I took leave they said in an almost supplicating tone of voice:

'Don't come here any more. We will let you know when order has been quite restored.'

I must say they were not the only ones to be alarmed—Dessouches ('Lifar, you've no need of me') . . . Nordling ('No, Lifar, don't come, the Communists will say I've been a collaborator') . . . José Maria Sert ('I don't know Lifar') . . . and how many others I had helped now found it convenient not to know me any more. I was an undesirable everywhere.

On my way out of the Opera I passed a group of people waiting downstairs. I just had time to notice a singer I knew aim a pistol at me. I kept on my way. Another singer I recognised as Chastoney and who, I knew, was already vice-chairman of the Opera purge committee, took the man's weapon away from him. I went on without turning round and reached the doors. But this incident revealed to me a great deal about the new and real—if temporary—masters of the institution to which I had devoted my life for so many years.

Only a few days passed before I heard that Roland Petit, then barely what is called a *petit sujet*—a tyro—in the Opera troupe and who had been my pupil and protégé, had put in for my job as ballet-master—and this on account of services rendered in the Resistance! I had often been invited with Jean Cocteau, and well cared for, in the restaurant Petit's father kept near the Central Markets. Petit had also opened a shop selling dancing-shoes and called 'Respetto'.

Petit's defection pained me, but I learned also that Rouché had not weakened and when replying to the wishes expressed by the *corps de ballet*, he had sent the candidate packing with these words, 'My dear fellow, the job is not for you—yet—you've got to earn a reputation as great as Lifar's—so set to work.'

Later on I was told that my dressing-room had been ransacked, the eyes had been poked out of the portraits and photographs on the walls, and the wreaths, trophies of the victories I had won for the Opera, had been urinated on. Such actions on the part of the stage-hands and the lower staff, whose interests I had always protected, dismayed me. But their deeds served to remind me of a certain side of human nature that I had almost succeeded in forgetting since the time of that revolution which caused me to flee my country. I rang up Rouché. He made humble excuses for the men's over-heated heads. He promised to save the remaining relics in my dressing-room and then advised me not to visit him unless he expressly asked me to do so.

In those days I suffered from all the drawbacks of isolation. However, many people got support from members of their families who had acquired merit on the other side of the barricades. In a similar way, after 1940 the same people had discovered with the Germans, relations or natural allies to protect them. So as the popular proverb so rightly tells us, in troubled times it never does any harm to have money and friends.

Through Gaston Palewski, a faithful old friend—whom I contacted by Boulos and who had been Paul Reynaud's secretary —I tried to approach General de Gaulle and explain my conduct to him. No reply.

At a reception given by Sert in September and held both to celebrate the Liberation of Paris and to honour the heroic Dru Tarter, Palewski was present. Dru Tarter had hidden in her little house at Barbizon about twenty British and American aviators. Later she was also honoured in America and on her house there will soon be a commemorative tablet recalling her courage. Dru Tarter, as an American citizen, had been arrested in Paris and sent, in 1942, to Vittel. I had to take steps to get her liberated and at the request of Georges Hilaire, secretary of State at the Ministry of the Interior, and of Jean Freysse, for we were all friends. Zeitschel agreed to act on condition that she did not indulge in any anti-German propaganda—and for this I was to be held personally responsible.

At Sert's dinner-party, Boulos, in proposing a toast to Dru

Tarter, said that when celebrating her heroism one should remember the steps I had taken which had been so useful to her. To my stupefaction she replied she did not know me!

The second political centre in the distracted country that France had become was the Soviet embassy. Gousovsky was at the head of the mission but Bogomolov was soon to take his place. Through my Georgians and Russians, through Gégélia, I was put into touch with and received at the embassy. This was a priceless victory for me. I remained for nearly two hours in the ambassador's office and described to him what the course of the war had been in France. I told him how determined I had been to serve my adoptive country along the lines of the mission entrusted to me and also how I had served my native land by my fame and by protecting its sons as far as had been in my power.

'We know how you helped our Resistants. We are proud of you.'

A little later on indeed I was sent a certificate—No. 13 of the anti-Vlassov Resistance in France.

The ambassador added:

'Now, in the light of a glorious victory many of the old points of view have changed. Come back to the country that will always be yours. I ask you this in the name of Russia.'

I eluded a direct reply by mentioning the tasks I had yet to accomplish and my need to know first of all what was the state of the Dance's development in the Soviet empire. The ambassador then changed both his tone and the subject.

'But tell me, Lifar, what is happening to Sacha Guitry?—they are making trouble for him here . . . you know we never forget that his father was in Russia and that he himself was born there. Listen, you're a good friend of his . . . so tell him this, that you are speaking on behalf of Stalin, and invite him to come to Russia. He would be protected there and would have everything needful for his work. He would have his father's old Théâtre Michel at Leningrad.'

I said I would be sure to pass on the invitation.

When, later, I did so, Guitry replied:

'I am French and I will stay in France.'

Then the ambassador got up and asked me to go with him to a reception given in honour of the Soviet generals Popov and Maximov. Once more I thought I was in a dream. In my eyes this embassy had been for years an accursed place, a symbol of all those prisons from which no man ever returned, where all sorts of tortures were inflicted and where the cries of the victims were stifled. But here I was chatting with the ambassador, strolling about in elegant rooms, and much safer than outside in the streets of Paris where plenty of good people had been persuaded that they had a grudge against me.

An attendant pushed open a double door and as we walked on the ambassador whispered, 'It is a reception for some of our generals who are passing through Paris.' I found myself suddenly transported, as it were, to the other side of a looking-glass. There was a huge drawing-room brilliantly lighted. Olga Adabache, who had been very helpful in the last difficult months, was there with her mother, a Communist and a Resistant very active during the hardest years of the Occupation. They did not hide their pleasure at seeing me.

Under life-sized portraits of Stalin and Zhukov (the future conqueror of Berlin) were lined up twelve generals in full-dress uniform all bedecked with gold and silver. I blinked my eyes. We were back in another age. In the Western armies such uniforms were no longer known. What had become of the old Red Army with no distinguishing badges, no decorations, no indications of rank—in fact no differences in rank. These powerful war-lords with the gleaming medals and their ribbons . . . why, here once more was the old imperial army of my childhood's days.

The ambassador led me up to the generals:

'Let me introduce Serge Lifar, an honour to his country and who, I hope, will soon be returning to his native land.'

I was made much of, questioned, congratulated—and I played up, but as I passed Zhukov's portrait I stopped and glanced up at it:

'God forgive me, but it's Suvorov! Yes, indeed, the same epaulettes as in the Tsars' times. Surely very many things have changed once more—that is the uniform of our parents' days!'

My remarks cast a chill over the company . . . then conversation started up again. That evening I felt it had been decided that I should be forgiven anything. Glory is sometimes a good counsellor. It was enough for the Soviet leaders that they had won the war. Henceforth they would seek to merge all the glories of Russia into their own glory. Though I was not duped about

their feelings, I was pleased by their intelligence. I speak of the
leaders, for as far as those who carried out the orders were concerned—even if they were generals—they were representatives
of the decent Russian people whom I could easily meet on equal
terms in a fraternal atmosphere of relaxation and merry-making.
The party went on for a long time. There was music and song.
Sometimes from out of the bottom of my glass a strange little
voice would squeak and this is what it said to me: 'The evening
of *Joan de Zarizza* . . . Goebbels on the steps of the Opera . . .
the British chasing your plane . . . Hitler, Hitler . . .' How far
off that voice seemed! There had never been any war. Stalin
had never met Ribbentrop.

I was still musing as I made my way back to my new hide-
out—220 rue de Rivoli—for I still had to be careful in my
comings and goings. There I found a note brought by one of my
liaison agents. It was signed by Jacommet, the chairman. On
Monday 13th November I must appear before the Paris Opera
Purge Committee there to answer for my deeds.

PART FOUR

'LIKE THE PHOENIX'

1

'VOX POPULI'

The day of my 'trial' arrived. I had learned that Schwarz, Ivanoff and Bardin had already been 'purged'. I knew that I was going to meet my judges not only in my own name but in that of all the artists of the Dance, of the whole *corps de ballet* who had maintained the prestige and the pride of artistic France during those gloomy, dangerous years.

My 'trial' before the Purge Committee of the Lyric Theatres dragged on for five weeks at the rate of one hearing a week. The sittings were to be held in the lyric artists' foyer at the Opera itself. On 21st November at half-past three I therefore presented myself at the Opera. I wore the get-up I had devised for my trip in 1939–40 (see p. 157)—top-boots, leather jerkin and beret. I carried a revolver and was accompanied by the men of my group, Georgians, Spaniards and Russians all armed to the teeth and with automatics under their arms and grenades in their hands. They prepared to wait around the place—after they had made it quite clear that if by mishap a 'stray bullet' should hit me they would without any warning at all blow up the whole Opera building. Their supply of arms and their ferocious appearance lent considerable weight to their words. A small delegation consisting of the general staff—Antonio, Skobline and Nijeradzé—entered the Palais Garnier with me and kept close so as to protect me. There was a crowd on the square —now known as the place Diaghilev—and there were faces at all the windows. There were plenty of stage-hands but also some unknown figures who seemed to have come up from the depths of the Parisian underworld. These filled the corridors and cluttered up all the staircase to the last step. As soon as I got into this mob I heard a voice shouting, 'Hands up.' I obeyed instinctively. Then the voice bawled, 'Higher.' Then, as so often has happened to me, my irritation gave way to a desire to play the buffoon, so I raised my arms higher and since I was in a dancing pose I began to perform my leaps and my *entrechats-six*, . . . an angry growl rumbled round the high walls. I saw automatics aimed at me. But the police had been summoned and now surged in. In those days the police were both disorganised and overwhelmed and those who had arrived seemed to be in a blind panic. But they tried to cope with the situation, and to disarm me. They surrounded my group and me and hustled us a little. I showed them my permit to carry arms. Antonio, who did not like the turns things were taking, clenched his fist and punched the police superintendent who happened to be within reach. For a moment it looked as though there was going to be a free fight. But after I had made a sign to him not to let matters get still worse, Antonio allowed himself to be led away.

A little group left for the military police station at the Invalides (the HQ of the 2nd armoured division and of the Paris military authorities), since as a captain commanding the 5th battalion of the Brittany F.T.P., Antonio had the right to be dealt with by the army. It so happened that General Leclerc met the party and asked what the matter was. Antonio told him. The general replied, 'How right you were to bash out at one of these policemen who so zealously served the Germans. You're free and you've got my permission to start all over again.'

The first session of my 'trial' then began. The committee tribunal consisted of fourteen members presided over by Jacomet, the government delegate. The vice-president was Gaudin who had taken the place of Chastonney who had resigned after a ukase had been issued by the Communist members of the commission—who wanted my blood. Jacomet had constantly to call his committee to order. Their attitude was so indecent and so aggressive that it showed quite plainly their minds were made up before they had learned anything from the proceedings. The tribunal judged *in camera* and its decisions were 'final and admitted of no appeal'.

I made an effort to appear quite relaxed. After all I was not being tried by an official court of my adoptive country. This

committee for 'professional purges' was something quite different. It was composed of people who until lately had been my
close acquaintances, and two of them, Siosa and Rozes, *danseuses*
of the *corps de ballet*. It was not up to me to defend myself and I
decided to take the whole proceedings as a joke, as a game
played between them and me. Otherwise this parody of a trial
would have seemed a tragedy to me. All I had been able to get
out of Gustave Roussy was this recommendation transmitted
by a messenger: 'Do not disclose anything, your mission still
exists.' For me, who knew all, this was too much of a good
thing. But I knew that Roussy was 'an outstanding member
of the Resistance' and in close touch with those nearest to
General de Gaulle who had protected Roussy and given him
back his job as rector of the University of Paris.

Indeed it would have been useless for me to speak, since no
one would have believed me and so my case would have been
made all the worse. So I resolved to keep silent. It would be
better for me to take refuge in humour. After all, was there not
something comic in my circumstances as there is in all real
human tragedies? And I kept on saying to myself, 'And there
was I all the time thinking I had Roussy to back me up and to
cover me!'

Then a completely trumped-up act of accusation was read
aloud. I saw at once that there had been a deliberate plot. But
I did not want to appeal to officials for fear that they might
sacrifice me for 'reasons of State'.

My examination was very short.

'Lifar, sit down.'

Then the witnesses came in immediately. About a hundred
had been selected and they were divided into three groups:
first the artists of the *corps de ballet* (all in my favour except
Ritz), then the dressers and finally the stage-hands. Almost all
of the latter—who during the Occupation had been good
fellow-workers—had become hostile and accusing. Thus the
social aspect of the proceedings was clear from the first. But
I must add that all these minor members of the staff had been
subjected to indoctrination and pressure from their Communist
Union . . . they had to live and to do so they had often to forget
that they themselves had during the Occupation 'collaborated'
in the Opera performances—and for that I could not find it
in me to blame them too much.

M.V.—U

But there was the dancer called Ritz. He was the first to be called and his case was much more serious. He had been taken prisoner in 1940 but had soon been liberated. He declared:

'Lifar belonged to the Gestapo.'

'What makes you say so?' asked the President.

'Oh, I don't know . . . but we were all sure of it . . .'

Even in such a court the effect produced by this remark was feeble enough. In fact there was some embarrassment. Ritz added:

'Then, when we went to the South of France last February Lifar met Admiral von Spiegel commanding all the Mediterranean theatre of operations and it was to him that Rommel went on his return from Africa. Moreover it was no doubt owing to contacts of this kind that Lifar was able to be the real boss of the Opera for four years.'

The committee thrilled with delight. I stood up at once.

'Sure enough. I was a perfectly contemptible creature and everyone knew it. But then why the devil did the witness quite recently, as he has just declared, travel with me though nothing forced him to?'

The witness wavered a little. The public growled. I went on:

'But since he has been talking about contacts and what one can get through them, will the witness just tell us how and why he came back so quickly from captivity?'

This time it was too much—Ritz stammered and stuttered. The committee thanked him. He cleared out very quickly.

The second witness was Yvette Chauviré. She made her entrance clad in a long white dancing-skirt and covered with shawls because it was so cold. She had been called by the prosecution. When she spoke it was to say that she laid no blame on Lifar for anything. 'Thanks to the *maître*,' she added, 'the Paris Opera was saved and did not cease to flourish.'

The President, who appeared disconcerted, thanked her. I turned towards her:

'My respects, mademoiselle.'

A member of the committee asked whether they would hear the evidence of Rouché and of Samuel-Rousseau who both would have a word to say in the case.

'Unfortunately no,' answered the President, 'they have both refused and have been excused from giving evidence.'

'What a pity,' I murmured gently, 'the chiefs cannot accept their responsibilities.'

Then quite spontaneously a member of the committee, interrupted:

'Everyone knows he was a friend of Hitler and the lover of Frau Abetz.'

'You did some peeping through keyholes?' I shot out at him.

'Death, death to the traitor Lifar,' roared the committee, evidently exasperated by my sally. The President rang his bell loudly in an attempt to restore order.

When things had calmed down, Yvette Darsonval came forward to say:

'We owe everything to Lifar, our master.'

After that the little girls of the *corps de ballet* appeared. They were in stage-dress. I was very moved to hear them come to my help. They said what they had to say with such vehemence that they were cut short and shown out. I also left the court when the hearing was suspended. I could hear the tumult and the imprecations hurled at me behind the door as I moved away still surrounded with the automatics of my bodyguard—by this time back from the Invalides.

The next week the proceedings started up again on the same day and at the same time. 'The Wednesday dances were then continuing.' I was happy to learn that a petition had been got up by the artists of the *corps de ballet*. It stated that during my time as master of the Opera *corps de ballet* I had never made any ill-considered political declaration and that my activities had had as sole aim the furtherance of our art and the enhancing of the National Dance Academy's prestige. All had with one accord signed the document—with the sole exception I have mentioned.

This time it was the turn of the dressers and stage-hands. The first witness called was Mme Tanguy, my own dresser. She came forward and declared—with a remarkably small vocabulary— that among the pro-German remarks she had heard me make were wishes for a German victory and insults to the Allies. Characteristic of my attitude was my statement, 'In the whole world there is nothing any good but God, Hitler and I.'

I could not help smiling though I did my best to keep a straight face. And when the President turned to me as though he was awaiting my comments I asked him for permission, which he granted, to put some questions to the witness. I turned towards Mme Tanguy.

'Madame, are you really sure that Hitler exists?'

A stupefied silence reigned. The witness was ill-at-ease since beyond the declaration she had learned by rote, she had nothing to say. She stammered a mistrustful 'yes'. I went on:

'And are you quite sure that I myself am standing in flesh and blood before you?'

I heard a still more embarrassed 'yes'. A slight rumble began to arise from the public. I leaned over towards the witness:

'But then there is God, madame, have you seen him? are you sure he exists?'

'Lifar to the gallows,' she yapped while all the court-room accompanied her with furious clamour and torrents of insults.

When some order had been restored, Mme Thiébault, head of the female staff, came to declare that this Mme Tanguy was such a bad dresser that I had been obliged to dispense with her services and to turn her over to Peretti.

The hostile declarations of some of those present could perhaps be explained by the fact that their careers had no future. Moreover, later on, some were to come to me and not only make excuses but also ask favours. Furthermore, in addition to the more easily comprehensible social factors, it was professional jealousy that was the main driving force that aroused a desire for vengeance within these so-called 'purge' committees set up for the various professions. Fame, I realised, suddenly enough, is the worst of poisons.

Now came the turn of the stage-hands. At the instigation of Jean Rieussec (a member of the committee and secretary of the Opera Communist cell), Daniel Pion and Paul Germain, the stage-hands, had signed the following petition:

'We the undersigned stage-hands must protest most strongly against all the petitions in favour of Lifar whom we consider as a traitor not only to his own country but also to France. Nevertheless, should the Purge Committee act on the evidence given in the defendant's favour, we demand the benefit of reciprocity.'

This petition got 48 signatures as against 44 of the *corps de ballet* (with such names as Darsonval, Chauviré, Lafon, Micheline Boudet, Dany Robin, Renault, Babilée, Efimoff, etc.), favourable to me.

They all trooped by—stage-hands, electricians, property-men—
each one repeating after the other the same declaration strictly
in the same wording. The first statement made some impression,
the second strengthened it, while the third created some astonishment. By the time the sixth had recited his rigmarole even those
most prejudiced against me began to feel embarrassed and to
realise there was something fishy about the performance.
The people behind them might at least have taken the trouble to
fabricate a special deposition for each man. In that way things
would have been incomparably more effective. I kept silent and
let them talk. But when the last of the lot had come and said,
'I heard him declare that if he were in power he would have
all the stage-hands shot', I got up and addressed the court.

'I have listened to all these gentlemen. They have most
excellent memories. However, it is a pity that regarding one
point they have one and all lost their memories entirely. Not one
of them has remembered that on the day of their strike during
the performance of *Joan de Zarizza* I saved them all from deportation. It would have given me pleasure to hear that at least one
of them recalled this incident.

'But let that pass. However, this phrase of mine they all
remember I cannot recall at all. But, after all, we can see that
memory may play us false. I may, as a matter of fact, quite
well have pronounced some such words, but I would just like
to refresh my memory—so when did I make this remark?'

Then, all together, 'After *Boléro* because there had been some
trouble with the scenery.'

Lifar: 'Oh, that's fine . . . but tell me *Boléro* was a great
success.'

All together: 'Oh, yes, I should say so, twenty minutes at least
of cheering and calls. You made us work that curtain!'

Then I snapped towards each of them in turn:
'And where were you when I made this remark?'
'Well, in my place near the second row of flood-lights.'
'And you?'
'In the flies.'
'And you?'
'With the machines in the basement.'

I made them all answer. Then I turned to the President and
his assessors who had watched carefully the whole proceeding
and I said:

'There you are, gentlemen, I am indeed most guilty. It was very wrong of me to complain of my stage-hands and of the way the stage was kept. For, marvellous to say, it is evident that at the very time *Boléro* was ending and the audience was shouting its delight in the immense hubbub you can imagine, twenty micros arose from the ground and by some means as yet unknown sped on their way to twenty stage-hands scattered about all over an immense building, and all for the sole and only end that these men might hear clearly the phrase I was going to address to them, the phrase that wished them all in front of an execution squad.'

My last words were lost in the uproar. From all corners came the cries: 'Swine, kill him, you won't be able to play the Smart Alec for long.'

The President had a difficult job in restoring order and then he announced Princess Olga Galitzine. She, tall and simple, had come to say:

'I was arrested by the Gestapo, I was beaten, I was tortured and I had my nails pulled out. And all this because the Gestapo had discovered the name of Lifar in my house and because Lifar figured on the Gestapo's black list and among the No. 1 suspects.' She showed her medical certificates. She held out her mutilated fingers. Then in deep silence she retired. But she had introduced some measure of dignity and real emotion into the assembly. After that I also withdrew accompanied by my escort.

During the following week Paul Germain got in touch with me and proposed that I should join the Communist Party . . . 'Come with us like Picasso and Roussy and we'll protect you, we'll save you. . . .' I rejected the offer and somewhat haughtily told him I was not for sale.

I asked one of the leaders of the Paris Bar, M. Charpentier, to take my brief. Henceforth he, and his junior, M. Silvestre, were to help me.

It was amid great excitement too that the third hearing was held. I must say that if one had been counting rounds as at a boxing-match, that round would have been one for me.

My friend Antonio, 'the Man with the Red Hand', the man on whose head the Germans had set a price of a million marks, Antonio Calvera, commander of the F.T.P., presented himself before the tribunal. He was self-possessed as are the men who have fought and won. By any reckoning he had done a great deal more than all the gentlemen of the committee. As soon as the President had called on him to speak, Antonio began by reading his own mentions in Orders—and those of all the members of his group. The President, who had never so much as heard of this sort of thing, and who I thought I could feel was trying to help me, was obviously acting as a judge and not as a partisan. So he proposed that everyone should stand up so as to pay tribute to such valiant fighters, such heroes. And in a great burst of enthusiasm all the Committee did as the President wished.

Then Antonio spoke and paid a warm tribute to Lifar. Antonio missed out nothing, he told of the asylum provided, the help given, the arms stolen and handed over. Then he ended and in a ringing voice declared, 'So now you understand that if Lifar had belonged to the Gestapo I would not be here to tell you what I have. He knew everything about my activity, he had only to betray me. It's he or I.'

All the members of his group, under oath, confirmed what Antonio had said.

Before declaring the proceedings over for the day the President shook Antonio's hand. I already saw myself acquitted.

Whether or not it was the effect of Antonio's evidence, but at the next, fourth, sitting of the committee, the atmosphere was no longer the same. I felt that Jacommet was less stern. He looked at me in a way that was more communicative, more penetrating. Between this magistrate and me there now existed a more human contact. And then, first of all, the proceedings were more ceremonious, more dignified. Antonio and his men remained at the entrance, outside the court-room.

This was to be the day of the pleadings. That same morning I had been musing at my window and thinking of the days I had just lived through and of the hours I was now going to endure. For as long as the case lasted I lived in the boulevard Haussmann and my room gave on to the rue des Mathurins. From my window I let my eyes wander over the mangificent, famous building of the Opera, so near to me—and so far off. It was fifteen years since I had become a member of the Opera . . . and then, suddenly, I shuddered. For the first time the statue of Apollo on the cupola was turning its back towards me. In spite of myself I could not help thinking that this might be a presage. I tore myself away from the window, shook off my musings and prepared for the struggle.

I went to the hearing accompanied by M. Charpentier and his junior. They were to aid me on this decisive day. Their role, however, was to be that of enlightening the wretched committee about the possible juridical aspects of the case. Furthermore M. Charpentier had had delivered to the President a note in which it was pointed out that the 'acts and deeds of Lifar during the Occupation were in no way liable to be the objects of judicial proceedings within the framework of existing laws and that they were not such as could be made a reason for prosecution.'

He wanted, however, to add a few words and asked to be allowed to address the court. He was a man of great force of character and he led off thus:

'It was I, gentlemen, who, in Algeria, was one of the drafters of the law instituting the purge committees—and that at the request of General de Gaulle himself. I am, therefore, very well acquainted with that law and also with the intentions of those who framed it.'

A murmur rippled through the committee, but it was not only one of esteem. These amateur judges took it rather ill that a professional should seem to be teaching them, giving them a lesson. Charpentier went on: 'I refused to defend Louis Renault since he had collaborated with the Germans in material matters and ones of grave consequence. Yet Louis Renault was a very old friend of mine. But Lifar, gentlemen, is in quite a different position.

'He is a foreigner, it is true, but I could wish that all Frenchmen had given as much to France as this foreigner has.'

The audience began to murmur. The President rapped on the table. Charpentier continued:

'Lifar's case is an exceptional one. It is not only a national case but an international one. He is now accused without his case having been examined or the charges against him investigated. He has been pursued by blind hatred.'

After having been so long repressed the committee seemed literally to explode. The members cried, 'Out with Charpentier.' The passion for revenge, the mob rule, swept away any respect for the advocate, the defending counsel, the man who had drafted the law that put them where they were, the collaborator of General de Gaulle. At that moment one could see all raw and naked the brutal force of a Communism that nothing can restrain, that overthrows all bourgeois ideals and values, to the cry of, 'Now it's my turn.'

I could not help shouting out, 'What insolence in the face of a distinguished Frenchman.' The President rebuked me sharply: 'Be quiet, you are the defendant, it's not for you to teach us lessons. I am in charge of the proceedings.' And carried away as he was with his excitement, he forbade Charpentier to speak any more and he left the court-room. M. Silvestre however, his colleague, remained.

I asked to be allowed to speak. I had to conduct my own pleadings and this I did for three and a half hours.

'You must hear me: listen to me carefully, gentlemen. Formerly when I expressed myself in my art, I was understood everywhere. Today for the first time I am going to make a speech.'

I recounted the story of my life. I spoke of my childhood and youth in Russia, of the Revolution, of how I had suffered hunger and experienced war—had been at close quarters with death. My adversaries might well be Communists, but I wanted to show them that although one was an artist that did not mean that one feared harsh realities or that one lived pampered and in luxury. One could be a dancer and all the same keep one's feet on the earth—in spite of what one of their idiotic Communist newspapers wrote. I told how I had left Russia, how I had lived years of poverty and grinding hard work. It did not cost me much effort to recall the rue Taitbout and the rue de la Victoire where, since I had no studio, I did my exercises on the pavements. 'My first audience was made up of the ladies of the street,' I was able to fling at them, and I added, 'I have always earned my living by my own work.' Then I went on to speak of the war. Although I was silent about the mission entrusted to me by Gustave Roussy, I did remind them of the time when the Opera's doors were closed, when the ballet troupe and the staff were thrown on their own resources. I explained how it was in their interest that I had reopened the Opera, their Opera, that I had paid out to them the first salaries they had received since the theatre was shut down—and that I had wanted nothing for myself. I could not resist the pleasure of recalling the words I had heard them jeer at our poor Glouglou when he refused Hitler's tip . . . 'You damned fool, you ought to have grabbed it, money does not stink.' Then I reminded them of that evening performance and of *Joan de Zarizza* and of how I had managed to get them off deportation to forced labour in Germany.

The Opera had played for the Germans. Yes, of course it had.

But on those occasions who attended to the lighting? Who raised the curtain? Who played in the orchestra?

'Gentlemen, whether you like it or not,' I flung at them, 'if I am a "collaborator" then so are you—just as much as I am.' They growled but they listened. I went on. 'We were all in the same boat, for better or for worse. You knew that in 1940—in the days of our friendship—when, very loyally, you backed up my efforts. . . .'

What then could have happened since that time, what could explain their total change of attitude? The war had become more harsh? Of course. I knew that better than any of them. They had heard my comrade Antonio declare that the man who had been in the outposts was myself. The Germano-Russian war? But I was a Russian and had received a certificate from my country.

A member of the committee shouted at me: 'If you were so influential it was because you were Hitler's friend and you received him at the Opera.'

I replied harshly: 'You know very well that I never received Hitler. Your comrades can bear witness to that. If I was in contact with the Germans, it was to help you, and to save you each time I heard that danger threatened.'

'And the one who was shot? You didn't help him.'

This time I lost my temper.

'It's you who were responsible for his death!' I shouted.

They tried to stifle my voice, but their uproar came too late. I did not let them rob me of speech. I bawled out as loud as I could and finally got a hearing once more. Real indignation possesses an irresistible force.

'Yes, it's you who are to blame for his death if you knew of the danger he was in and did not tell me about it. I was among you every day. It was quite easy for you to keep me informed. Maybe I could have saved him as I did so many others. You killed him by your silence. His blood is upon your heads.

'And now you have the nerve to throw that in my face. Well, it's too late. He did not die because he was a stage-hand at the Paris Opera. He fell like a hero defending a cause he felt was sacred—and as a member of the Communist Party on a special mission.

'And I was the first to introduce a Soviet ballerina to Paris—ten years ago when everyone hid his face in horror at the very idea of such an invitation.

'You talk to me about my articles, of my article on Kiev, my native city. But in that article I spoke of my art and sang the praises of my Russian birthplace. How many Jews have I hidden, protected, assisted, saved? You do not mention these things but you have heard tell of them at earlier hearings. How many of the Resistance found welcome and help at my home? Welcome and help given at the risk of my liberty, of my life. You do not even whisper a word about that. But voices and evidence do not count when they are favourable to me.

'And why am I here today?

'I myself have the definite impression that I am here as a scapegoat, an animal that must be slaughtered so that others may go free. If there are any accusations to be made, I will make one: I accuse a rotten society. I demand to be judged only on my acts.'

I moved towards the bench with my hands held out.

'There is no single drop of blood on my hands.'

I ended by repeating what I had believed, my mission for my art, for France, for my country. I said how proud I was that my *corps de ballet* had, in such sad times, given proof of their loyalty and their gratitude. I added that, in any case, I would never forget happier times when they themselves had been my assistants and my friendly companions. They could prevent me from carrying on my profession, but they could not prevent me from being proud of having put my fame as a dancer at the service of France and 'of this house, their House, the Opera of Paris'.

I sat down amid dead silence.

The President said: 'We knew you were a great dancer but we did not know you were also a great orator. Thank you.'

And he shook hands with me.

Then he declared the hearing of the case was over. I think that if the 'verdict' had been pronounced there and then, I would have had a good chance of being acquitted. But I was not to hear the court's findings until the following week.

The verdict was obviously dictated from outside. It was voted *nem. con.* (save for one voice, that of André-Gaudin, the Vice-President) and was . . . 'Death' . . . but as it did not lie in the committee's power to inflict a capital punishment, I was given the maximum sentence they could impose . . . 'Exclusion for life from the Opera and from State theatres.'

❦ 2 ❦

'LIKE THE PHOENIX'

On that evening of the 'verdict' I left Paris. I went to seek refuge at Haute-Barde near Bordeaux and in the house of a friend Jean Beau whose family was, during those days, the only one to remain entirely faithful to me. I had at that time only one wish. To forget everything. 'Exclusion for life . . . ' I was obsessed by the vision of the Apollo statue turning his face away from me. Was it really all over with me? At forty years of age? Icarus—ten years only had elapsed since the creation of *Icare*—was he already struck down for having dared to fly too high, too near the sun?

Possibly. As it was a child saved me.

Jean Beau had a son. A baby of some twenty-six months. He was called Patrick. It is a difficult thing to explain what I want to convey now. It was the sight of that infant and it was the mute friendship we struck up that brought me back once more to zest for life. It was life at its source, still fragile but already so impetuous, which gave me back the taste for living. I could not leave his side. I watched him open himself to life, watched him feel, taste, touch. I realised another dimension of existence. Something died down in me . . . the fierce urge to disappear, to give up. I decided to fight, to win, to reconquer my ruined world.

As early as 1945, Delpierre, the leading figure at Monte Carlo, then Eugène Grunberg and, most of all, Constantin Népo, the husband of Yvette Chauviré, had offered me the job of directing the 'Nouveau Ballet de Monte Carlo'. I accepted and Népo took advantage of a lecture on the meeting between

Michelangelo and Leonardo da Vinci to introduce me to all the theatrical celebrities he had invited. I was enthusiastically welcomed. At the first sign I made there flocked to my side those comrades who knew they would find once more with me their art's liveliness and boldness. Chauviré of course, and then Algaroff, Golovine, Skouratoff, René Jeanmaire, Janine Charrat, Olga Adabache, Kalioujny, Trailine, Audran.

The intrigues, of course, were not long in making their appearance. On the day that Prince Louis of Monaco was to visit the theatre, the musicians and stage-hands, without any warning, went on strike. I had myself to borrow the firemen's ladder. Moreover at that time a photograph was taken of me during a meeting of the trade union that was exceedingly ill-timed. No doubt it is hardly worth while mentioning that the Monte Carlo syndicates had got their orders from Paris. The director then asked me not to go to the theatre. But I refused and was backed up by the *corps de ballet* who demanded my presence and threatened not to dance if I was not there. And their menace was so urgent, so inspiring, that it snow-balled. The casino croupiers, the firemen and even the cabmen also threatened to go on strike in order to support me. So impressed was he by these marks of sympathy that the director gave me permission to go to the casino but I must be disguised, rigged out with a beard, and to this I could not consent. Finally, after interminable discussions and palavering, the musicians and stage-hands at last agreed to work. Once again the *corps de ballet* won the day. And that 1946 season was to prove the most productive in all the history of the Dance. *Dramma per musica* on a cantata by Bach and with Cassandra's décors must rank among the most elegant of ballets. The Parisian critics who flocked to Monte Carlo hailed us as having created 'the home of the Dance in Europe'.

On 5th May 1946 there was presented—also at Monto Carlo —the new Georgian ballet *Chota Roustavelli* which, owing to the events at the end of the war, I had been prevented from putting on at the Opera. From far and wide there came a discerning public to witness the performance. I felt at once that contact with life had again been made. From the moment I appeared on the stage a breach was broken in the wall of mis- understanding. Now I had but to go forward. I had proved that the Dance was not dead in Europe. Into the domain of the Dance

I had driven a paralysing blow at intrusive cultural influences from America. When, later on, during the 'World Congress for the Defence of Culture' I had to reply to the Americans in *Le Manifeste du Choréauteur*, I declared: 'France accepts advice from no one. She gives it.'

The season was indeed brilliant. The Aga Khan and the Begum—always most generous towards the Arts, the Dance and dancers—were lavish in their support of my enterprise which, however rich in prestige it may have been, was poor in financial resources. Their help lent new life to my ballet.

After Monte Carlo the troupe left for Italy where, with stoical endurance, it performed in adverse conditions. In Switzerland the protests started up again, led by the Press of which the *Courrier de Genève* was the most virulent. Still, all the same, I danced in *Giselle* with great success.

Next we went to London where we performed at the Cambridge Theatre directed by Pomeroy. The boycott went on. In spite of my friends' support—one of them, Oliver Baldwin, did me the honour of inviting me to look on at a sitting of the House of Commons—the Covent Garden dancers had to watch our performances incognito from the topmost gallery. But I did not give up. I was even interviewed by the B.B.C.—an odd event since it was they who had condemned me to death in 1940. Finally I decided to invite Her Majesty the Queen who graciously accepted; programmes were printed, and posters put up. Then on the eve of the performance the Lord Chamberlain asked me to call off the gala. I was dumbfounded and it needed all the efforts of my friends—and among them especially Lady Cunard— to induce the Lord Chamberlain finally to reveal the reason for his strange action. The explanation was that Mr Pomeroy could not be allowed to receive the Queen because during the war he had supplied to the British troops quantities of objects of, let us say, a confidential and prophylactic nature. I had with a very heavy heart to call off the royal performance. I danced all the same but I had to wait several years before I could regain my position in Britain.

In the month of October 1945 I had again appeared before a purge committee, this time one sitting at the Ministry of National Education. This body, in view of the excessively severe sentences inflicted by the earlier purge committees, constituted a sort of appeal court for the revision of such judgments. The atmosphere of the new court was quite different from that of the former one. The documents in the files were really examined. The chairman of the new committee was M. Côme who had returned gaunt and as thin as a skeleton from Buchenwald. His assistants were M. Szyfer, a victim of Nazi violence, and M. Quinault, the ballet-master of the Opéra-Comique. The committee took into consideration the fact that I had never been arrested, that no legal proceedings had been taken against me before any French Court of Justice and that there had never been any question of handing me over to any civil court. At the time when the attention of France and of all Europe was attracted to the great trials which epitomised the tragic history of the war years—Pétain, Laval, Nuremberg—my name was never even mentioned nor any role I might have played recalled. As though by enchantment I seemed to have disappeared altogether.

On one occasion, however, my name was mentioned and that was during Jacques Rouché's trial. His lawyer demanded my expulsion. Rouché was acquitted.

When I met him a short time afterwards he said to me, 'You must understand, Serge, I had to save my honour, my position, my children . . .' All I could reply was, 'And my honour, then, doesn't it count for anything?' And then on 13th August, 1942, he had signed a photograph of the *corps de ballet* . . . 'To my choreographer, to Serge Lifar, thirteen years of friendship.'

After due deliberation the committee congratulated me and added, 'In consideration of the state of public opinion, and in your own interest, we ask you, M. Lifar, to accept a leave of absence of one year.' The committee reported in this sense to M. Capitant, then Minister of Public Education, who ratified the sentence. So there I was condemned to a cessation of professional activity for one year dated from 1st November 1944. The minister said to me, 'It's worth while accepting this in order to appease wide-spread public opinion and the passions that have been unleashed.'

Thus from 1st November 1945 I was free once more to pursue my profession in France. But I was still the victim of uncommonly violent press campaigns. At this time, indeed, my name was so taboo that it did not appear on the Opera posters even when my ballets were being performed. But the extreme case of wilful and even ridiculous neglect was afforded by the omission of Lifar's name from a book glorifying the Opera Ballet and appearing over the name of M. André Billy of the Académie Goncourt. This snub surpassed even the campaign of ferocious hostility displayed in newspapers inspired by political passion and bent on gaining cheap notoriety by blaspheming history.

Happily some choreographic critics protested against this travesty of the truth and they fought for me by imperilling their own security. I shall never forget the names of those whose action so warmed my heart—Jean Dorcy, Maître Pourchet, Anatol Schaikévitch, Léandre Vaillant, Pierre Michat, Jean Laurent, Guillot de Rodes, Jean Silvant, André Boll and Berlioz.

During that year I sent to my friend Darius Milhaud, then in America, the scenario of a ballet *Phoenix* for which I asked him to compose the music. The work was a glorification of the rebirth of France. Milhaud replied that he was indignant at getting my letter. He called me anti-Semitic: such was the opinion of the French colony in the United States—he accused me also (wrongly) of having written for *le Pilori*. Some months later, Milhaud, back in France, renewed his friendship and esteem for me. Shortly afterwards he wrote, with Philippe de Rothschild, a ballet for which they asked Salvador Dali to do the décors and me to direct the choreography.

Despite the difficulties I kept obstinately on my way, strengthened by the conviction that I had right on my side and by my unfaltering love for the Parisian public. In all this I was not without some merit. For instance, on 17th September, 1946, I was invited to dance at the Palais de Chaillot. The occasion was a gala performance got up by the committee formed to raise funds for a monument to those killed during the Liberation of Paris. On the 19th of the same month there was to be another gala in the same place and organised by the newspaper *La Cause Géorgienne*. This performance was under the patronage of the USSR ambassador in France, Alexandre Bogomolov who had given his consent on 23rd August. I may add that for both galas the house was sold out in twenty-four hours. But on 14th September a group of 'resistants', deportees wearing the striped uniform of the concentration camps, mayors girt with their official sashes, walked in procession through Paris to protest at my presence in the Pleyel gala. Some people even threatened to blow up the hall. As I did not want to be the cause of any disturbances in the life of Paris I wrote to Luizet the Prefect of Police and declared that I would not appear at the gala.

Luizet sent me a letter expressing his regrets. But then all the ballet stars decided spontaneously that they would not dance either, so the performance was called off as also was that at the Palais de Chaillot—this latter at the request of Bogomolov himself.

Nevertheless, the Georgian group in Paris—with whom it will be remembered I was in close touch—met Molotov who was then in Paris as Soviet representative to the United Nations. Molotov at once telephoned to Stalin who answered that the performance should not be countermanded. We may keep in mind that Stalin was a Georgian and would be flattered if the Georgian ballet which had triumphed at Monte Carlo and in London should be shown in Paris. Stalin also asked Molotov if I had obtained a Soviet passport. On Molotov's saying 'No', the master of Russia commented, 'But let him take it, I'm not his impresario.' However, when Bogomolov at last called on Le Troquer, then Minister of the Interior, and asked for the performance to be permitted, it was too late, especially as the troupe had been broken up.

But on 27th November, 1946, and ironically enough backed by Luizet himself, I did, all the same, dance at the Salle Pleyel in Paris. Seven appearances on the stage, seven *pas-de-deux* with seven of my Opera stars who had wanted to take part in my come-back. The warmth of the welcome given me by the Paris public, my beloved public of then and always, swept away all opposition. I realised that Destiny had given me the green light.

Georges Hirsch had succeeded Lehmann—who himself had succeeded Rouché[1] as administrator of the Réunion des Théâtres Lyriques. As soon as Hirsch had got the Opera well in hand he contacted me and during a luncheon at the Restaurant Drouant he told me very clearly that his personal plan and wish were to see me, despite all the partisan opposition, back at the Opera and breathing new life into the choreographic 'body' which was becoming anaemic.

Furthermore on 16th July, 1947, the *corps de ballet* had addressed this letter to M. Hirsch.

'The *corps de ballet*, which only a short time ago appeared to be dismembered, has under your able guidance been reconstituted, reorganised and completed. It has gained new prestige

[1] Rouché died in 1957 and the artistic world paid him touching tributes.

M.V.—X

which, however, some people are determined to contest. Now, for some months past, in the works of the repertory, in the ballets of such a high quality as *Sérénade*—presented by M. Balanchine whose choreography has revivified the whole ballet season—our members have been able to give expression to their technical abilities.

'Thus, although we are certain that the favour of a wide public has been renewed to us, we have also the feeling that, for lack of new creations, we are no longer the vanguard of the ballet troupes and that the torch we have held aloft for years may pass definitely into the hands of other troupes.

'M. Balanchine is soon to leave the Opera and after his departure the ballet will run the risk of falling once more into a state of stagnation which would be fatal to it. Again, a number of temporary engagements, which would inevitably be of an empirical character, would not offer a reasonable and definite solution to the problem that presents itself. It is not, then, without some anxiety, that we look forward to a future that would leave us without a creator, an animator. Thus we have to give up the prerogatives, the world-wide fame enjoyed by our *corps de ballet*.

'We think, sir, that in order to assure that all your efforts —which tend so rightly to raise our ensemble to the peak of choreographic art—may have their full effect, the Opera owes it to itself to have a master who—by his permanent innovating spirit and his incontestable creative power—would allow the ballet to give full expression to its qualities, and also would attract the attention both of an international élite and also of a wider public both French and foreign. Thus the ballet could assert its authority and prove that—contrary to what some people allege—it has not fallen into desuetude and decay.

'It is only these artistic preoccupations which induce us fervently to hope for the return of Serge Lifar. The fact is that he, whether one likes it or not, remains the most gifted and the most inventive of present-day choreographers and it is also he who has given most freely of himself for enhancing the reputation of our ballet.

'All the other artists—and they were French—who by the action of the purges were removed temporarily from our House have again resumed their old functions, at the expiry of the sanctions pronounced against them and without meeting with the slightest obstacle. That, alone of the Opera artists—and those elsewhere—Serge Lifar should be, owing to the incomprehensible relentlessness of some people, still subjected to ostracism, constitutes an evident iniquity. Furthermore, this measure so disproportionate to the offence, would have, in the final analysis, consequences much more baleful, by depriving it of the indispensible leaven of renewal, for the *corps de ballet* than for the person it is sought to harm. You are aware that troupes have been formed with the object not only of rivalling but of supplanting the Paris Opera ballet—and this not only abroad but here in Paris itself. These competing companies which are striving to lessen our fame are insistently demanding—so as to attain their objectives—the services of the man they consider the most remarkable choreographer of today, that is to say, Serge Lifar who, however, we feel sure, has only one wish and that is to be allowed to devote himself entirely to the development of our ensemble.

'We know, sir, that for you also artistic considerations come before all others and that is why we beg you to grant our request which is expressed solely in order that the ballet and therefore the Opera itself may enjoy a future of great and long-lasting brilliance.'

Among those who signed were: L. Darsonval, M. Bardin, M. Renault, M. Lascar, C. Vaussard, L. Mail, M. Bozzoni, J-P. Andréani, G. Bessy, M. Lafon, X. Kalioujny, Descombey and Lacotte.

I most readily agreed to forget past miseries and to consider a return to the Opera. I was, moreover, touched by Hirsch's courage. But then, I must admit, he never went back on his word. He was always most loyally by my side in the battle that was soon to be engaged. He acted rather mysteriously but highmindedly. He was faithful without really knowing who I was.

In July 1947 I handed over to the Marquis de Cuevas the *Nouveaux Ballets de Monte Carlo* about whose future I had been concerned—and I signed a contract with Hirsch. This bound me once more, as from 1st September 1947, to the National Academy of Music and Dance. I would not myself reappear on the stage until public resentment had entirely died down but I did at once take in hand the National Ballet again.

I was much moved at finding myself once more in my old 'home'. I approached it with a beating heart as a lover draws near to the dwelling of his lady-love. I raised my eyes: this time Apollo was greeting me. The bad, old days had vanished. My first encounter was with the head janitor Ferrari. He embraced me and welcomed me like the prodigal son on his return to his father's roof. The whole Opera had got the news that I was coming back. People were on the look-out for me in every corner, but none yet dared to show himself. The story that I had got my old job back streaked through the building like wildfire. More than one of the staff was wondering what my attitude to him would be. Without doubt some of them, but they must have known little of me, feared I would feel an urge to revenge. In each recess, at each window, within each hollow shadow I sensed eyes on the watch. I walked on to the rotunda where I knew the whole *corps de ballet* was waiting for me. Then for a short pause I stopped. Would not the passage of time have made some difference? Would there not be a certain coolness in the welcome? There was the need to get accustomed once more. I pushed open the door. It was an explosion. I could see nothing more. All the *corps de ballet* was mobbing me, thronging me, acclaiming me. There was my faithful army composed of those who had always supported me. And loyal among the most loyal—Max Bozzoni, Léone Mail, Serge Ferraut, Andrée Lelièvre, the latter maybe most of all, the ballet leader who had carried on a ceaseless battle, undertaken innumerable initiatives, organised petitions so that I might come back to the Opera. All embraced me. No, time had made no difference. Fidelity was linked to fidelity. Henceforth victory was certain.

My contract, as I have said, did not come into force until 1st September and until that date I went to the Opera only for rehearsals. But that did not matter much. There I was among my artists and at home—and on the posters appeared '24th September *Le Chevalier et la Demoiselle* by Philippe Gaubert, choreography by Serge Lifar'. On this evening which was to be the first of renewed contact with my public, I went before the performance to Drouant's with Georges Hirsch, M. and Mme Jacques Ibert who had already, back in 1943, talked to me about his ballet *Le Chevalier errant*. It must be admitted that this work was a very difficult one to stage, so much so indeed that no fewer than five producers (among whom was J. L. Barrault) and some choreographers had been obliged to turn it down . . . we were discussing plans for the future when a message came that

Hirsch was wanted on the telephone. When he got back to us he was deathly pale. I did not have to ask him what was the matter. He just let drop: 'The stage-hands have gone on strike . . .' He did not need to explain anything to me. I realised quickly enough he was in grave danger. Were we, he and I, to crash on the rocks when in sight of port? . . . Was he going to ruin his career for having come over to my side? To the side of one whose name . . . 'Long live Lifar' or 'Lifar to the gallows' . . . still aroused violent currents of opinion.[1] He added only, 'Keep calm, the battle is engaged' . . . and then he went off to the fight.

Three hours later Hirsch reappeared and ordered champagne. He seemed to have had a merry fight. He told us about the evening's events. The iron entrance gates had remained shut. Two thousand people who could not get in were massed on the Opera square. Among them were the Aga Khan and the Begum as well as other prominent persons. Some of the younger members of the crowd wanted to force their way in. Cries resounded, 'Kill the stage-hands.' Then came to greet the public the dancers, Jean Babilée leading them, the *danseuses* in short skirts, even the 'little rats' (the youngest apprentice dancing girls), and they made it clear that they had been against their will prevented from appearing on the stage under my direction. The 'little rats' themselves were in their 'tutus' (short frilly skirts), and a great roar of ovation welcomed them. There reigned an atmosphere of enthusiasm and riot.

The next day work and rehearsals began again. The following week—strike. The strike went on for a month. The Press was for the most part violent in comments.

The situation got more and more tense. Hirsch demanded a frank and recorded consultation with the unions. Out of the eight different sorts of employment represented by the Opera workers, seven voted against the strike. One only—that of the stage-hands—voted unanimously for the strike. And that was enough to hold everything up. The authorities must intervene.

---

[1] In 1949 at Saint-Etienne I experienced a last spurt from the volcano of hatred which was nevertheless becoming quiescent. Some unknown individuals, thinking no doubt to cover themselves with glory by a very tardy Resistance, wanted to force me to go and salute a monument to the memory of Resistance martyrs. They had no need of violence to get me to perform this act.

Jaujard, the Director of Fine Arts, attempted negotiations. All I could do was to wait, since the kindly protection Pierre Bourdan extended to me was ended by his tragic death from drowning in the South of France. And I was saddened by seeing the relations between the stage-hands and the artists—who were also prevented from practising their profession—deteriorate, as also those between these ill-directed men and the public. The police had to protect the men from the anger of the crowd. One may feel astonished that Paul Germain, the delegate and one of their toughest leaders, should by now be the administrative chief of the technical staff of the United National Lyric Theatres. After a month Jaujard and Hirsch at last came to an agreement and signed a formal document with the stage-hands. Lifar might carry on his job as *maître de ballet* but, on the other hand, he must never himself appear on the stage of the National Opera . . . and all the same I had been a member of the syndicate of producers since 1946. Now at last the ballet performances could start up again. On the first evening the performance had just begun, the theatre was still lighted up for fear of possible demonstrations, when I slipped into the centre box. Someone in the crowd recognised me and pointed me out. Then the whole audience rose up and turned towards me—soon the artists on the stage and the musicians joined in the long ovation. The President of the Republic, Vincent Auriol, who was present in his box took part in this collective greeting.

Later on my positions as *maître de ballet* and of choreographer and of professor were given back to me and, at the same time, I managed to get set up at the Opera a choreographic institute— that was a project I had cherished for a long time.

But I still had to regain my place as a dancer.

I was caught up by a quarrel of world-wide significance. For the centennial festival of New York held in 1948, the Paris Opera was invited to the United States and Canada. It was to figure in the programme of a French delegation led by the chairman of the Paris Municipal Council, then Pierre de Gaulle, brother of the general. We were to perform at Montreal, Chicago, and then at New York and Washington. I was to take a plane and follow the troupe which had gone on ahead. In order to do this and to get an entry visa for the United States I had to get

an attestation (No. 24,977) from the Ministry of War and this
document must be signed by Colonel Poupard as proof that I
was in order with my adoptive country since the American
embassy at Paris had denounced me as a Soviet agent. But
in America there had just appeared a book by the famous impresario Hurok—whom I have had occasion to mention several
times. In this book the great impresario Hurok—insufficiently
informed about me as about my ballets—repeated the worst
of the calumnies spread abroad about me—I had received
Hitler, I had welcomed the capture of Kiev by the Germans
and had even gone there to dance while the town was in flames
and the inhabitants being massacred. All this nonsense no longer
found acceptance in France but in America it threatened to
unsettle people's minds and therefore to imperil the success of a
French official tour. All the same everything went off well at
Montreal whereas at Chicago our success was brilliant.

However at New York the climate was stormy. For some
ten days Walter Winchell, the celebrated commentator on
one of America's most important radio chains, had been carrying
on a campaign based on the theme 'Serge Lifar, Hitler's shadow,
is among us'. And every day he started up with his *Leitmotif*
which reminded me of Jean Hérold Paquis's outbursts during
his one o'clock to two-thirty radio talks. This sort of thing—
'War widows, you can put on crape for your husbands, your
sons and your brothers who fell in the war. Serge Lifar, Hitler's
man, is among us.' And all the while he was surreptitiously
denouncing me to the authorities as a Russian and a Communist.
I was also asked to point out those stage-hands of the troupe
who might be Communists, and this I indignantly refused to do.
But feeling was running high.

While I was in New York I refused to attend any of the
official receptions and meetings. I stayed in my hotel on Fifth
Avenue near where the Opera performances were to take place.
I was guarded by four armed 'gorillas'. I made myself as small
and unobtrusive as possible in the hope that the commotion
would die down. Finally the evening of the performance arrived.
All New York was there despite the anonymous threats which
had been received announcing the theatre would be blown up;
Henri Sauguet's *Mirage* had a triumphant reception. For thirty
minutes the applause for Chauviré and Michel Renault kept up;
the crowd shouted for Lifar . . . Lifar . . . I hid myself away in a

corner of the theatre. After the performance of *Suite en blanc* the audience stood up to clap . . . then some of my comrades discovered me, dug me out and dragged me on to the stage to acknowledge the acclamations. The theatre did not blow up. Everyone was happy. We had won a victory.

But once back in France I remembered with a shock that I could not appear on the stage. I had almost forgotten this ban while I was in America. But now during the Opera dance evenings there were scenes. Cries from the audience . . . 'Lifar on the stage' . . . it was up in the top gallery that some unknown people —who afterwards let me know their names—among them were Mlles Harau and Michot—encouraged the most vocal and rousing cries of enthusiasm.

In the January of that year 1949 I was 'summoned' by a Communist cell in the Opera. This time I went alone. We argued for two hours. They said to me, 'Of course, Serge, we admire you as a dancer but we thought you were a Nazi and belonged to the Gestapo.' I explained everything to them and repeated, but more calmly, what I had declared to the purge committee. Finally they said, 'Let's forget all this row, Serge, you're a worker just as we are, you're a pal. You were very decent about us in New York. We'll let you carry on with your job.' And we shook hands.

For the 2nd February 1949 *L'Après-midi d'un faune* was billed. Before the performance there was to be a little ceremony which for some time past had become a tradition—the procession of the *corps de ballet*. The huge interior of the Opera was crammed from the orchestra stalls to the very last row of the gallery. There was electricity in the air, the excitement of waiting. First of all appeared at the back of the brilliantly illuminated Foyer de la Danse the 'little rats' of the Opera. They came forward to the footlights, bowed to the public already thrilled by anticipation, then they split into two rows which moved towards the wings, one on the courtyard side and one on the garden side. After that appeared the second quadrilles who curtsied in the same manner, then the first quadrilles the *coryphées* (leaders of the ballet), after them the so-called 'small subjects' followed by the 'great subjects' whose appearance alternated with that of the soloists and the stars. For them the applause, which had been loud and continuous, redoubled.

Then, in their turn, came the men in similar order. All were dressed in Romantic costume—black tights and white blouses; the 'great subjects' . . . the leading dancers . . . the stars in white tights . . . In the Foyer de la Danse I drew near to the door of the 'cave' when I saw my shadow which a searchlight threw lengthened into the recess; from that pool of light I heard thousands of voices roaring, calling me by name. Finally I came forward and showed myself dressed entirely in white, star and ballet-master. Then the storm of applause thundered louder than ever. I walked forward slowly on the immense stage, alone amid the crowd that called for me. They had missed me as much as I had missed them. I bent forward and ran for the last few yards that separated me from the footlights. Both public and artists remained standing and cheering me . . . it seemed endlessly. I could have died in such a moment.

So the Dance went on. I created ballets which were danced in the four quarters of the globe. I selected new stars who were to be the pride of the world of Dance—Nina Viroubova, Liane Daydé, Michel Renault, Bessy, Motte, Thibon.

In 1947, at a party given for me by Etienne de Beaumont, I met Georges and Nora Auric. When they had congratulated me Nora asked me to commission a ballet for the Opera from Georges. I was enthusiastic about the idea and mentioned it to Hirsch who said that to his great regret he could not accept the proposition unless Auric would consent to write the score without a fee since the Opera was very short of money. So it came about that I paid the fee amounting to half a million francs. We asked Cocteau to write the scenario and Bérard to do the décors, and the costumes. Such were the origins of *Phèdre* which has been called the outstanding piece of this century. I was often at Auric's home in the place Beauvau while he was composing. At the Opera rehearsals the musicians Jacques Metan and Harsany read the score at sight for me.

The piece was created in 1950 at the Opera. Nora Auric was delighted enough to write to me, 'For our Serge with loyalty and affection', and she was also proud to show the portrait she painted of me.

Just as I had been able to open the doors of the Opera wide for Auric, so I was happy to be able to get Chagall in 1958 for

M.V.—Y

the décor of Ravel's *Daphnis et Chloé*. These marvellous scenic décors are far removed in style and subject from Chagall's ceiling for the Opera. But it is true that I shall always be shocked by the obelisk on the place de la Concorde—its appropriate place would seem to me to be the Place de la Défense. In 1962 at my invitation Picasso prepared for the Opera his décors for the ballet *Icare*.

On 3rd May 1956 I was also received by General de Gaulle at 5bis, rue de Solférino (then his Paris office). Our conversation lasted no less than fifty-five minutes, during which time I told him the story of the mission confided to me by Roussy and I also mentioned the latter's real role. After I had handed to him that chapter of my book which deals with Hitler's visit to the Paris Opera, the General said to me as I took leave of him, 'I am glad to shake hands with you both for myself and also for France.'

Later on, General de Gaulle wrote me this letter:

Cher Maître,
As you are leaving the Paris Opera to which you have devoted all your artistic activities for so many years and to the greater renown of our National Ballet, I should like to say to you once more how much I admire your great talent and also to express to you my thanks for the part you played in the diffusion of French culture abroad.

Please accept, *cher Maître*, the expression of my compliments and best wishes.

(signed) Ch. de Gaulle.

I now felt the moment was coming for a separation between the dancer and the choreographer, my two aspects, my 'double-headed eagle' as someone said of me. I no longer took on any important role in the ballets. Little by little I handed on my parts to the numerous star dancers I had formed and trained during the twenty-seven years I spent at the Opera. I did not want to bow myself off. I wanted to fly off.

On 5th December 1956 I danced the ballet I cherish above all others. It was the last role I had kept for myself, that of Albert in *Giselle*. I knew only that this was to be my last appearance on the Opera stage. Still alone. But all my heart was in my role, all my heart devoted to my public. I danced as I had never danced before. Within me were both emotion and a limitless detachment. I had reconquered everything—my dancers, my ballets, my universe, my public. And I owed all that to the dancer I am.

While I was dancing I saw again flash by my dark years and My years of bright light. So many events in the life of one man! Gustave Roussy had killed himself at the moment his shady dealings were about to be revealed. And this freed me, so to speak, from an evil spell which had weighed heavy upon me for years.

There had been dark deeds and jealousies around me, but how much enthusiasm too! And how many secret understandings! I owed so much thanks to so many people.[1]

But in the last analysis it is to the people of Paris that I owed everything. They had always supported me, encouraged me, called for me, acclaimed me—the modest public immune to all the propaganda who thronged to the box-offices to get tickets, and who mingled with the university students—always my enthusiastic admirers—at the stage entrance to see me, to encourage me again and again.[2]

---

[1] On 27th September 1968 Serge Lifar (then aged 63) signed his third contract as *maître de ballet* of the Paris Opera.
[2] In 1965 the King of Sweden decorated me with the Order of Vasa.

EPILOGUE
(But not the End)

D.M.
PUERI SEPTENTRIONIS
ANNORUM XII QUI ANTIPOLI
IN THEATRO BIDUO
SALTAVIT ET PLACUIT

To the Divine Manes
of the Northern youth
aged twelve years who
at Antibes in the theatre
danced two days and pleased.

*(From an inscription on a 2nd century
Roman tombstone at Antibes)*

So here I am after forty years and arrived at the end, if not of
my adventures, at least of my career as a dancer.

In the springtime of 1961 I saw my country again. During
a month's visit I was to fly over thousands of miles, see once
more the four capitals of the USSR—Moscow, Leningrad,
Tiflis and Kiev my own home.

When I landed in Moscow and set foot on Russian soil it
seemed to me as though all my life abroad had faded away, was
only a blurred memory. No, nothing had happened. I had quit
my native land only a few hours before. I did not rest for a
minute. I wanted to see everything . . . the Lomonossov University—a gigantic skyscraper—on Mount Lenin, the Bolshoi
Theatre, the Tretiakov Gallery with its sumptuous ikons by
Rublev, the celebrated St Serge monastery at Zagorsk, Ark-
hangelskoie with the former palace of Prince Yusupov now a
museum. At Klin I visited Tchaikovsky's house.

Then I flew off to Leningrad—St Petersburg—Pushkin's
city, the museum-city. I admired its fine avenues, the Neva in
its granite bed, the Peter-and-Paul fortress, the Admiralty, the
Winter Palace, the Hermitage. I saw *le Lac des cygnes* at the
Marie Theatre (today called the Kirov), *Pétrouchka* at the Michel

Theatre. And I could not help thinking—this is really the most beautiful city in the world.

I crossed a continent to discover the capital of Georgia, Tbilissi, Tiflis where Greek, Roman and Slav civilisations meet and mingle in a southern setting . . . the exuberant atmosphere, the luxuriant vegetation, the nonchalant and relaxed way of life. Here at the foot of grandiose mountains you are already in the Orient.

And now came Kiev. Before my eyes, my childhood rose again. There was my Dnieper and its broad curving course, the isles where once I lay and dreamed, the sky and the fast fleeting clouds, the heights overlooking the stream . . . up them I had climbed so often to lose myself in musings before the infinite horizon; the church of St Andrew and not far off the St Sophia Cathedral. Yes, time was abolished . . . and there were also our superb Kreshchatik, my high school, the University, the opera.

Now I was in my own street, the Irinskaia. I stopped—there was my home . . . memories of my parents, of my childhood, the newspaper we published at the high school, my St George's Cross, the first dancing-shoes I wore when I had begun to learn dancing with Bronislava Nijinska at the Kiev Opera.

I went to the cemetery—the railing, the cross, two small oblong mounds of earth . . . the tombs of my father and mother. I remained standing in the wind. The nightingales were singing. Somewhere in the distance a trumpet sounded, there was the echo of a roll of drums, the sigh of a violin. Then came a procession. It passed close to me. The coffin, after the custom of my country, was open. An infant was being buried. My very dear Swedish friend Lilian Ahlefeldt had tears in her lovely eyes. She was by my side, for she had accompanied me on my pilgrimage. I was happy not to be alone in the world, but I realised that a whole cycle of my life was ended. Now I could fly off again to the West.

In the plane that brought me back I felt how proud I was to be a Russian, to have remained a Russian . . . proud of Russian culture, proud of Russian might whether of the Empire, of the Emigration, of the Soviets . . . it was the Russia of always, eternal Russia.[1]

[1] While I was in Russia I met Mme Furtzeva, the Minister for Cultural Affairs, and in 1969 the Soviet Government invited me to visit Moscow and Leningrad. This was my third visit to the USSR.

Today, when I have relived all my career in order to recount it, I am fulfilled . . . a life then is made up of so many efforts, so many passions, so many dreams come true, so many creations. And all this is purified just because it has been told.

At last I am myself. I am already that other person, still myself, a dancer in life, a dancer on the stage.

 INDEX